W9-ASB-554

*Wage Justice*

Women in Culture and Society

*A series edited by Catharine R. Stimpson*

Sara M. Evans and
Barbara J. Nelson

# *Wage Justice*

Comparable Worth and the
Paradox of
Technocratic Reform

The University of Chicago Press

*Chicago and London*

Wingate College Library

The University of Chicago Press, Chicago 60637
The University of Chicago Press, Ltd., London

© 1989 by The University of Chicago
All rights reserved. Published 1989
Printed in the United States of America

98 97 96 95 94 93 92 91 90 89 54321

Library of Congress Cataloging-in-Publication Data

Evans, Sara M. (Sara Margaret), 1943—
    Wage justice : comparable worth and the paradox of technocratic
reform / Sara M. Evans and Barbara J. Nelson.
    p. cm. — (Women in culture and society)
    Includes index.
    ISBN 0-226-22259-4
    1. Minnesota—Officials and employees—Salaries, etc. 2. Local
officials and employees—Salaries, etc.—Minnesota. 3. Pay equity—
Minnesota. 4. Wages—Women—Minnesota. I. Nelson, Barbara J.,
1949–    . II. Title. III. Series.
JK6157.E83 1989
331.2'15—dc19                                                88-39871
                                                                  CIP

⊗    The paper used in this publication meets the minimum requirements of the American National Standard for Information Sciences—
Permanence of Paper for Printed Library Materials, ANSI Z39.48–
1984.

This book is printed on acid-free paper.

**SARA M. EVANS** professor of history at the University
of Minnesota, where she also directs the Center for Advanced
Feminist Studies. She is an editor of *Feminist Studies,* coauthor,
with Harry C. Boyte, of *Free Spaces,* and author of *Personal Politics.*

**BARBARA J. NELSON** is professor in the Hubert H.
Humphrey Institute of Public Affairs at the University of Minne-
sota, where she also codirects the Center on Women and Public
Policy. She is the author of *American Women and Politics* and
*Making an Issue of Child Abuse,* which is also published by the
University of Chicago Press.

For Harry
and
For Mandy

# Contents

# Foreword

Think of a supermarket. No matter how glossy or dingy, no matter whether it sells *radicchio* or iceberg lettuce, a supermarket is an arena in which two forces meet: those of production and distribution and those of consumption. Wisely, scrupulously, *Wage Justice: Comparable Worth and The Paradox of Technocratic Reform* explores the supermarket of America. It asks how the productive wage earner, especially a woman, might be paid more fairly. Equity matters, not only as an abstract principle and potential good, but as a concrete condition of existence. For greater equity helps more people to live more freely and sociably. Among other things, they can pay for better goods for themselves and their families at a supermarket check-out counter.

In the 1960s, many feminists, policy analysts, and public officials believed that "equal pay for equal work" would generate economic equity. Despite new laws that embodied this belief, women's wages kept on being significantly less than those of men. One reason for the doggedness of the gap is the fact that many men and women still do not do the same sort of work. On the contrary, occupational segregation guarantees that they will do different sorts of work. In the United States, race and ethnicity further determine who does what and for what reward. However, not all white men are fat cats for whom the market pours cream. As the United States zips and stumbles from a manufacturing to a service economy, white men lose the high wages of manufacturing jobs. The struggle for pay equity becomes more painful and complex.

In the 1970s, most notably in the state of Washington, a second strategy for confronting wage discrimination, "equal pay for work of comparable worth," emerged. At once straightforward and radical, comparable worth is "the principle that jobs dissimilar in nature can be compared in terms of knowledge, skill, effort, responsibility, and working conditions, and that jobs equivalent in value in these terms should be paid equally" (p. 7). Men and women might not do the same thing, but if their work is similarly demanding and valuable, they ought to have similar rewards. By the mid-

ix

1980s, at least twenty states had begun to study and to adapt the theory of comparable worth, even as the federal government was becoming a bully pulpit of conservative opposition. Minnesota was among the state leaders. In 1982, it passed a State Employees Pay Equity Act; in 1984, a Local Government Pay Equity Act, which required local jurisdictions to respond to the principles of comparable worth. The 1984 statute was harder and messier to implement than that of 1982. The Minnesota School Boards Association, for example, was helpful, but the Association of Minnesota Counties was not.

Lucidly, *Wage Justice* analyzes the Minnesota experience: the laws, the policies they represented, the politics of their passage and enactment, and their consequences, both unintended and intended. The process did reveal the depth of the connections between jobs and gender. The salaries for many did improve. In 1983, the base salary for a Clerk 1 working for the state of Minnesota was $11,922, only 17% above the poverty line of $10,178. Over the next four years, without the pay equity act, the base salary would have risen to $13,675, 22% above the then-current poverty line. However, with pay equity, that Clerk 1 took home $15,931, 42% above the poverty line.

If *Wage Justice* were only the first major study of comparable worth in action, it would be unparalleled. It is much more as well. Sara Evans and Barbara Nelson are scholars of broad and steady vision who place comparable worth in context. *Historically,* it is a late-twentieth-century development in the mingled histories of women and work, feminism and labor legislation. A pervasive feature of these stories has been feminism's struggle against the assumption by judges, legislators, and trade unionists alike that wage workers were men, naturally. *Theoretically,* comparable worth provokes an argument between the two powerful schools of contemporary economic thought: the neoclassical, which derides comparable worth as an intolerable intrusion into the operations of a neutral market, and the institutional, which can support comparable worth as a tolerable adjustment of the operations of a market that preexisting structures, beliefs, interests, and agents drive. Each of these analyses carries with it a concept of gender, which, in turn, shapes decisions and notions about public life. For neoclassical theory, a woman's inferior wages are the result of her choices, tastes, and preferences. For institutional theory, such wages are the result of the devaluing of women and minorities. *Ideologically and politically,* comparable worth has become a battleground between liberal/progressive types, who often call on institutional theory, and conservatives, who often call on neoclassical theory. Ironically, as Evans and Nelson show, employees of all ideological and political persuasions tend to support comparable worth, unless they feel compelled to salute "the free market" and to spurn whatever "feminism" supports.

A paradox haunts Evans and Nelson as they reason their way through the past and present, theory and practice, ideology and politics of comparable worth. Its purpose is to help bring about fairer wages for everyone and greater symmetry between the equal political rights of a democracy and the compensations of workers within that democracy's political economy. However, in Minnesota and elsewhere, elites have decided how to achieve this purpose, most commonly through job classification schemes that enhance managerial powers. Inadvertently, comparable worth shows "the simultaneous necessity and difficulty of using technocratic means to achieve a just and democratic social transformation" (p. 164). Comparable worth, then, is more than a struggle for pay equity; more than the conviction that markets are not always super; more than the belief that human beings are able to alter such markets if they choose. Comparable worth demands that a democracy confront the dilemmas of democracy in the postindustrial world.

For scholars and citizens, *Wage Justice* is an honorable guide to our rich, multiply divided polity.

CATHARINE R. STIMPSON

# *Acknowledgments*

The idea for *Wage Justice* emerged in the fall of 1983 when it became clear that Minnesota's comparable worth efforts were going to provide a national laboratory for social change. The rich and varied women's studies community of the University of Minnesota matched social innovation with academic interest. The project germinated at the Center for Advanced Feminist Studies (CAFS) and grew to full flowering under the aegis of CAFS and the Humphrey Institute's Center on Women and Public Policy. Our first thanks go to our friends and colleagues in this community, who sustained us and our research. Nancy Johnson, the Assistant Director of the Center on Women and Public Policy, coordinated this massive research project (which covered twenty states and twenty-four local jurisdictions). For wonderful friendship and a magnificent job, our deepest gratitude goes to Nancy.

Legions of people helped to make the Comparable Worth Project successful. Anne Truax of the Minnesota Women's Center and Regina Strauchon of the University's Personnel Department joined us on the original Coordinating Committee. Anne Truax also coordinated our conference, "Comparable Worth: Minnesota and the Nation," held October 17–19, 1985. Lori Graven of the University's Department of Professional Development and Conference Services made every detail of the conference mesh. Richard Arvey, Clarke Chambers, Kathryn Chaloner, Laura Cooper, Tom Dewar, Arvonne Fraser, and Barbara Laslett formed the University Research Advisory Committee, and were especially helpful as we designed the survey of state of Minnesota employees. Rossana Armson and Ron Anderson of the Minnesota Center for Survey Research directed the employee survey with expertise and enthusiasm. Charles Backstrom generously consulted on survey design issues.

Our research assistants were superb. Our heartfelt thanks go to Lavon Anderson, Susan Bickford, Kathryn Carver, Elizabeth Conway, Linda Harris, Laurel Haycock, Alissa Hummer, Sarah McGrath Johnson, Gary Keese, Janet Larsen, Julie Luner, Renee Monson, Barbara Naramore, and

Amy Sandberg. So too, we had excellent secretarial support from Linda Baumann, Ellen Carlson, Donna Kern, Debra Tornes Leon, Lynne Mills, Karen Schuster, and Louise Straus.

For believing in the importance of determining what happens when new policies are implemented, we gratefully thank all of our funders. Our gratitude goes to Judith Healey, formerly Vice President of the Northwest Area Foundation and now President of the Minnesota Foundation; Terry Tinson Saario, President of the Northwest Area Foundation; the Minnesota Women's Consortium; and Robert Michael and Heidi Hartmann of the Panel on Pay Equity Research of the National Academy of Sciences. At the University of Minnesota we would like to thank warmly Thomas Anding, William Craig, and Thomas Scott of the Center for Urban and Regional Affairs; John Wallace of the Office of the Academic Vice President; Robert Holt, Judson Sheridan, and Patricia Swan of the Graduate School; Harlan Cleveland, Royce Hanson, and G. Edward Schuh of the Hubert H. Humphrey Institute of Public Affairs; and John Clark of the Conflict and Change Center. Sara Evans's participation in the project was also supported by a W. K. Kellogg National Fellowship.

Our most enduring debt of gratitude is to the scores of women and men who answered our questions over a period of five years. With patience, interest, and good humor they allowed us to interview them, observe meetings, and examine their materials.

And to our families, we say thank you for understanding the cycles of research and writing. A collaboratively written book makes more evident the collaboration of our loved ones in the broader struggle for justice.

# 1  *Introduction*

After years of toys for boys, now we're
going to have justice for women.
*Minneapolis City Council Member
Kathy O'Brien, 1987*[1]

On September 30, 1983, the Minneapolis City Council
unanimously declared its intention to develop a new comparable worth
wage policy in response to labor and feminist pressures for wage justice
in public employment. A twenty-four-member Advisory Committee on
Pay Equity, composed largely of elected officials and union representatives
from five salary-setting jurisdictions (the city itself; the Minneapolis Park,
Library, and School Boards; and the Minneapolis Community Development Agency), accepted its charge "to review the existing classification
system, identify patterns that indicate a lack of balance of 'job value'
between male-dominated and female-dominated job classes, and recom-
mend a program to resolve any inequities."[2] In other words, they adopted
a comparable worth policy with the goal of eradicating sex-based wage
discrimination. In the midst of their deliberations, in April 1984, the state
of Minnesota passed a law requiring all political subdivisions within the
state to adopt a similar policy. By August the Minneapolis Advisory Committee unanimously proposed that the city implement a plan to raise the
wages of the lowest-paid female-dominated jobs in city government. But
the unanimity both on the Council and in the Advisory Committee masked
deep disagreements about the meaning of comparable worth in practice.

The committee divided sharply between the majority, which advocated
a complete overhaul of the city's job classification system, and a minority,
which believed the goal of ending sex-based wage discrimination could be

1

reached more simply and cheaply by an analysis of the existing system. Majority and minority reports reflected months of debate: Should the city rationalize its entire pay system, raising the pay of any job that fell below the average, or focus on rectifying low wages for women that were attributable to historic discrimination? Would the city be legally liable if it used an old, somewhat outdated classification system? Would the anxieties accompanying a major reclassification be blamed on comparable worth and make a politically popular policy unpopular?

The dominant coalition consisted largely of representatives of management interested in rationalizing an antiquated classification system for city employees and of male-dominated unions which feared that pay equity would disadvantage them. The proposed study met these diverse needs. It would create new job descriptions and classifications for all city jobs, replacing the outdated system. In the process, by creating a more "scientific" and "rational" system, a new study would gain credibility in the eyes of blue-collar employees who believed the old classification system was biased against them.[3] Clerical workers, led by representatives from the American Federation of State, County, and Municipal Employees (AFSCME) and City Council Member Kathy O'Brien, submitted a minority report. They knew a comparable worth analysis of *any* job evaluation system was likely to demonstrate approximately a 20% disparity for the lowest-paid women, especially clerical workers, and they wanted quick results in the form of comparable worth raises. AFSCME also viewed the introduction of other, more bureaucratic agendas as footdragging and a subtle form of opposition. When it became clear that quick and simple methods would not prevail, O'Brien proposed that the Council make a commitment to retroactive raises as a guarantee that the goal of wage justice would not be eclipsed in the longer process of a reclassification study. The Council agreed to set aside $750,000 for pay increases retroactive to July 1, 1985.[4]

The complexities surrounding the creation and implementation of comparable worth policies that surfaced in Minneapolis have been virtually ignored in recent public and scholarly debate. Most discussions of comparable worth focus on such questions as: Should it be attempted? Is the market system fair? Does wage discrimination against women exist? If there is discrimination, should government intervene in wage setting to correct it? Minneapolis had moved from the abstract consideration of the issue to such concrete concerns as how comparable worth can be best accomplished and what the consequences are of various choices. In a sense the former set of issues remained a subtext of the latter, muted in part by the liberal political culture of Minneapolis with its commitment to governmental activism in the interests of fairness and equity. But arguments within the Advisory Committee on Pay Equity focused explicitly on a new set of questions about choices of technology, levels and kinds of employee participation, the proper role of unions and of collective bargaining, the budgetary implications of each option, and the longer-term effects on specific local interests of both managers and employees. The sides of this new debate were not neat—union members, feminists, politicians, bureaucrats could be found on various sides. Their inability to agree on clear definitions reflected not only philosophical differences but also deeply held perceptions of conflicting interests and political realities.

The implementation of comparable worth for state and local employees has proceeded farther in Minnesota than in any other state in the nation. In 1982 Minnesota passed the State Employees Pay Equity Act, which established equitable compensation relationships as "*the* primary" wage-setting consideration for employees of the state of Minnesota.[5] The total cost of the complete, four-year (1983–87) implementation in new salary money added to permanent salary costs was $22 million, or 3.7% of the 1983 baseline salary.[6] This sum provided the necessary wage increases for underpaid female-dominated classes, making Minnesota the first state to pass and fully implement a comparable worth wage policy for state employees. The Local Government Pay Equity Act, passed in 1984, broke new ground by requiring all local jurisdictions to make comparable worth "*a* primary" consideration in compensation and prescribed a process by which jurisdictions could determine if pay inequities exist.[7] The Act gave localities a timeline by which they studied wage practices for comparable worth inequities, devised a remedy if one was needed, and received immunity from prosecution in state courts. The immunity ended August 1, 1987. Localities were expected to fund comparable worth raises from local revenues. By August 1987, 90% of local governments had completed their analysis and embarked on an implementation plan (averaging 2.6 years).[8]

By virtue of covering the entire public-sector work force (14.3% of the nearly two million people employed in Minnesota in 1987) the new wage policy was a visible and significant change, a change that other states and localities were investigating, though without the same integrated state and local approach.[9] As Map 1.1 shows, by August 1987, twenty-eight states had done either full or pilot job-evaluation studies and twenty states had begun to make some kind of pay equity adjustments. In addition, scores of local jurisdictions outside Minnesota had also enacted comparable worth, either through legislation or collective bargaining. (A 1987 survey by the National Committee on Pay Equity indicated comparable worth activity by at least 166 localities in twenty states.)[10] Outside Minnesota, local-level implementation tended most often to be initiated through collective bargaining.

National efforts at comparable worth had little support in the 1980s. In the early years of the Reagan presidency, national legislation, even that designed for federal workers, had little chance of success because of the ideological opposition of a Republican Senate as well as presidential hostility. Congressional hearings in 1982 and 1984 provided a national forum for the growing debate. On January 6, 1987, with the Democrats in control of both houses of Congress, Democratic Representative Mary Rose Oakar of Ohio and forty-four cosponsors seized their opportunity and introduced H.R. 387, a bill to conduct a pay equity study of the federal wage and classification system. The Compensation and Employee Benefits Subcommittee recommended the bill to the House Committee on Post Office and Civil Service. Controlled by the Governmental Affairs Committee, the Senate companion bill, S.5, was sponsored by Republican Senator Dan Evans of Washington, Democratic Senator Alan Cranston of California, and thirty-four cosponsors. Both bills remained in committee. National supporters agreed that the time was not right for further congressional action.

Although national efforts remain stalled, the experiences of states and localities in implementing comparable worth adds a new, more grounded quality to the discussion. Careful and systematic analysis of the implementation brings new actors onto the stage, highlights complexities overlooked in more abstract discussions, and begins to resolve some of the hypothetical assertions, and the dualism, of those who claim that it is either the "issue of the 80s" or the "looniest idea since Looney Tunes." For the rest of this century, the new question is: *How well does comparable worth work?*[11]

*Wage Justice,* based on extensive data from the Minnesota experience as well as comparative information from other states and localities, explores both this practical question and the broader theoretical issues it raises. Between 1983 and 1987 the state and local jurisdictions in Minnesota offered a massive natural experiment in which a variety of policy options were pursued. Our book focuses on this time period, that is, from the introduction of the state legislation through the initial implementation period of the local legislation—the three-year period protected from state court intervention. The book is a detailed analysis of policy initiation;

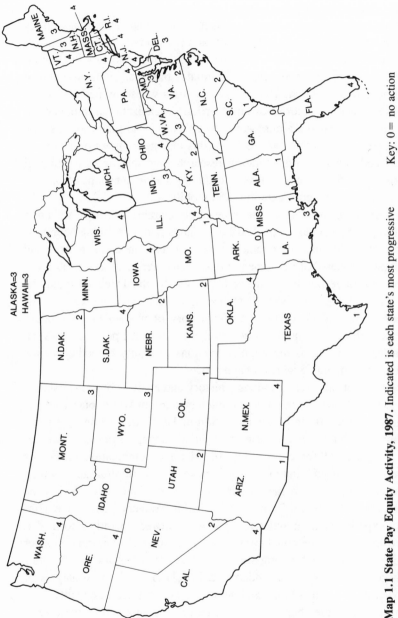

**Map 1.1 State Pay Equity Activity, 1987.** Indicated is each state's most progressive stage, with pay equity adjustments being the most advanced. Only action taken by the state legislature or governor's office is considered. (Source: "National Committee on Pay Equity: State Update" [Washington, D.C.: National Committee on Pay Equity, 1987], 1.)

Key: 0 = no action
1 = research/data collection
3 = job evaluation study
4 = pay equity adjustments

decision making in legislatures, councils, and administrative offices; and the crucial initial stages of implementation where the shape of policy is actually defined.

Our purpose is to show the consequences of comparable worth policy at three levels: for individuals directly and peripherally involved, for organizations favoring and opposing the efforts, and for society in general. Our emphasis on consequences differentiates this analysis from much of implementation research. Unlike many studies whose immediate aim is the development of theories of inter- or intra-organizational implementation, this study has the aim of advancing theories and practices of social interpretation and action. We feel that this change in direction is an important addition to implementation research, one that ties the study of governmental actions more closely to the normative questions of participation, democracy, representation, and mobilization.

In addition to introducing the issue of comparable worth, this chapter also frames the paradoxes of distributive justice in a declining economy, horizontal justice in a hierarchical world, and technocratic reform and democratic values that implementation reveals. Practical action on comparable worth responds to and reshapes the troubled debate about the meaning of equity in advanced technological societies. We extend this inquiry in discussions of the specific history of women in the modern economy (chapter 2) and the concerns that economists, political analysts, and historians bring to the popular versions of equity embodied in the concept of comparable worth (chapter 3).

The heart of the study provides a history and analysis of the legislative process (chapter 4), the process of implementation in Minnesota state government (chapter 5), and implementation in 1,607 local Minnesota jurisdictions (chapter 6). From these local jurisdictions, a sample of twenty-four was selected for close study, based on a combination of factors including size of jurisdiction, form of government, rural/urban/suburban character, population characteristics, and region of the state. Within the historical and theoretical frames established in chapters 2 and 3, the Minnesota experiment illuminates the paradoxes of technocratic reform discussed in this and the concluding chapter (chapter 7). The final chapter also assesses the case for comparable worth in light of its practical realities and argues that it must be understood in relation to other strategies of empowerment within a broad and democratic conception of equality.

Throughout these chapters, the research draws on a wide repertoire of data and methods. The different methodologies are described in the chapters on the legislative process, state implementation, and local implementation. In terms of data, interviews with elected and appointed officials, public managers, union officials, women's labor groups, union rank and file, representatives of women's organizations, and members of the business community[12] (including vendors of job evaluation systems) provided a detailed understanding of the actions and motivations of policy choice and implementation unavailable in quite the same way from any other source. In addition, we observed many public and private meetings of participants holding very different views on comparable worth. In 1985 the University of Minnesota Comparable Worth Research Project hosted an international conference at which state and local practitioners from the United States and provincial officials from Canada could exchange their views and experiences on implementing comparable worth. The records of this conference became an important, early source of information on local trends. The list of the interview participants is found in Appendix A. We also collected public and private documents from the state of Minnesota, nineteen states also implementing comparable worth, and twenty-four localities in Minnesota, and we assembled a fifteen-year clipping file from the *New York Times, Washington Post, Wall Street Journal, Minneapolis Star and Tribune,* and *St. Paul Pioneer Press Dispatch.* To determine the effects of adopting a comparable worth wage policy on employees both receiving and not receiving these raises, we directed a survey of 493 state of Minnesota employees. The first data ever to assess the consequences of initiating a wage policy change of this type, the survey informs the discussion of state-level implementation.

## *Defining the Policy*

To unravel what is at stake in this highly complex debate we must first begin with a clear definition. Within the broader goal of eliminating wage discrimination, comparable worth is "the principle that jobs dissimilar in nature can be compared in terms of knowledge, skill, effort, responsibility, and working conditions, and that jobs equivalent in value in these terms should be paid equally."[13] Though there are several methods for identifying and correcting underpaid jobs, by the late 1970s most definitions of comparable worth presumed the use of job evaluation technology. In this frame, comparable worth is a wage policy requiring equal pay within a jurisdiction or firm for male- and female-, majority- and minority-dominated job classifications that are valued equally in terms of skill, effort, responsibility, and working conditions regardless of the sex or race of job incumbents.[14] In practice, implementing this policy requires the application of a single job-evaluation system to all job classifications within the jurisdiction or firm. The single job-evaluation system measures in detail the skill, effort, responsibility, and working conditions of every job classification and combines the scores in each area to produce a single overall score for every classification. Job classifications with equal overall scores are considered to have equal value to the jurisdiction or firm. Under a comparable worth wage policy, classifications of equal value are paid equivalently whether they are predominantly male or female, white or minority. All individuals holding jobs within classifications of equal value would not be paid the same wages, however, because seniority, merit, or the quantity or quality of work done would continue to differentiate individuals' wages within equivalent classifications. Likewise, comparable worth analyses are done on a firm-specific basis. The values and wages of each firm are determined individually, as is the long-standing practice with the equal pay for equal work policy.[15]

Job evaluation systems provide the basic data around which arguments for and against comparable worth have been constructed. Proponents argue that a comparison of male- and female-dominated job classes exposes the extent to which discrimination against women has depressed female wages below the market standard. For example, in the state of Minnesota prior to the comparable worth adjustments, zookeepers (predominantly male) were paid substantially more than childcare workers (predominantly female), though their scores in the state's job evaluation system were almost the same. This example and others found in table 1.1 illustrate typical differences in state governments between such female and male job classes as nurses and pharmacists, or secretaries and delivery van drivers. As figure 1.1 shows, no female-dominated class in Minnesota, in 1981, was paid at or above the average wage for male-dominated jobs with the same scores.

Similar methods can be used to demonstrate discrepancies in the wages of jobs in which racial minorities are concentrated: in many public work forces (such as New York and New Jersey state governments and several local governments in California) both forms of discrimination are being investigated under the rubric of comparable worth.[16] Such an analysis was not possible in Minnesota, where less than 4% of the population was made up of racial or ethnic minorities at the time when the comparable worth analysis was undertaken there. The state-level public labor force actually had a slightly higher percentage of racial and ethnic minorities than the state population as a whole (3.8% in 1984 and 4.1% in 1986).[17]

TABLE 1.1
**Ten Largest Male and Female Job Classifications, State of Minnesota, 1981**

| No. of Incum- bents | % Female | Job Class or Title | Hay Pts. | Current Salary (Monthly Maximum) "Male" Classes | "Female" Classes |
|---|---|---|---|---|---|
| 448 | 97.8 | Clerk-typist 1 | 100 | | $1,039 |
| 411 | 88.1 | Clerk 2 | 117 | | 1,115 |
| 805 | 98.8 | Clerk-typist 2 | 117 | | 1,115 |
| 135 | 0.7 | General repair worker | 134 | $1,564 | |
| 303 | 99.7 | Clerk-stenographer 2 | 135 | | 1,171 |
| 192 | 99.5 | Clerk-typist 3 | 141 | | 1,171 |
| 485 | 74.6 | Human services technician, senior | 151 | | 1,274 |
| 1,335 | 0.1 | Highway maintenance worker, senior | 154 | 1,521 | |
| 184 | 99.5 | Clerk-stenographer 4 | 162 | | 1,307 |
| 310 | 100.0 | Clerk-typist 4 | 169 | | 1,274 |
| 402 | 72.1 | Human services specialist | 177 | | 1,343 |
| 462 | 6.3 | Highway technician, intermediate | 178 | 1,646 | |
| 282 | 94.7 | Licensed practical nurse 2 | 183 | | 1,382 |
| 393 | 15.8 | Correctional counselor 2 | 188 | 1,656 | |
| 518 | 2.1 | Highway technician, senior | 206 | 1,891 | |
| 128 | 0.0 | Heavy equipment mechanic | 237 | 1,757 | |
| 132 | 0.8 | Natural resources specialist, conservation | 238 | 1,808 | |
| 169 | 0.6 | Principal engineering specialist | 298 | 2,347 | |
| 165 | 2.4 | Engineer, senior | 382 | 2,619 | |
| 180 | 0.0 | Engineer, principal | 479 | 2,923 | |

*Source:* Minnesota Council on the Economic Status of Women, *Pay Equity and Public Employment; Report on the Task Force on Pay Equity* (St. Paul: Minnesota Council on the Economic Status of Women, 1982), 20.

While the evidence of differential pay for male- and female-dominated jobs is strong, proponents and opponents offer sharply differing explanations. What one side views as a cumulative history of discrimination and bias the other understands as the workings of market forces and individual choice which legislation can only distort, not remedy. Proponents of comparable worth locate the problem in the dramatic segregation of the modern labor force by sex and race, and in the consistent devaluation of work associated with women and minorities. While equal pay for equal (i.e., the same) work and affirmative action have removed some discriminatory barriers since the 1960s, the continued predominance of women in low-paid, female-dominated jobs justifies a comparable worth remedy. Like charges for surgical procedures which start high and drift up over time even as they become more common and less time-consuming, women's wages have remained low relative to men's because that is how they began.[18] Opponents of comparable worth argue, however, that unfettered market forces—particularly since the 1960s—do not discriminate but instead reflect a series of personal preferences, particularly on the part of

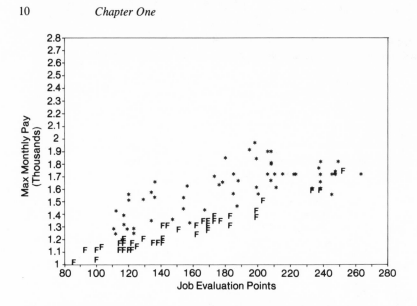

**Fig. 1.1 Distribution of Minnesota State Government Job Classes by Pay Scale and Evaluation Points, 1981.** (Source: Minnesota Commission on the Economic Status of Women, *Pay Equity: The Minnesota Experience* [St. Paul, 1985], 12.)
Key: * = male-dominated job classes (over 80% male incumbents)
   F = female-dominated job classes (over 70% female incumbents)
   (balanced classes not shown)

women. They point to factors which differentiate female workers in terms of education, experience, and seniority, and to women's familial responsibilities, to explain their placement in the economy.

While the two sides debate the origins and nature of the apparently unbridgable gap between the full-time, year-round earnings of women and men—women have earned approximately two-thirds of the male earnings since at least 1955, when the federal government began to keep such statistics—comparable worth addresses one specific portion of that gap: the difference between the earnings (or wages) of men and women in equivalently rated jobs according to a given job evaluation system. The specific goal of comparable worth is important to remember, because the debates surrounding this policy frequently soar into high abstraction and global claims.[19] Any clear definition must reflect the practical realities of comparable worth as a policy as these realities existed in the 1970s and 1980s and as they are planned for the 1990s, as well as the policy's historical roots in management practices and labor legislation in the twentieth century.

Many states and localities, including the state of Minnesota and its local jurisdictions, call their comparable worth policies "pay equity," a term that conveys the *goal* of eliminating wage discrimination rather than the *process*.[20] In the eyes of many proponents, "pay equity" captures rhetorically their deeper and less technocratic intentions and it claims for their "side" the fundamental value of fairness. "Equity" is a word with ancient roots in the Latin *aequus* (equal). It entered the English language in the fourteenth century to mean "fair dealing," a definition which deepened by the sixteenth century to "natural justice." This latter meaning took on specific legal content through the Chancellor's Court in England, which evolved a separate body of law from the common-law system. The chancery operated not on precedent but on the basis of commonly held notions of "equity," and it provided remedies for persons (including women) severely disadvantaged under the common law. By the nineteenth century the rules of law and of equity effectively merged into a single court system both in England and in the United States.[21]

The rhetorical choice of the term "pay equity," then, makes strategic sense for advocates of a policy intended to remedy the effects of historic discrimination against women. Consistent with most of the scholarly literature, we prefer the clarity of the term "comparable worth" to describe the specific policy. We use "pay equity" to describe accurately the name of the policy in Minnesota.

## *Paradoxes of Technocratic Change*

Because the practical realities of comparable worth depend on the application of modern business-management technology, its consequences can be paradoxical. The concept of equity, for most proponents of comparable worth, is one part of a broadly democratic and egalitarian vision that would also embrace numerous other strategies to open up vocational options and greater participation. Yet while comparable worth is a means of achieving wage justice in the sense of a nondiscriminatory "fair share," it does not address, and in practice may not be congruent with, other key democratic values.

That such paradoxes exist does not constitute a good argument against comparable worth. They simply serve as a reminder that social change tends to be piecemeal and complex, and that single-issue reform strategies always come up short. Thus, we would argue that comparable worth should not be understood as an alternative to mechanisms for eliminating discrimination, such as affirmative action (as many have asserted), but must instead be seen as one of many avenues to the broader goals of an equitable society and wage justice. We outline below three central paradoxes as a prelude to our closer examination of the historical, economic, and political dimensions of the case for a comparable worth policy.

## Redistributive Justice in a Declining Economy

One of the greatest ironies of the comparable worth movement lies in the economic context in which it must compete for resources. As we shall argue, comparable worth promises to accomplish for female-dominated clerical and service workers what the organization of the CIO in the 1930s did for male jobs in heavy industry in terms of raising wages and workers' standards of living. This has powerful implications for women's capacity to live autonomous lives, supporting children (as millions already do) without the hardships and degradation of poverty. It enhances women's capacity for active citizenship as well, providing them with the "independence" America's founders believed indispensable for the virtuous citizen.[22]

Since the mid-1970s, however, the male wage that provides the measure against which women's wages can be described as discriminatory has been in decline. This downward pressure on wages, particularly in the unionized basic industries, is related to the movement of industries into the Third World, where wages and working conditions resemble those of nineteenth-century America, and to the shift in growth within the United States economy from the highly unionized industrial sector to the service sector. Between 1972 and 1986 the average weekly earnings of private nonfarm workers declined nearly 14%, with earnings of young men (20–24) down almost 30% after increasing continuously for the previous twenty-five years.[23] In such a context, advocates of comparable worth and other forms of wage justice may find defensive hostility among their most important potential allies, as well as a constantly eroding standard against which to measure female or minority wages and earnings.[24]

## Horizontal Justice in a Hierarchical World

Because comparable worth emphasizes a kind of horizontal equity, that is, equal pay for work of equal value, it does not address vertical inequities embedded in work hierarchies, that is, differently valued jobs, and their relative differences in pay. For example, the fact that doctors' earnings are often five times as great as nurses' would not be addressed in a comparable worth analysis, since no valid job evaluation system would rate the jobs of doctor and nurse the same. Job evaluation systems as the key technological tool for implementing comparable worth bring with them a complex and much-debated value system. Originally devised to "capture" employer values and to replicate the market, job evaluation evolved in the 1930s and 1940s as a business method of rationalizing internal pay systems.[25] It therefore incorporates many of the hierarchical assumptions that are challenged by comparable worth advocates.

While some proponents of comparable worth have in recent years engaged in strenuous efforts to devise unbiased systems of job evaluation, others join in the assertion by critics of comparable worth that the entire exercise is subjective and that there is no such thing as "intrinsic worth" to any job. Such an argument has three aspects: (1) jobs do not have intrinsic social worth; (2) jobs do not have intrinsic worth to a firm; (3) jobs in firms do not have intrinsic worth but do have subjective value to that firm. Most comparable worth advocates agree that the third position is sufficient for their purposes and indeed that job evaluation was originally designed to discover precisely that subjective value so that a firm could use its wage bill to pay for those activities and qualities that it valued most. Their only concern is that such subjective values should not contain systematic biases against women or minorities.[26] This leaves intact, however, the fact that any plan reflecting employer values and market assumptions will reinforce hierarchy. Thus comparable worth is not, as some critics claim, a plan for all jobs to be paid exactly the same. Rather, the idea that some jobs are worth more than others is reinforced under comparable worth.

## Technocratic Reform and Democratic Values

If most workplaces are inherently hierarchical, they are also generally undemocratic, and comparable worth will not make them less so. In many cases, organized campaigns for comparable worth provide democratizing and empowering experiences as women and minorities rethink the value of their own work and challenge the hierarchy of values enshrined in the wage scale. Unlike the great union organizing campaigns to which they may be compared, however, they do not have the character of a social movement demanding an ongoing role in the process of wage negotiation. Rather, most often comparable worth advocates demand the institution of a highly specialized management technology, job evaluation, and a mathematical analysis of similarly rated male- and female-dominated jobs. The skills required to accomplish these tasks are in fact not difficult to acquire, but they are usually less common among organized workers than among managers, and they hardly exist among unorganized workers.

While the Minnesota model is more elite-dominated and less driven by

grass-roots activism than some others, as long as the policy remains defined in terms of the managerial tool of job evaluation, the implementation
process will pose similar problems. Following a successful campaign for
comparable worth, power and decision-making generally shift in the direction of technical expertise. The choice of technicians often remains
in the hands of employers and the process of job evaluation becomes
management-dominated. Indeed, managers frequently see an opportunity
to rationalize personnel systems (job descriptions and classification as well
as pay plans), an agenda that further complicates employee and public
perception of just what comparable worth is and is not. In Minnesota,
strong unions have gained some right to participate in the choice of a job
evaluation system, but it remains legally a management prerogative not
subject to collective bargaining. On the other hand, many methods of job
evaluation require a substantial amount of employee participation, the
consequences of which we will explore.

### *Setting the Stage*

Comparable worth emerged as a policy option during World War II and
entered the political agenda in the middle 1970s. It represents a marked
shift from previous methods of overcoming the effects of discrimination
(such as affirmative action or busing) that were designed to eliminate barriers to equality of opportunity. Like protective legislation earlier in the
twentieth century, it intervenes to correct abuses that neither the market
nor labor organizations have effectively prevented. But unlike protective
legislation, it easily extends to most workers who are substantially underpaid regardless of sex or race. Like the minimum wage, it provides a
nonmarket mechanism for wage-setting, though unlike the minimum wage
it does use the market (for white male wages) as an essential reference
point. Finally, like other bureaucratically enforced reforms (such as affirmative action) in which employers must monitor and report on their own
behavior it has been subject to the subversive influences of bureaucratic
manipulation and "human resource management." Yet comparable worth
is also an issue which repoliticizes wage relations against the grain of
bureaucratic and technocratic methods by calling attention to the fact that
wage-setting has always been profoundly political.

Comparable worth emerged out of the widespread feminist and minority activism in the early 1970s which called attention to economic, social,

and legal inequities. For a fuller understanding of the origins and ramifications of comparable worth, we must turn to the history of women's participation in the modern economy and the legal and political responses that participation has provoked for more than a century and a half.

# 2    *The Historical Legacy: Women, Labor, and Politics*

> Plenty of employments are open to
> [women]; but all are underpaid.
> *Caroline Dall, 1860*[1]

The central concern that drives comparable worth is the persistent wage gap of approximately 33% between women and men employed full-time year round.* Much of the feminist, minority, and union activism in the 1970s focused on the serious consequences of inadequate wages for the growing number of female-headed households in which women bear financial as well as emotional responsibility for children and other dependents.[2] Many of these same issues have appeared throughout the history of labor legislation in the nineteenth and twentieth centuries. An examination of this history can expose both the structural underpinnings of the problem comparable worth proposes to address and the ways in which American political culture shapes the debate. It also places comparable worth in the broader context of American feminism as a stream of thought and activism toward the goal of equality for women.

An approach to the origins of comparable worth that locates the issue in policy traditions of both labor legislation and feminist activism has been largely absent from the writing on the subject. In this chapter we show the linkages, and occasionally the ironies, of this double legacy that

---

*This concern was prompted in part because antidiscriminatory measures in the 1960s and early 1970s appeared to have some effect on racially based wages as the differences between black and white wages declined significantly. At the same time, the gap between male and female wages remained roughly the same. Thus, the majority of the research on comparable worth has consistently focused on gender. Recently, the technology has been used to discover and change wage discrimination based on race as well.

has fostered the emergence of comparable worth as "the issue of the eighties."[3]

## Women and Industrialization

The emergence of wage labor accompanied the growth of commercial markets and capitalist industrialization in the late eighteenth and the nineteenth centuries. As historians have recently recognized, these structural changes in the economy which fueled massive transformations in the fabric of American life were strongly gendered from the outset. Industrialization shaped, and was shaped by, new forms of family life—more emotional and affectionate, smaller, centers of consumption as well as of production—and a vibrant, individualistic, competitive, and sometimes violent public political life. The republican political ideology of the American Revolution presumed that citizenship was a right of white men. "All men are created equal" excluded from consideration women, children, slaves, and Indians. Republicanism in that time not only meant "equal rights to participate" but also entailed a theory of property that valued economic independence and rough equality of "property" as the foundation for active and responsible citizenship. Grafted onto the economic theories of Adam Smith, some versions of republican individualism also presumed not only that economic actors were male but that competition (the essence of the market) was an essentially male characteristic.[4] In this configuration, women's duty was "republican motherhood," that is, the bearing and raising of future citizens. Increasingly, the association of women with home (no longer a center of production but instead sharply separated from the market) and with children engendered the middle-class domestic ideology we associate with Victorianism.[5]

Ironically, when the first factories opened to produce woolen textiles, few men were willing to leave farming to work in them. Francis Cabot Lowell, a factory owner in Waltham, Massachusetts, actively recruited young white women by developing a system of dormitories to assure them and their parents of a proper, "homelike" atmosphere. The result was an early industrial labor force of young, white, single women.[6] Such women continued to dominate the textile industry into the twentieth century.

The cultural power of domesticity never prevented women from working for wages (particularly single white women, free blacks, and later freed slaves, and immigrants), but it assured that the economy would distinguish finely between "men's work" and "women's work" and that women would receive substantially lower wages than men. Employers assumed that women were only temporary workers, leaving the labor force upon marriage, and that their income was a secondary supplement to the family economy.[7] In 1820 women's earnings were approximately a third of the earnings of men. By the late nineteenth century they had risen to 54% of men's earnings. "Occupational segregation and low wages for women's work were thus the very bedrock on which U.S. industrialization was built."[8]

As the economy changed, so did women's work patterns, though the degree of occupational segregation remained fairly constant. The concentration of white women in domestic labor began to decline as young white women found alternatives in factories and offices. Black women, however, remained concentrated in agricultural and domestic labor until World War II. Historian Alfred Chandler has traced the emergence in the late nineteenth century of "managerial capitalism," as the scale of American industry grew to encompass a large stratum of middle managers who allocated resources and coordinated economic activities previously controlled by the market.[9] Such massive enterprises required extensive internal communications and record-keeping, which generated a growing demand for clerical workers.

With the introduction of the typewriter in the 1870s, clerical employment rapidly shifted from male apprentice-like work which might lead to a high position in the firm to work done by a highly substitutable female labor force.[10] During the same period, educated women, barred from professions such as medicine and law, created a series of "female professions." Responding to an intense demand for public-school teachers, women feminized teaching, even though their pay was about half that of the male teachers whom they rapidly replaced, and they invented the professions of nursing and social work in the latter half of the nineteenth century. In each case the "female professions" justified their existence with reference to the female qualities of nurture and selflessness rooted in domestic ideology. This association between women's paid labor and their unpaid work in the home provided further justification for the very low pay women's professions commanded.

### Origins of Labor Legislation

The plight of women workers, however, remained relatively invisible in the middle years of the nineteenth century, as unions, legislatures, and courts colluded in the mistaken notion that workers were, by definition, men. The origins of labor legislation lay in the efforts of industrial workers to control abuses through the political system when collective bargaining efforts failed. In the great struggles between owners and workers that raged throughout the nineteenth century the legal power of the state became contested terrain. Workers sought and occasionally won legislation to require that they be paid regularly and in cash, and to place a ceiling on hours and a floor under wages. They fought for a ten-hour and then an eight-hour day and for a "family wage" sufficient to support a male worker and his wife and children. The "family wage," of course, had serious and paradoxical consequences for women. As an ideal, it presumed the middle-class image of the female role as housewife, devoted to home and children and removed from productive, market-oriented labor. Thus it undermined the wage demands of working-class women in the labor force and simultaneously damaged the self-esteem of male workers who consistently failed to achieve a sufficient family wage. It also strengthened the barriers against female access to more highly skilled craft occupations. A "family wage" was by definition a "manly wage." When (mostly male) workers won favorable labor legislation, however, the courts regularly annulled it.[11]

Court decisions reveal the confluence of economic, political, and gender ideology within entrepreneurial republicanism. In 1886 the Pennsylvania Supreme Court declared unconstitutional a law requiring payment of wages in cash rather than in company scrip redeemable only at the company store. The court waxed passionate in its defense of a concept of rights and citizenship tied closely to property and to manhood. The law, it charged, "is not only degrading to his [the employee's] manhood but subversive of his rights as a citizen of the United States. He may sell his labor for what he thinks best, whether money or goods, just as his employer may sell his iron or coal, and every law that proposes to prevent him from so doing, is an infringement upon his constitutional privileges and consequently vicious and void."[12] Similarly, later opponents of a proposed child labor amendment charged that such a law would endanger the family and, implicitly, the proper roles of women and men. *The Manufacturer's Record* (voice of the Southern Association of Science and Industry) editorialized in 1924 that the amendment would undermine parental authority to the extent that it would "keep boys under 18 years of age from driving up the cows" and "the mother would have no right to teach her daughter to do any house work whatsoever, whether it be the sweeping of floors or the washing of dishes."[13]

Not only did the courts presume that workers were male but also, in their view, the maleness of workers appeared to be compromised by state protection and intrusions into the market. Political and legal defeats, in turn, informed the rise of a new, craft-oriented unionism in the 1890s which in many ways reinforced the links between manhood, work, and freedom from the state. The American Federation of Labor (AFL) drew on an older artisanal consciousness to organize highly skilled craft workers. Suspicious of the state, they relied primarily on their own economic power and tough collective bargaining with specific employers. They also policed the boundaries of their crafts against the intrusion of unwanted outsiders: women, and frequently ethnic and racial minorities as well. The combination of judicial intransigence and union hostility helps to explain the logic of the reformers' shift in the late nineteenth century toward focusing on the problems of working women and children, workers for whom "protection" was less of a cultural threat.[14]

### Female Reform and Protective Legislation

This strategic shift toward protective legislation made cultural sense not only in its appeal to jurists but also in relation to the growing power of female reform movements based on domestic ideology. Female progressivism built its critique of the "male" public arena (the state and the economy) from the perspective of domesticity, reclaiming in a different context the marginalized communal dimension of eighteenth-century republicanism. "Home Protection" became the banner under which the Women's Christian Temperance Union (WCTU) sought to eradicate saloons, reform prisons, initiate kindergartens, support parent-school associations and missions for homeless women, and win the vote for women. Frances Willard, president and chief strategist of the WCTU from 1879 to 1898, drew on middle-class women's commitments to clubs and missionary societies and their social definition as moral guardians of the home to bring thousands into public political activity for the first time. The consequence was a redefinition of politics. In the name of the moral values of the home, female political culture had assumed responsibility for the destitute and homeless. In the long run, women demanded that the government assume this responsibility, a major step towards the modern welfare state.[15]

The fight for protective legislation for women and child laborers was one of the principal links between middle-class and working-class reformers. It reflected, from the perspective of union women, failure of the labor movement to organize effectively among working women or to respond to women's own initiatives.[16] Working men also feared that women would get better conditions than they did. For example, the ten-hour day had been established by organized male workers in the building trades as early as 1840, and by 1890 an eight-hour day was standard in collective bargaining agreements in many cities. According to Judith Baer, "[protective] legislation did not reduce women's hours below men's, but brought them—at best—to that level."[17]

The demand that working women be protected by law from exploitation and unhealthful industrial conditions, however, had important cultural consequences. It introduced into law and judicial decision-making a focus on women workers as different from men and justified discrimination based on that difference.[18] The arguments developed to provide legal grounds for protective legislation (and to overcome jurists' adherence to an extreme version of freedom of contract) issued directly from politicized domesticity in their emphasis on motherhood and female weakness and need for protection. Following a series of state court decisions, the U.S. Supreme Court upheld in 1908 an Oregon law limiting women to a ten-hour work day. The arguments marshalled by Louis Brandeis and Josephine Goldmark of the National Consumers League linked protection of women to the national welfare because of women's maternal function. In *Muller v. Oregon* the Court accepted the reasoning that "women's physical stature and the performance of maternal functions place her at a disadvantage." Women required protection "from the greed as well as the passion of man" for the future of the human race.[19] Only two years before, the Court had ruled in *Lochner v. New York* that "[limits on] the hours in which grown and intelligent men may labor to earn their living, are mere meddlesome interferences with the right of the individual."[20]

Following *Muller v. Oregon,* states rapidly passed protective laws, beginning with the regulation of hours. Ironically, these precedents were set to remedy conditions affecting industrial workers at a time when the changing economy was rapidly drawing women into other sectors. After 1900, there was a dramatic decline in the proportion of women in domestic and industrial labor with the rise of the new "pink collar" clerical and service sector. Yet the debate around protective legislation (which remained unchallenged by the courts until the 1960s) continued to define a deep division among feminists. Those in the League of Women Voters, the National Consumers League, and other progressive organizations continued their battle for protection through the 1920s and 1930s as part of a broad program of reform. They were challenged in those decades by the

National Women's Party under the leadership of Alice Paul, which espoused a version of feminism rooted in the basic republican concepts of citizenship, equal treatment, and economic independence.

The earliest versions of this "republican feminism" can be traced to the writings of individual women during the American Revolution, to the Seneca Falls Declaration in 1848 ("We hold these truths to be self-evident, that all men and women are created equal"), and to Sarah Grimke's classic statement: "I ask no favors for my sex. I surrender not our claim to equality. All I ask our brethren is that they will take their heels from our necks and permit us to stand upright on that ground which God designed us to occupy."[21] In the early nineteenth century feminists bypassed the inequalities and economic dependence of women in the family except to advocate laws granting married women the right to own and control property, an advantage in a commercial age when a husband could not lose assets held in his wife's name. By the late nineteenth century, however, theorists like Charlotte Perkins Gilman had begun to argue that without economic independence women would remain unable to exercise civic rights such as the vote in any meaningful way.[22]

The most direct descendant of this perspective in the twentieth century has been the struggle for the Equal Rights Amendment, initiated in 1923 by the National Woman's Party following the achievement of woman suffrage in 1920. Leaders like Alice Paul spoke eloquently for women's rights to equal participation, equal legal protection, equal access and opportunity. Attacking protective legislation, they emphasized the humiliation as well as the concrete wrongs created by laws which treated women as weak, dependent, and childlike. But their republican vision was a thin and highly individualistic one. The civic purposes of economic independence were lost as "public" became identified with massive bureaucracies, and citizenship lost the implicit communal overtones and became simply individual exercise of "rights" like voting and free speech. Opponents, sensing this, viewed the first ERA as a selfish attempt on the part of professional women to enhance their opportunities at the expense of working-class women.

On both sides of the battle over protective legislation, however, feminists had come to view the state as the source of the solution. This dependence on the state created dilemmas as well as opportunities for feminists in a political culture that strongly supported the ethos of individualism. Progressive-era feminists essentially wanted to wed mother nature (in the form of an ideology of separate endowments) to a father state (in the form of protection). But father state was also the patriarch that had often left men with only limited legal rights to act collectively in the workplace against an unstable capitalism, and had opposed both economic and political rights for women. This complicated push for protective legislation continued in the courtrooms and legislatures through the middle years of the twentieth century, years when a broad-based women's movement did not exist.

In 1938, with the passage of the Fair Labor Standards Act, the Congress and the courts finally accepted the legitimacy of regulating hours, wages, and working conditions for all workers. Proponents and opponents in the 1937 hearings expressed views not unlike those currently under debate around comparable worth. Would such as interference in the market create unemployment, inflation, and economic disorder? Was interference necessary, reasonable, and just? Was regulation constitutional?[23] Defenders of protective legislation continued to maintain that laws like those regulating women's hours, night work, wages, and working conditions would be struck down by the courts if applied to men and should therefore be maintained against threats such as the ERA. But the nineteenth-century fusion of politics, economics, and gender had lost its hegemonic force. It was no longer persuasive to identify work with manhood and rugged independence and women with dependence, weakness, and state protection. Too many men were helplessly unemployed and too many industrial workers had joined the Congress of Industrial Organizations (CIO) with the assistance of federal protection for opponents of regulation to maintain that a worker's manhood would be harmed by state intervention. And too many women had joined the labor force for them to be portrayed as pitiable anomalies.

## Women and the Twentieth-Century Economy

The steadily growing number of women entering the labor force after about 1870 had changed the context for all of these debates by mid-century. In 1900 only one in five adult women worked outside the home and these women were predominantly young and single. By 1940 the ratio was one in four; by 1950, one in three, of whom most were married and over thirty-five years old. By 1980 the majority (52%) of women had joined the labor force. What could be portrayed as an unusual and perhaps desperate condition in earlier years had become the norm. And the problem of women's low wages had taken on new proportions.

Historians and economists debate the causes of these changes. Cer-

tainly the managerial revolution and the growth of the service sector drove
much of the economic change in the twentieth century, creating jobs open
to women—clerical and secretarial work, jobs in hospitals, schools, communications industries, and public accommodations. Economic growth
and rising productivity raised real wages for both women and men significantly. Economist Barbara Bergmann argues that the quadrupling of
women's real wages since 1890 explains their willingness to enter the
labor force.[24] Others point to the changed supply of female workers due
to increased longevity and decreased fertility, resulting in significantly different life patterns no longer defined by the rhythms of pregnancy, child-
birth, and lactation.[25] As shown in figure 2.1, the result of these changes
has been that each successive cohort of women has joined the labor force
in greater numbers and with greater persistence over time.

The emergence of a managerial elite within large-scale industries and
of scientific management gradually changed wage-setting practices. The
late nineteenth- and early twentieth-century American economy was characterized by extreme competition. Industrial and financial giants emerged
at the expense of hundreds of small and moderate-sized businesses. Business practices designed to manage vertically integrated corporations on a
new scale sought to replace cutthroat competition with greater predictabil-
ity and control.[26] Where previously the competitive market had determined wages, large-scale businesses began to look for ways to rationalize
their pay systems in light of growing specialization and internal promotions. New forms of management and industrial organization, in place by
the early twentieth century, placed a premium on the analysis of tasks for
the purpose of making production more efficient and predictable. By
World War I, professional management consultants provided advice on the
reorganization of corporate structures and governments as well.[27]

From time-motion studies, planning departments, and careful attention
to allocation of tasks and lines of responsibility, it was but a short step to
the creation of systems of job evaluation which could rank jobs in terms
of their relative value to the corporation, for the purpose of setting wages.
At the government level, the rationalization of wages began with the Bureau of Municipal Research in New York which introduced Frederick Taylor's ideas regarding efficiency and scientific management: "Taylor's insistence upon the exact measurement of tasks [found] a parallel in the
Bureau's campaign for job standardization in public employment. This
involved the orderly arrangement of titles and salaries tied to accurate
'work values,' so as to enable the public executives to supervise employees closely."[28]

The first job evaluation system to assign points as a measure of job

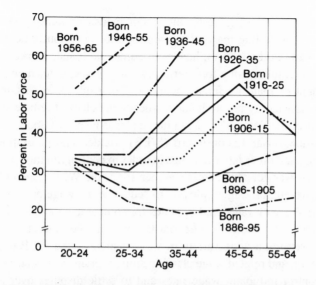

**Fig. 2.1 Labor Force Participation by Age of All U.S. Women Born 1886–1965.**
(Sources: Barbara R. Bergmann, *The Economic Emergence of Women* [New York: Basic Books, 1986], p. 23, in Linda J. Waite, "U.S. Women at Work," *Population Bulletin* 36:2 [Washington, D.C.: Population Reference Bureau, 1981], 8.)

worth was developed in 1925 by Merrill R. Lott.[29] During the 1930s, the use of job evaluation became increasingly focused on rationalized wage structures and effective wage administration in response to the growth of industrial unionism. But before the Second World War, however, no one advocated using job evaluation systems to rectify market-based discrimination. It was quite legal, and rather common, at that time to pay men and women differently for exactly the same jobs. And major companies like Westinghouse explicitly priced female jobs below comparably rated male jobs. The Westinghouse wage administration manual explained:

> The gradient of the women's wage curve is not the same for women as for men because of the more transient character of the service of the former, the relative shortness of their activity in industry, the differences in environment required, the extra services that must be provided, overtime limitations, extra help needed for the occasional heavy work, and the general sociological factors not requiring discussion herein.[30]

Job evaluation, then, had evolved by the end of the 1930s as a management tool, useful in wage administration but also in hiring, placement, supervision, and other managerial tasks.

It was the economic exigencies of the Second World War which forced the problem of women's wages onto the political agenda. By 1943, with the active assistance of government, major industries were forced to recruit women, including married women, into jobs previously held exclusively by men. Union leaders, however, feared that female workers would be paid less, resulting in a long-term lowering of wages for men and the displacement of male by female workers. Their efforts to sustain wage rates were assisted by research and advocacy in behalf of female workers by the staff of the Women's Bureau in the Department of Labor.

The National War Labor Board (WLB) wielded enormous power in wage setting and other labor disputes in order to control inflation and labor unrest in the war economy. In November 1942, the WLB issued General Order No. 16 authorizing employers to "equalize the wage or salary rates paid to females with rates paid to males for comparable quality and quantity of work."[31] According to one War Labor Board hearing officer, in the process of settling a wide variety of wage disputes, "the WLB turned to job evaluation and related wage classification programs as a necessary tool both to control intraplant wage rates and to settle disputes over alleged intraplant inequities. It was then that job evaluation and other wage classification systems began their tremendous growth and expansion."[32]

The decisions of the WLB, however, remained ambiguous. It declined to use an equal pay principle for traditionally female jobs on the grounds that wages assigned to women only were "presumed to be correct."[33] In 1945 the United Electric Workers (UE) brought a case to the WLB charging that General Electric and Westinghouse systematically devalued the work of women in female job classifications. They used the companies' own job evaluation systems to prove their case and received an affirmative decision from the WLB on virtually the same grounds as later comparable worth cases. The decisions were never implemented, however, as the WLB's authority ended after the war.[34]

While some trade unions, led by the Women's Bureau of the United Auto Workers (UAW) and women in several other CIO unions such as the United Electrical Workers, with their allies in the U.S. Women's Bureau in the Department of Labor continued to defend protective legislation and to oppose the first ERA, in the postwar era they turned to the state level to lobby for equal pay legislation. Despite some encouraging precedents established during the war and a few labor contracts specifying "equal pay for equal work," the gap between male and female wages actually increased. In 1939, full-time working women earned 62% of the wages their male colleagues received. Immediately after the war the figure dropped to 55% and by 1950 it was 53%.[35] This may reflect in part the resegregation of the labor force that rapidly occurred following the war as women were forced out of higher-paying industrial jobs and back into lower-paying industrial and service work. Several states passed equal pay laws between 1945 and 1960, including some with "comparable worth" language, though there is little evidence of enforcement in such terms.[36] This shift away from protection and toward the problem of discrimination drew heavily on the precedents established by laws against racial discrimination.[37] At the same time, advocates of the ERA, centered around the small and aging inner circle of the National Woman's Party, opposed equal pay legislation because of their suspicion and hostility towards the U.S. Women's Bureau.[38]

The passage of the Equal Pay Act in 1963 achieved the first national legislation forbidding discrimination against women workers. It came during a Democratic administration in which the labor movement enjoyed considerable influence, and followed the report of the President's Commission on the Status of Women, which reintroduced women's rights onto the national political agenda. In its original formulation, the Equal Pay Act would have set a standard similar to "comparable worth" by requiring equal pay for "work of comparable character on jobs the performance of which requires comparable skills." The secretary of labor at the time, Arthur Goldberg, argued that comparability could be determined through the use of job evaluation systems. The act was amended to change "comparable" to "equal" and to define "equal work" as jobs of "equal skill, effort, and responsibility and . . . performed under similar working conditions." Without the final clause, even "equal work" could have meant work valued equally by a job evaluation system. But with it, the courts interpreted the law narrowly to mean virtually identical work. For example, a female nurse who could show that she was paid less for the same work done by a male nurse could win a case under the Equal Pay Act. But if she were paid less than a male pharmacist whose job was rated equally with hers in their employer's job evaluation plan, she would have no recourse. The Equal Pay Act also provided exceptions for unequal pay based on "merit, seniority, quality, and quantity of production, and any other factor other than sex."[39] These exceptions are known as the affirmative defenses of unequal pay.

Effective enforcement of the Equal Pay Act was assured by its passage as an amendment to the Fair Labor Standards Act (FLSA), administered by the Wage and Hour Division of the Department of Labor. By the same token, coverage was restricted to workers already covered under the FLSA (61% of all wage and salary earners).

In the early 1960s, women benefited far more, however, from the rising political power of the civil rights movement than from previous labor leg-islation. The original draft of Title VII of the Civil Rights Act of 1964 prohibited discrimination in all aspects of employment on the bases of race, color, religion, and country of origin. An amendment offered by Democratic Representative Howard Smith of Virginia added "sex" to the list. Smith, an opponent of the act itself, appeared to offer the amendment as a joke, with the intention of weakening the chances of passage. He did so, however, in part at the instigation of constituents who were members of the National Woman's Party. A long-time supporter of the ERA, he, and many feminists at that time, combined an opposition to civil rights for minorities with advocacy (of a chivalric sort) of women's rights.[40] What-ever Smith's intentions, with the leadership of Democratic Representative Martha Griffiths of Michigan, women members of the House strongly backed the amendment and won. The only female opponent in the House was Democratic Representative Edith Green of Oregon, who accepted the view of the Women's Bureau that the amendment was a hostile move which could undermine support for the bill as a whole.[41] Indeed, only one of the men who supported the amendment to include "sex" actually voted for the Civil Rights Act itself.[42]

When the bill reached the Senate both President Johnson and the Wom-en's Bureau, in the interest of swift passage, decided not to oppose the inclusion of "sex."[43] The bill finally passed with a "technical amendment" proposed by Republican Senator Wallace F. Bennett of Utah providing that employers could "differentiate upon the basis of sex in determining the amount of wages or compensation . . . if such differentiation is autho-rized by the [Equal Pay Act]."[44]

Interpretations of the Bennett Amendment have become central to those interested in legal strategies for implementing comparable worth. Does it in fact limit the scope of Title VII to the provisions of the Equal Pay Act? More specifically, is Title VII, through the Bennett Amendment, limited only to those jobs covered by the Fair Labor Standards Act? Is Title VII restricted to cases involving "equal" or identical work? Or does the Ben-nett Amendment only incorporate the four affirmative defenses of unequal pay (seniority, merit, quality or quantity of goods produced, and factors other than sex), thus opening the door to comparisons of different but equally valued jobs? In the late 1960s, however, this legal debate remained in the background. The Equal Employment Opportunity Commission, charged with enforcing the Civil Rights Act, virtually ignored sex dis-crimination cases on the assumption that the inclusion of "sex" was a bothersome "joke."[45]

The accomplishment of the civil rights movement in terms of public policy in the 1960s was to make equality of rights and opportunity a part of the political consensus that had emerged in the postwar era. These were added to other components of the welfare state, which included a commitment to government intervention in the economy to maintain high consumption/high employment, basic rights for (presumably male) workers, and a much more generous social safety net for the (presumably female, or juvenile) dependent poor.[46]

The extension of equality of rights and opportunity to women, however, was accomplished only with the visible activity of a reborn feminist movement in the late 1960s and early 1970s. The founding of the National Organization for Women (NOW) in 1966 brought together professional women, political activists, and members of the UAW Women's Bureau.[47] The emergence of a radical women's liberation movement a year later galvanized a younger generation of college-educated activists to challenge the gendered definitions of both public and private life in fundamental terms.[48]

NOW's initial focus on the enforcement of Title VII emphasized equality of opportunity, challenging the legality of segregated want ads and demanding affirmative action in hiring and promotion. Revived feminism, in both its liberal and radical approaches, was in many ways very individualistic, often an unknowing heir of Alice Paul in its demands for *access* to economic opportunity and reproductive freedom. This explains the centrality of the ERA as a symbolic demand. Title VII had undermined the legality of most protective legislation, and as women began to file claims not only against their employers but also against their unions, key union leaders dropped their opposition to the ERA by the late 1960s and early 1970s. With the ancient breach between advocates of women workers and self-defined feminists healed, the ERA passed Congress in 1972. While politicians and feminists battled over the ratification of the ERA in the subsequent decade, however, a combination of political and economic changes shifted policy alternatives away from individual opportunity and towards the problem of wage justice.


### Emergence of Comparable Worth as "The Issue of the Eighties"


During the 1970s labor-force participation became normative for adult women. That shift, a product of continuous change throughout the century, represented a major structural change. The majority of families no longer fit a nuclear, male-supported model. As figure 2.2 shows, labor force participation-rates of each successive cohort in the twentieth century far surpassed the expectations of women themselves at least until 1973. According to economist Claudia Goldin, "no generation of young women in America could have predicted solely from the experiences of their elders what their own work histories would have been."[49]

Increased labor force participation for women had been driven since the Second World War by the fact that many families could enter the middle class only with two incomes.[50] In addition, the growth in female-headed households multiplied the numbers of women seeking jobs. Figure 2.3 reveals that divorce rates, rising through the century, soared in the sixties. Together with increasing rates of out-of-wedlock births, divorces created a large pool of female-headed, single-parent households. Subsequent studies demonstrated the economic devastation of divorce for young mothers, whose standard of living on average fell 73% (compared to men, whose standard of living following divorce rose 42%).[51] In 1978 Diana Pearce's study coined the term "feminization of poverty" to describe the

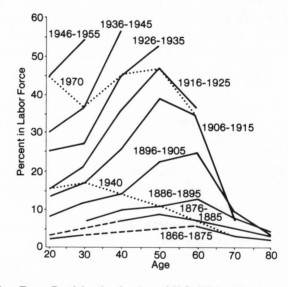

**Fig. 2.2 Labor Force Participation by Age of U.S. White Married Women Born 1866–1955.** (Source: Claudia Goldin, "The Earnings Gap in Historical Perspective," in U.S. Civil Rights Commission, *Comparable Worth: Issue for the 80's* [June 6–7, 1984], vol. 1, p. 9.)

*Note:* Dashed lines denote missing data. Data for 1890 to 1920 are for native-born women with native-born parents. Dotted line is cross-section.

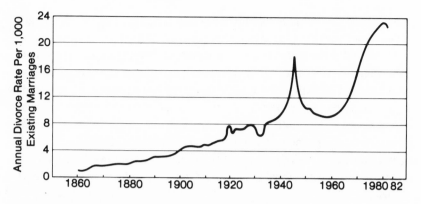

**Fig. 2.3 U.S. Divorce Rates, 1860–1982.** (Source: Barbara R. Bergmann, *The Economic Emergence of Women* [New York: Basic Books, 1986], p. 52, adapted from Arland Thornton and Deborah Freedman, "The Changing American Family," *Population Bulletin* 38:4 [October 1983], p. 7.)
*Note:* Divorces per year per 1,000 existing marriages.

growing underclass of women and children unable to sustain a minimal standard of living.[52]

While the economic burden of female heads-of-household became an increasingly visible issue, real wages for all workers began a serious decline in the mid-1970s, and income inequality rose.[53] The service sector continued its rapid growth in response to technological innovations, generating relatively low-paid jobs in traditionally female-dominated fields. But the economy as a whole began to stagnate as the manufacturing sector began to shrink. Between 1958 and 1968 there were four million new jobs in manufacturing; in the next decade there were less than one million. From 1978 to 1983 the manufacturing sector lost three million jobs.[54] One economist has argued that "this stagnation and decline was contemporaneous with the slowdown in U.S. productivity growth, the transformation of the employment base towards service jobs, and perhaps the growing hostility of whites towards redistributive and other policies aimed at improving the socioeconomic position of minorities."[55]

Women and minorities thus faced serious problems in deciding how to address questions of equity and justice in the political climate of the 1970s and 1980s. Affirmative action and equal opportunity fell on hard times while they also appeared to benefit only a few. Comparable worth was one attempt to reach a broader constituency and shift the ground of the debate towards a policy that would be effective and successful.[56] Several factors coalesced to place comparable worth on the political agenda despite an increasingly hostile political climate. Most important was the self-organization of women at many levels of American society.

Mobilized at the grass roots by a variety of organizations, women and minorities began to make new demands on employers, unions, and government alike. A skilled and knowledgeable network of women in government at national, state, and local levels increasingly lent their support to efforts to resolve a number of the demands made in the name of women. A shared agenda emerged from this politically powerful coalition as it debated the problems of working women in union halls, working women's organizations, professional associations, government agencies, and courtrooms.

Women's influence within the labor movement grew visibly in the 1970s. In part this was due to a decline in the traditionally male union strongholds of heavy industry, which began to lose members and political clout. The only unions experiencing significant growth were those organizing clerical and service workers and the traditionally female professions of teaching, nursing, and librarianship. Furthermore, the self-organization of working women both inside and outside unions raised new and stronger voices defending their interests.

In 1974 clerical workers in Boston and Chicago created a new kind of workplace organization modeled on community organizations rather than on labor unions. Their goal was to tap into and politicize the female networks within offices. In Chicago, for example, Women Employed conducted a nationally televised sit-in at a law office that had fired a secretary for refusing to make coffee. Both Women Employed and 9 to 5 in Boston adroitly used Title VII and affirmative action guidelines to build campaigns against discriminatory employers and to win legal victories.[57]

At the same time, women in traditional labor unions created their own organization, the Coalition of Labor Union Women (CLUW). Structurally, CLUW was conservative, remaining within the labor movement and refraining from independent action, particularly in the area of organizing. Yet CLUW broke down the isolation of women within specific unions and forced the labor movement to recognize women as an important constituency for the first time. Organizers of the founding meeting developed their network initially through associations outside the labor movement itself. The director of the Women's Bureau under President Nixon, Libby Koontz, initiated a series of lunch meetings with labor union women that began to build networks across specific union affiliations. And Olga Madar of the UAW recalled meeting Addie Wyatt of the meatcutters through an organization in support of the farmworkers' strike. The appearance of

3,000 women at CLUW's founding meeting in Chicago when only 800 had been expected signalled the intensity of women's interest and need for solidarity.[58]

In the highly feminized service sector, the growth of unions such as the American Federation of State, County, and Municipal Employees (AFSCME), the Service Employees International Union (SEIU), and the Communications Workers of America (CWA); the networks and greater voice in the AFL-CIO generated by CLUW; and the emergence of clerical workers' organizations were major factors in the emergence of a comparable worth strategy. For female-dominated unions and clerical workers' associations comparable worth provided not only material benefits for current members but also a key issue around which they could organize new members.

Professional women began to assert their interests as well. By the late 1960s, the proportion of women in most professions had begun to increase, reversing a forty-year trend. Feminized professions found a new assertiveness that demanded respect, autonomy, and adequate remuneration for teachers, nurses, and librarians, often through the process of collective bargaining. Members of traditionally female professions were among the first workers to raise the issues underlying what came to be called comparable worth. For example, librarians at the University of California at Berkeley conducted a study in 1971 which showed that librarians earned 25 to 27% less than persons in other (predominantly male) academic nonteaching positions.[59] Similarly, teachers' unions in Minnesota and elsewhere began to bargain for uniform pay scales, thus eliminating the differential between high school teachers (mostly men) and elementary teachers (mostly women). In several places, notably Washington state and San Jose, California, management job evaluation studies that were quickly implemented with substantial raises for female managers caught the eye of labor organizers and precipitated demands for similar reclassifications of clerical workers.[60]

The emergence in the late 1960s and early 1970s of the new feminism reflected in new labor organizing and grass-roots activism had important political consequences in the form of specific legislation and legal interpretations. The Equal Employment Opportunity Commission (EEOC) began to enforce Title VII prohibitions against sex discrimination more vigorously. Title IX of the Education Amendments of 1972 and the Women's Educational Equality Act provided greater educational opportunities for women and support for female athletics. The ERA passed Congress in 1972 and the Supreme Court ruled in 1973 that abortion in the first trimester of pregnancy was a constitutionally protected private decision between a woman and her physician. State commissions on the status of women and new organizations such as the National Women's Political Caucus and the Women's Equity Action League nourished networks of powerful women, providing intersections between politicians, professionals, unionists, and grass-roots activists.[61]

Commissions and local groups churned out studies in state after state documenting women's legal and economic disabilities. A recurrent conclusion of these studies was that "equal pay" was not a successful strategy. The wage gap between full-time working women and men had remained unchanged since World War II. Despite dramatic increases in female employment, full-time women workers continued to take home less than 60% of the average male wage.[62] In puzzling out the reasons, researchers pointed out that women and men rarely worked in the same jobs and therefore the Equal Pay Act was not applicable in most instances. Unions with large proportions of clerical workers began to urge studies of job segregation and pay practices.

## *Explicit Demands for Comparable Worth*

In 1973 women's organizations in Washington State approached the Washington Federation of State, County, and Municipal Employees with a concern that state pay practices, keyed to prevailing wages, discriminated against women. Republican Governor Dan Evans responded with a request that the two state personnel boards conduct a study "to identify those job classifications predominantly and traditionally held by women where salaries fall below job classifications typically filled by men having a comparable level of skill requirements and job responsibilities."[63] The report in January 1974 set the pattern for subsequent comparable worth studies.* It plotted male jobs and female jobs, defined as classes that were

---

*Debates about the validity of the study also set future patterns. The governor appointed an Advisory Committee to oversee the study, composed of representatives of business, labor, the governor's office, the personnel systems, and women. An Evaluation Committee of eleven state employees and two private-sector members then worked with the consultant to assign points and rank the jobs. The Advisory Committee also suggested that Norman D. Willis and Associates, the firm conducting the study, hire a female consultant. In a later critique, economist June O'Neill referred to the Evaluation Committee as "thirteen politically chosen individuals," implying that the resulting rankings, to which she took exception, might be explained in this way. Helen Remick, "Major Issues in *a priori* Applications," in Remick, ed., *Comparable Worth and Wage Discrimination*, 102; June O'Neill, "An Argument Against Comparable Worth," in U.S. Civil Rights Commission, *Comparable Worth: Issue for the 80's*, 183.

two-thirds or more of one sex, on a graph which had points from the job evaluation system drawn along one axis and salaries along the other. Regression lines, drawn for male and female jobs, demonstrated the difference between pay scales for men and women (see figure 2.4).

This pilot study led to a full-fledged "Comparable Worth Study" conducted by Norman D. Willis and Associates that was completed in December 1974. That study demonstrated a 20% average salary difference between equivalently rated male and female jobs (defined as classes with 70% or more men or women). Governor Evans hailed it as "a landmark study not only for state government but for industry, other governments in the state of Washington and perhaps even a landmark study insofar as the United States is concerned."[64] In 1974, AFSCME representatives in Minnesota also bargained for an agreement that the state would conduct a job evaluation study to determine whether there were internal inequities in pay, but the study was not conducted.

In 1976 AFSCME in California sent business agent Maxine Jenkins to its local in San Jose, California, where female employees were known to be unhappy about their wages.[65] With strong leadership from city librarians, the union's women's caucus conducted its own study and produced a position paper in 1977 entitled "Women Working: Eliminating Sex Dis-

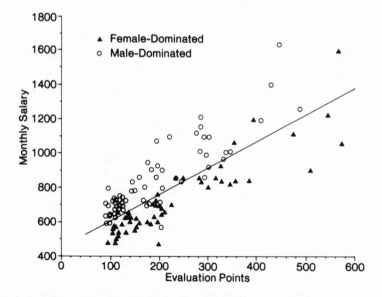

**Fig. 2.4 Distribution of Washington State Government Job Classes by Pay Scale and Evaluation Points, 1974.** (Source: Helen Remick, "Major Issues in A Priori Applications," in Helen Remick, ed., *Comparable Worth and Wage Discrimination* [Philadelphia: Temple University Press, 1984], 103.)

crimination from the Pay and Personnel Practices of the City of San Jose."
By 1978, with a woman mayor and female-dominated city council, the
union demanded an "equity standard" for city pay practices. In 1979, city
management reluctantly agreed to fund a study based on the Hay Associates' point-factor system.[66]

The issue of the wage gap was further dramatized in the mid-1970s by
a National Organization for Women campaign emphasizing that women
earn fifty-nine cents for every dollar earned by men. Pins, bumper stick-
ers, and posters bearing the "59¢" slogan were highly effective in generating widespread recognition of women's low wages.[67] The use of aggregate wage differential figures as an organizing device, however, proved
misleading and complicated the public education task of comparable
worth advocates. Aggregate data combine two separate problems into one
figure. One problem is the position of women in the labor force as a
whole, their predominance in lower-skilled jobs and their absence from
management and high-status, high-salary professions. The other problem
is the relatively low pay of female-dominated jobs in comparison to the
pay for equivalent jobs occupied by men. Each problem, one could argue,
is a product of historic discrimination, but the forms of discrimination are
different as are the remedies. For the former, access to education and affirmative action can ensure equality of opportunity. For the latter, the policy
proposed is comparable worth.

As job segregation and women's low wages received increasing attention, litigation soon followed when collective bargaining failed or was
unavailable. When nursing administrators in Denver recognized in 1973
that their salaries were lower than those of other city and county administrators, they joined with the Colorado Nurses Association (CNA) to initiate a suit on behalf of all the nurses working for the city and county of
Denver. Following the tradition of *Griggs v. Duke Power Co.* the CNA
took a "disparate impact" approach to Title VII by arguing that the "facially neutral" policies of the Denver Career Service Board, which established salaries for city and county employees, had a disproportionate impact on women.[68] CNA lawyer Craig Barnes asserted that the board's
procedures "were so infected with bias that there was no way that they
could come up with a nondiscriminatory result. And so the process resulted in disparate impact across the board against women."[69] Though
their case became famous for its comparison of nurses with tree trimmers,
the CNA lost in District Court and again in the Tenth Circuit Court of
Appeals. Judge Winner of the Appeals Court ruled that, though the plaintiffs had proved discrimination, the law could do nothing about it. By the

time of his ruling in 1978 the term "comparable worth" was increasingly in use. In *Lemons v. City and County of Denver* Judge Winner called comparable worth a "pandora's box" which would open up government regulation of the entire wage structure.[70] The U.S. Supreme Court refused certiorari in 1980.

The same year that Denver nurses first consulted their lawyer, lawyers for the International Union of Electrical Workers filed an EEOC complaint claiming wage discrimination. In the subsequent suit, filed in 1974, lawyer Winn Newman did not use the rhetoric of comparable worth but argued that Westinghouse discriminated by devaluing women's jobs in a segregated labor force. Like the Denver nurses, Westinghouse workers challenged restrictive interpretations of the Bennett Amendment and emphasized wage discrimination by using statistical measures modeled on successful minority cases. The Third Circuit Court of Appeals ruled in favor of the plaintiffs in *International Union of Electrical Workers v. Westinghouse Electric Corporation* on the grounds that the Bennett Amendment did not limit Title VII to cases where the work performed was essentially the same. The Court argued that

> the claimed policy of the employer in deliberately setting wage rates lower for those job classifications which were predominantly filled by females than for job classifications which were predominantly filled by males would, if proven, be a violation of the Civil Rights Act of 1964 even though the jobs predominantly held by women were not the same as the jobs predominantly held by men.[71]

In 1981 the Supreme Court, following the *Gunther* decision (see below), declined to review the case.

Cases which reached the courts came out of a massive number of complaints received by the EEOC. By the late 1970s there were signs that the EEOC itself was moving toward an interpretation of Title VII compatible with comparable worth. In 1977 the EEOC chair, Eleanor Holmes Norton, commissioned the National Academy of Sciences study to examine "the issues involved in a 'comparable worth' concept of job compensation."[72] By that time the terms of the debate around "comparable worth" had become clear both in the legal debates over Title VII and in the use of job evaluation systems to determine which jobs should be considered "comparable." Advocates, wishing to consolidate their efforts into a broad strategy for change, created the National Committee on Pay Equity in 1979. In so doing, they signalled the newly emerging rhetorical preference for "pay equity" rather than "comparable worth."

The intellectual case for comparable worth, in both legal and economic terms, received full statements in the late seventies and early eighties with the publication of two classic studies. Lawyer Ruth G. Blumrosen spelled out in the *University of Michigan Journal of Law Review* the case for consideration of labor force segmentation as a legal basis for sex-based wage discrimination.[73] And the report of the Committee on Occupational Classification and Analysis of the National Academy of Sciences concluded "that the substantial influence of institutional and traditional arrangements makes it impossible to view current wage rates as set solely by the free play of neutral forces operating in an entirely open market, no matter how attractive such a theoretical formulation may be."[74] Published in 1981, *Women, Work, and Wages: Equal Pay for Jobs of Equal Value,* edited by Donald Treiman and Heidi Hartmann, concluded that "one approach, which needs further development but shows some promise, is to use existing job evaluation plans as a standard for comparing the relative worth of jobs."[75]

While litigation and research proceeded, labor actions in favor of comparable worth also occurred. In San Jose, the completed Hay Associates study became available in December 1980. Prudence Slaathaug, AFSCME Local 101 business agent, called it "absolute dynamite. People had it photocopied and routed throughout the city in about five minutes."[76] Union leaders expected a quick response from the city council, which had voted 14% raises for 366 managerial positions on the basis of a similar Hay Associates managerial study released in May.[77] Labor negotiations foundered, however, on the complexities of implementation and management's fiscal caution in the wake of Proposition 13, which slashed property taxes. The result was the first comparable-worth strike, and as such it received immediate national attention; but there were others as well. In 1981 employees of the Anoka-Hennepin Independent School District 11 in Minnesota also went on strike to protest the fact that secretarial pay was lower than the wages paid to school custodians, but they did not name their grievance comparable worth. Strikers who publicized their actions as comparable worth struggles, however, received national attention as, for example, when members of the Yale Clerical and Technical Workers Union, Local 34 of the Federation of University Employees, walked out in 1984 on the grounds that their pay was discriminatory.[78] They became the first private-sector clerical union to strike for pay equity.[79]

The publicity generated by comparable worth strikes sparked further grass-roots activism. Unions, such as an autonomous clerical union in Contra Costa County, California, which for many years had demanded increased affirmative action and equal opportunity, seized upon comparable worth. One activist, already frustrated with the differentials between men's and women's wages, explained, "The comparable worth issue came up when San Jose went on strike. I became a lot more enlightened, and pretty outraged."[80] Similarly, women in an AFSCME local in Hennepin County, Minnesota, and members of the Minneapolis chapter of Working Women, an organization of clerical workers, conducted their own studies in 1983 and began campaigns to eliminate wage discrimination by sex.[81] The appearance of grass-roots social movements for comparable worth clearly speeded dissemination of this policy. But the more dominant forms of activism tended to be elite-controlled litigative and legislative strategies. Even union negotiations for comparable worth proceeded in some areas without the mobilization of the rank and file.

Two key court cases broadened the potential for litigation on sex-based wage discrimination. The Supreme Court handed down a landmark decision in 1981 in *County of Washington v. Gunther,* which broadened legal interpretation of the Bennett Amendment.[82] The case had been brought by female prison guards in Oregon who argued that their wages were unfairly lower than those of male prison guards. Theirs was not an equal pay case, however, since their work differed from that of male guards in important respects. In a narrowly constructed decision which explicitly avoided the issue of comparable worth, the Court ruled that the Bennett Amendment to Title VII incorporated only the four affirmative defenses of the Equal Pay Act rather than the Act as a whole. In other words, seniority, merit, quality and quantity of work, and factors other than sex were accepted as reasons to have different wages, but the absolute requirement for substantially equal jobs was not. *Gunther* was hailed by advocates of comparable worth as opening the door to Title VII litigation.

The same year, AFSCME in Washington State filed a suit charging sex-based discrimination. Economic reversals and a more hostile administration had led the state to ignore the Willis study and refuse to implement its recommendations. Governor Dixie Lee Ray publicly ridiculed comparable worth as "apples and pumpkins and a can of worms."[83] In frustration, the union filed an EEOC complaint and then hired lawyer Winn Newman to sue the state. In 1983 Judge Jack Tanner of the U.S. District Court ruled in *AFSCME v. State of Washington* that the state of Washington had discriminated against women by systematically paying female-dominated job classes lower wages than comparably rated male-dominated classes.[84] The case made headlines across the country for two reasons. It broke new legal ground with a successful argument for sex

discrimination based on statistical demonstrations that facially neutral policies had a "disparate impact" on women; the argument in this case paralleled arguments made successfully in Title VII cases involving minority
rights. Media attention, however, was probably captured even more by
Judge Tanner's award of more than ten years of back pay, which some
estimated to be as high as half a billion dollars.

*Gunther* and *AFSCME v. State of Washington* encouraged proponents
of comparable worth to broaden their efforts. Legislation joined litigation
and labor negotiations as a strategy to win comparable worth. In rapid
succession many states outside of the South established comparable worth
study commissions, passed comparable worth legislation, and even began
to distribute comparable worth raises. These laws focused, as we have
mentioned before, primarily on the state-level public work force. No legislature was willing to require comparable worth of the private sector,
although a number of states, most notably California, have studied it.

In the wake of all this hostility, comparable worth became, not surprisingly, a hotly contested, partisan issue. In 1984, the Reagan administration, following the lead of private sector opposition, shifted from quiet to
active opposition, while Democratic presidential candidates Walter Mondale, John Glenn, and Gary Hart espoused comparable worth.[85] Agencies
which had pressed for comparable worth, notably the Equal Employment
Opportunity Commission and the Civil Rights Commission, became bas-
tions of hostility. In January 1984 the Justice Department recommended
that the administration challenge Judge Tanner's order and support the
state of Washington in its appeal. Michael J. Horowitz, counsel to the
director of the Office of Management and Budget, argued that comparable
worth benefited white middle-class women at the expense of Blacks.
"There is nothing the Reagan Administration has done that holds as much
long-term threat to the black community as comparable worth. The maintenance man will be paid less so the librarian can be paid more."[86] Such
assertions were clearly a tactic to divide the natural constituency for comparable worth in recognition of increasing insistence by advocates that the
concept could be applied to race as well as sex. The result was a series of
articles about the consequences of comparable worth for racial and ethnic
minorities. Economist Julianne Malveaux, for example, argued persua-
sively that, while comparable worth would not solve all the economic
problems of Blacks, it would make a major contribution to Black women
and to Black men employed in female-dominated fields.[87]

The Civil Rights Commission held a series of hearings on comparable
worth in June 1984, making no secret of the opposition of Staff Director

Linda Chavez and Chairman Clarence Pendleton to the issue. Anxieties about the gender gap during the 1984 election silenced opposition from that time until November, but Pendleton grabbed headlines with his "Looney Tunes" statement immediately after Reagan trounced Mondale and Ferraro.[88] The following spring the Commission's Reagan-appointed majority voted 5–2 to reject comparable worth as a remedy for sex bias in the workplace.[89] Two months later the EEOC voted unanimously to reject "pure" comparable worth cases, where there was no evidence of intentional discrimination.[90]

The loss of administration support paralleled the fate of the Washington State case in the courts. In 1985 *AFSCME v. State of Washington* was reversed by the Ninth Circuit Court of Appeals. Plaintiffs subsequently decided not to appeal to the Supreme Court and to accept an out-of-court settlement with the state which achieved their goals but without the enormous back-pay settlement.

Nevertheless, tremendous momentum for comparable worth as a policy in state and local jurisdictions had been generated in the early 1980s. By August 1987, 28 states had begun the process of conducting a job evaluation study and 20 had moved further to budgeting and implementation. In addition, 167 local jurisdictions outside Minnesota had adopted comparable worth policies as well. Greater levels of public controversy in the mid-1980s slowed the process of diffusion and redirected it. No longer did litigative strategies appeal to proponents who realized that district court decisions after *Gunther* and especially after the reversal of *AFSCME v. State of Washington* did not support a comparable worth interpretation of Title VII. Emphasis turned to political solutions including legislation and, secondarily, labor negotiations. This switch of emphasis increased the number of arenas where comparable worth was debated, as proponents attempted to move the policy consensus on this issue to a point where public opinion and experience with the policy would lead to national legislation or more favorable court rulings. More arenas of action meant more arenas of conflict, however. In the next chapter we discuss what is at stake in the comparable worth controversy. As we shall see, comparable worth is a good example of a policy where proponents and opponents argue from different assumptions and reach different conclusions.

# 3    *What Is at Stake?*

A substantial portion of the earnings gap can be attributed to the different qualities and quantities of human capital acquired by boys and girls before they enter the labor market. Few boys, but many girls, expect to become homemakers. Later in life, such a girl might decide to take a job . . . . Her investment in homemaking skills will not pay off in the labor market. She will generally be limited to relatively unskilled, low-paying jobs. Her situation may be unfortunate, but it is the result of her own choice.

*Critic of comparable worth[1]*

I will not concede that women freely choose to invest less in themselves and freely choose to take low-paying jobs. . . . Either [women] are socialized into believing they should be subservient to men, or they are discriminatorily excluded from valuable training programs.

*Advocate of comparable worth[2]*

What is at stake in the comparable worth movement? At the very basic level, the stakes are the interpretation of the wage and earnings gaps between women and men, and minorities and whites. Women working full-time earn, in the aggregate, up to 33% less than men working full-time; and full-time minority workers earn up to 25% less than full-time white workers. Why does this occur?

At the more general level the stakes are about the social construction of causation. How much of our destinies do we control as individuals and how much is the result of large social forces as they play themselves out in our lives and through our choices? As an issue, comparable worth encompasses not only deep divisions of opinion about what workers should be paid (and thus how they will live) but also about how society will *know* what workers should be paid (and thus how society justifies the payment decision).

42

## Earnings Differentials

As we have seen, the current comparable worth movement began in the 1970s with the growing recognition that, largely because of occupational segregation by gender, women working full-time, year-round received roughly two-thirds of men's full-time, year-round earnings. When arrayed by race and ethnicity as well as gender, the earnings differentials gave further credence to the widespread feeling that the economic deck was stacked against people of color and women. In 1980, as the comparable worth movement became more prominent nationwide, the median earnings of white women employed full-time, year-round averaged 59.3% of the earnings of white men, and Black and Hispanic women received, respectively, 55.3% and 40.1% of white men's earnings. Black men earned 70.4% and Hispanic men earned 69.4% of white men's earnings. By 1986, the equivalent figures for women showed some slow but encouraging gains, with white women earning 64.2%, Black women 56.2%, and Hispanic women 53.3% of white men's earnings. Black men's relative earnings increased very slightly to 70.5% of white men's earnings while Hispanic men's earnings decreased slightly to 63.9% (see table 3.1.)[3]

Recently there has been a great deal of confusion over whether the wage gap between men and women has decreased rapidly toward the end of the decade of the eighties. In 1987, the Bureau of the Census published a report showing that the *hourly* wage gap had closed to 70%, which looked like a dramatic change when compared to the 59% with which many people were familiar.[4] This early figure of 59% referred to the gender comparison of all median full-time, year-round wages. In 1986, the same

TABLE 3.1
**Median Earnings of Year-round Full-time Workers by Sex, Race, and Hispanic Origin, as a Percentage of White Male Earnings, 1980 and 1986**

| Worker Groups | Annual Median Income | % of White Male | Annual Median Income | % of White Male |
|---|---|---|---|---|
| | 1980 | | 1986 | |
| White men | $19,720 | — | $26,617 | — |
| White women | 11,703 | 59.3 | 17,101 | 64.2 |
| Black men | 13,875 | 70.4 | 18,766 | 70.5 |
| Black women | 10,915 | 55.3 | 14,964 | 56.2 |
| Hispanic men* | 13,790 | 69.9 | 17,008 | 63.9 |
| Hispanic women | 9,887 | 50.1 | 14,191 | 53.3 |

*Sources:* See chap. 3, n.3.
*People of Hispanic origin may be of any race.

comparison of all women's to men's median full-time, year-round wages shows that women earned 65.0% of what men earned. Hourly wage comparisons tend to obscure the fact that women work fewer hours than men, both by choice and because of the unavailability of full-time work. Yearly comparisons tend to obscure the fact that managerial and professional workers, mostly men, tend to work a longer number of hours in their full-time week than do workers with other kinds of jobs.

The trends in the relationships between the earnings of men and women and whites and minorities are also important to an understanding of comparable worth. After the Korean War, white women's earnings first declined and then held steady against white men's earnings. Minority women's earnings made gains against white men's earnings, making minority and white women's earnings more similar. Minority men's earnings made big advances, coming 40% closer to white men's earnings in the period between 1955 and 1975.[5] As the decade of the 1970s closed, however, the distance between minority men's earnings and white men's earnings began to grow larger again, in part because of the loss of manufacturing jobs that had employed a relatively high proportion of minority men.

The earnings of public employees are somewhat different than those for the labor force as a whole. Contrary to popularly held beliefs, the wages and earnings of public employees vary greatly over time and between places. The public sector employs relatively more minorities and women than does the private sector. Statistics from 1980 show that women employed full-time, year-round by the federal government make 62.8% of what men make, and state and local women similarly employed make 71.5% of men's earnings.[6] It is important to remember that public wage-setting is different from that in the private sector. Especially at the state and local levels, the public sector tends to be a countercyclical employer, adding to its work force when the economy is sluggish. Wage levels tend to be administered in many jobs that have no private counterparts.[7]

These earnings differentials do not, of course, tell the full story of the racial, ethnic, and gender variations in economic conditions. A more complete picture of the relative economic position of various groups includes information about employment, governmental transfers, wealth, and family composition. Blacks and Hispanics are, respectively, 2.4 and 1.7 times as likely to be unemployed as are whites, and the figures are much worse for Black and Hispanic teenagers. Individuals without jobs, regardless of the cause, are likely to receive some sort of transfer payment, such as Social Security or AFDC. In 1985, 62 million adults received at least one kind of transfer. Almost 55% of recipients were women, 12% were Black, and 5% were Hispanic. White men received the most money in transfers, averaging $6,475 per year compared to the $3,474 transferred to Black women.[8]

The race, ethnicity, and gender breakdown for wealth is even more stark. As defined by the Census Bureau, wealth equals the ownership of savings, housing, automobiles, stocks and similar items, minus debts. In 1984, the median net worth of all white households was $39,135; of all Hispanic households it was $4,912; and of all Black households it was $3,397. White households had almost twelve times the wealth of Black households. The median net worth of white and Black female-headed households showed an even more extreme relationship. The median net worth of white female-headed households was $22,500 compared to $700 for Black female-headed households, a ration of 32 to 1. These last figures indicate a general pattern: households headed by a woman alone are more financially precarious than two-adult households, especially for minorities.[9]

While not the whole story, earnings differentials do provide a powerful message in helping many groups understand and organize around their economic status. But earnings ratios do not refer to wage differences in jobs of equal value as defined by a comparable worth analysis, although there is occasional confusion over this issue. Rather, a great many factors explicitly *not* related to equivalent jobs contribute to the earnings ratios. From the perspective of the worker, men and women and whites and minorities often have different schooling, job skills, and work histories. From the perspective of the economy, men and women often hold different jobs. Occupational segregation is the watchword of most workers' job experience. According to 1980 census data, women, regardless of race or ethnicity, were likely to work in occupations that were two-thirds filled by women, and men were likely to work in jobs whose incumbents ranged from 69% to 79% male, the exact percentages depending on their race or ethnicity.[10]

Another way to think about occupational segregation is to move from the census figures, which describe the national composition of an occupation, by gender, race, and ethnicity, to figures about individual firms or jurisdictions, which describe the gender, race, and ethnic composition of specific occupations within that firm. In a study of gender segregation in 400 work organizations in California, James N. Baron and William T. Bielby found that "over 59% were *perfectly* segregated by sex—that is, workers of one sex were either excluded entirely or were concentrated in job titles filled exclusively by the same sex." Baron and Bielby report that the kinds of industries underrepresented or excluded from their study (insurance, trucking, construction, and retail trade) are likely to be *more* sex-segregated than the organizations included; thus they probably understate their findings about the percentage of perfectly sex-segregated occupations within individual workplaces.[11]

Occupational segregation is directly associated with gender, race, and ethnic differentials in overall earnings. As the proportion of women or minority members in an occupation increases, wages decrease. An analysis of the expanded occupational codes of the 1970 census showed that for every additional 1% of women in an occupation, yearly salary declined $42, making an all-female job average about $4,000 less per year than an all-male job. This is not a comparable worth analysis, however, but was instead a study of the aggregate income effects of all-female occupations, regardless of the skill level, education, or working conditions associated with the job.[12] An "over-concentration" of minorities in an occupation can have a similar effect. An analysis of employees working for the state of New York in 1982 showed that occupations where Blacks or Hispanics were at least 40% more prevalent than in the state's overall labor force appeared to be underpaid by 1.59 salary grades (roughly $7,950) when compared in a comparable-worth job content analysis to occupations predominantly held by white men.[13]

Occupational segregation is not the only structural characteristic affecting gender, race, and ethnic patterns in wages. Additionally, white women and minorities tend to be employed by smaller firms and in less robust sectors of the economy than do white men, and smaller firms and less robust sectors pay lower wages. In addition, whatever the occupation, women, most notably women of color, tend to be lower-paid incumbents within it as well. It was all these differences, but especially the fact that women and men often hold different jobs where equal pay for equal work would not apply, that led to the comparable worth approach.

## Neoclassical and Institutional Economics

### The Neoclassical Approach

How occupational segregation and earnings differentials are interpreted depends on one's views about how the economy functions in general and how discrimination functions in particular. Explanations of the economy cluster in two categories: neoclassical models and institutional models. In its pristine form, the neoclassical model makes three stringent assumptions: workers have perfect mobility; capitalists are competitive; information is costless. These assumptions contain radically individualistic views about a populace unconnected to one another, to their past, to communities of place, or to institutions of any kind. The neoclassical market posits a world without history or memory.[14] Like the Protestant Reformation, in which these economic beliefs were born, much of neoclassical economics is about the fall from grace, that is, about why the economy does not work in the ideal, individualistic fashion and how the distortions brought about by combinations of people or firms lead to a less than efficient distribution of goods and services.[15] The rise of the liberal philosophy of the individual male citizen added a secular political component to this economic perspective.[16]

The great power of the neoclassical view is that it emphasizes scarcity and presents a model which combines production and distribution into one function. Scarcity is an idea somewhat out of political and economic fashion, but the neoclassical model is based on the enduring fact that human history has been defined by the scarcity of both "necessary" and "luxury" goods, however these categories are defined. For neoclassicists, scarcity drives the engine of productive choices. Because of both natural and socially constructed limitations of supply, decisions must be made about how much of a specific good will be made, what mix of goods will be produced, and how goods will be distributed. Neoclassical economists posit that all of these decisions constitute one process in which individuals register their preferences for goods through consumption. The amount of goods produced and their distribution become a seamless web. Leaning heavily on utilitarian thought, they consider that this distribution is the (theoretically) most advantageous in that it supposedly produces the greatest good for the greatest number.[17]

Within the neoclassical economic framework, wages are understood to equal the additional net revenue the worker adds for the employer. Workers choose the kinds of jobs they prefer by comparing the skills they possess and their preferences in working conditions against the skills and working conditions required by jobs. Wage disparities among equally productive employees are hypothesized to be short-lived in this situation. The fundamental presentation of this view argues that if an employer pays wages below a worker's or group of workers' net contribution to the employer's revenue, other employers have an incentive to hire the low-paid workers away from the first firm.[18] By offering higher wages than the first employer, the other firms get good workers at a good price. Competition for the workers from the first firm, now shorthanded, will ultimately drive wages up to the net revenue point. Under the conditions of the three neo-classical assumptions, inefficient wages, whatever their causes, will not endure. Concomitantly, the existing wage is understood to equal worker's net contribution to revenue, although this contribution may be figured over a long enough time to smooth over wage differences that might be dictated by the business cycle, and may embody a set of additional assumptions about how workers and firms jointly negotiate the long-term matching of human capital, training, and firm loyalty.[19] The neoclassical approach does not necessarily predict a labor force integrated as to race or gender, however. As long as capitalists have equal access to financial markets and new firms are not excluded from entering production, segregated firms in competitive markets paying roughly equal wages can develop.

Monopolies, oligopolies and other combinations, including social collusion, change this pattern. Noting that discrimination in hiring and wages exists, Gary Becker suggested that the socially (i.e., not economically) derived "taste" for discrimination on the part of owners, managers, or workers means that the cost of hiring members of the disvalued group equals the wage plus the disutility of having the disvalued persons be part of the work force.[20] In the tradition of Becker, Aldrich and Buchele state that "this disutility can be measured as the decrease in women's [or minority] wages that would be necessary in order to make the employer indifferent between an equally qualified man and woman [or white or minority]."[21]

If this taste for discrimination is universal and strongly held, the result, as suggested above, can be *segregation by firm* within sectors of production. Further, if the universal and strongly held social views about the disutility of hiring members of a particular group vary by the type of occupation, then *occupational segregation* can result. Specifically, if employers hold the culturally prevalent view that women, for example, are the most appropriate workers for jobs that are similar to tasks usually undertaken by women at home (e.g., nursing, teaching, cleaning, organizing), then women will be employed more frequently in these types of occupations because employers have a low socially-derived disutility for hiring them for this type of work. Aldrich and Buchele additionally suggest that men's and women's wages are closer in these low disutility female jobs than they are in higher disutility male jobs.[22] Barbara Bergmann modifies this position by suggesting that occupational segregation causes crowding in women's (and by extension minority) jobs, increasing the pool of workers and decreasing their wages.[23] Some economists, like

Bergmann, emphasize women are crowded into these positions by employer choices, others that women flock to these jobs because women choose positions which allow themselves mobility in and out of the paid labor force as childbearing, childrearing, and household labor vary.

Within the neoclassical approach, human capital economists attempt to explain earnings differentials by demonstrating such differences in the characteristics of workers as schooling, training, uninterrupted attachment to the labor force, longevity in particular jobs, hours worked, and similar considerations. Most of the research used in the comparable worth policy debate has focused on female-male earnings differentials, rather than on minority-white differences. A review of the human capital literature on gender-based wage differences undertaken by the Committee on Occupational Classification and Analysis of the National Academy of Sciences found that, in 1975, the most thorough cross-sectional human capital analysis available accounted for 44% of the earnings differences between women and men.[24] This means that if women earn 60¢ to a man's dollar, almost 18¢ of the difference can be explained by differences in worker characteristics. Of course, some of these worker characteristics, like education, reflect processes that have historically discriminated against women. It would be difficult to disentangle the effects of this discriminatory history from the actual skill differences in the 18¢-worth of human capital explanations.

Some human capital economists also assert that women's lifetime wages are depressed by intermittency, i.e., moving in and out of the paid labor force as childrearing and household labor vary. Many, like Solomon Polachek, assert that women choose this pattern of labor force attachment.[25] As a result of the demand for this type of employment, women tend to concentrate in jobs allowing for intermittency, a fact that further depresses women's wages by increasing the pool of workers and decreasing their wages. Research by Paula England and Mary Corcoran and others confirms that intermittency does depress female lifetime wages, but that this penalty is the same in female- and male-dominated occupations, undermining the oversupply/concentration argument. England also questions the role of women's choices in these theories, a topic to which we shall return.[26]

Overall, the human capital approach to cross-sectional earnings differentials has been questioned from a variety of perspectives. First, a large body of research repeatedly shows that all groups of workers do not receive the same value (in wages) for the same increment of human capital (say, education). Second, the assumptions of neoclassical economics fit specific groups of workers differently. While no workers have perfect mobility and information, women workers have less geographical mobility and less job-related information than do men.[27] Third, the pure human capital approach ignores the explanatory force available from the examination of the economic consequences of institutional arrangements.

## *The Institutional Approach*

In contrast, institutional models of the labor force, while acknowledging human capital and supply-and-demand factors, give greater weight to the organization of firms, industries, and sectors; to managerial discretion; and to business relations with government in understanding how the economy works. One advantage of institutional models is that they do not confound production and distribution, emphasizing that production and distribution very often require different sets of decisions. Another advantage of the institutional approach is that it emphasizes the relative power and at least partial intentionality of economic actors. This approach takes as a given that institutions can marshal and deploy huge resources. For example, David Gordon, Richard Edwards, and Michael Reich argue for a theory of the social structure of accumulation that acknowledges that the process of capital accumulation is neither impersonal nor mechanistic.[28] Their approach emphasizes the importance of individual capitalists and employees who make their investment and labor decisions as members of their larger societies, where beliefs and actions have made it common to assume that female and minority workers are less expensive to hire. As Ruth Milkman has shown in her history of male and female employment in the automotive and electrical assembly industries, women were hired as cheap labor when owners and managers wanted to keep labor costs low. Both industries were oligopolistic, but in the auto industry, where wages were a relatively small part of production costs, women were rarely hired, especially at Ford, because Henry Ford disapproved of women working outside the home. In contrast, the electrical assembly industry hired many more girls and women. In 1933, at hearings on the Codes of Fair Competition held under the National Industrial Recovery Act, Charles Keaveny of General Electric suggested that women were hired in electric lamp production *because* they could be paid a lower wage than men.[29] Such a policy was driven by the fact that although electrical manufacturing became increasingly mechanized, control over wages was necessary in an industry that was so labor-intensive. Histories of the cotton textile industry, the federal civil service, tobacco processing, teaching, librarianship, and clerical work show a similar pattern of hiring women or people of color as cheap labor in labor-intensive industries or industries undergoing rapid expansion.[30]

The institutional approach highlights two points, one emphasizing the difficulty of determining a worker's contribution to net revenue and the other emphasizing the variation in quality of jobs. In many circumstances employers rarely know the actual contribution of workers to the net revenue of the firm. Indeed in large multicompany corporations it may not be easy to tell what constitutes "the firm" to which a particular worker is adding value. Does the women who dips candies for Godiva Chocolates add value to that company, or to Campbell Soup, the multinational corporation that owns Godiva? Similarly, it is not sensible to think of the contributions to net revenue of many kinds of service and professional workers like custodians or engineers. Neither is it appropriate to ask about the net revenue contribution of workers who produce on a straight cost rather than competitive basis, like some health providers or defense contractors, or of some public employees whose services are provided below cost.[31]

In the absence of information that would allow employers to know the real productivity of individual workers, information that would be very costly to obtain, employers have judged workers not as individuals contributing to net revenue but as members of the social and demographic groups—those of sex, race, age, etc.—to which they belong. This practice permits two kinds of discrimination: statistical discrimination, in which a person is judged on the average employment characteristics of the groups to which she or he belongs; and error discrimination, in which a person is judged on the *false* beliefs about the work-related traits of the groups to which she or he belongs.[32] The difficulty of obtaining relevant information on the contributions of employees to net revenue indicates that the assumptions and conclusions of the pure neoclassical approach are suspect when it comes to the elimination of discriminatory wage rates.

The institutional approach also emphasizes that all jobs are not equal. The quality of job varies and the distribution of social groups over high- and low-quality jobs is an important consideration in the institutional approach to discrimination. Two conceptualizations of the labor market, segmented and internal labor-market theories, help to explain the differences in the quality of jobs and which workers will hold them. Segmented labor-market theories divide the economy into primary jobs with high pay and low turnover in oligopolistic firms, and secondary jobs with low pay and high turnover in competitive sectors. Primary jobs are further divided between the independent primary segment made up mostly of white males employed as professionals, managers, and technicians; and the subordinate primary segment made up of a more racially and sexually mixed group of semiskilled, blue-collar and white-collar workers.[33] Treiman and Hartmann described this situation well when they said that "in many firms it is typical for managerial jobs to be dominated by white men, for professional jobs to be dominated by whites, although not so exclusively by white men as managerial positions; for clerical jobs to be dominated by women, for craft and laboring jobs to be dominated by one sex or the other and sometimes by one race or ethnic group; and for most service jobs to be dominated by women and minority men."[34]

A variety of institutional practices, most notably internal labor markets, solidify the relative positions of groups within this hierarchy. An internal labor market is an administrative unit, like a firm, where labor pricing and allocation are governed by rules and customs, as well as, and often in place of, reliance on market wages.[35] Specifically, each job in a large firm is connected to its own "job ladder" for promotion as part of the structure of the firm's internal labor market. Any job segregation occurring at the "port of entry" continues up the job ladder. The job ladders for the positions customarily dominated by women and racial and ethnic minorities are quite short. Thus, initial shunting into low-wage jobs is reinforced by limited promotional opportunities.[36]

Institutional economists approach comparable worth from the perspective of wanting to discover how occupational segregation occurred historically and what part of the earnings differential is explained by institutional factors in addition to human capital factors. When occupational characteristics are added to personal characteristics the explanation of the earnings difference changes. An occupational approach shows that the gender composition of an occupation is an important predictor of earnings, often the most important occupational or individual predictor of earnings. The National Academy of Sciences study found that 35–40% of gender difference in earnings was attributable to occupational segregation, if fairly fine definitions of occupation were used.[37] Aldrich and Buchele modified the NAS approach, suggesting that when male-female differences in wages within occupations are eliminated, 30% of the wage gap was explained by occupational segregation.[38] June O'Neill, an opponent of comparable worth, found that after adjusting for differences in schooling, training, part-time work, and environmental conditions, wages declined 1.5% for every 10% increase in the proportion of women in the occupation.[39] In other words, after controlling for schooling, hours worked, and working conditions, O'Neill found that wages in occupations filled totally by women were 15% lower than occupations filled totally by men.[40]

*Macroeconomic Consequences*

Most of the economic discussion of comparable worth has centered on the microeconomic questions of wage rates for individual workers. But wage rates have economy-wide consequences that have also been raised in comparable worth policy discussions. Economists of different schools agree that under certain circumstances comparable worth wage increases might increase unemployment for the recipients of the raises, or members of their categories, i.e., women or minorities. Again, most of the discussion has focused on gender with two hypotheses shaped by the neoclassical approach being presented: if comparable worth were implemented, either (1) lower-wage male workers would be hired to replace higher-wage female workers or (2) fewer women workers would be retained.[41] A modification of the first hypothesis, shaped in part by the institutionalist approach, suggests that men and women may not be highly substitutable workers in the short run because jobs are socially designated as more proper for men or women and because the work culture on the job comes to reflect the values associated with men or women more generally. Institutionally sensitive economists modify the second hypothesis by suggesting that the wages in an occupation, firm, or sector depend on the competitiveness of production, itself partially dependent on the relative importance of wages in total production costs. In oligopolistic industries with low to moderate wage to total expenditure ratios, comparable worth is not likely to cause significant disemployment.

Because only a few jurisdictions and firms have implemented comparable worth, it is difficult to evaluate the propositions concerning employment effects. The most encompassing analysis has been done on the Australian economy. In Australia minimum wage rates for each occupation have been determined by state and federal wage tribunals since the early 1900s. Before 1975, each occupation's minimum wage was determined as though it supported a workingman and his wife and children. When an occupation was deemed to be female, the wage rate was explicitly and legally fixed at 75% of what it would have been if it were a male occupation. A decision in 1972 by the federal tribunal made equal pay for work of equal value the wage-setting standard and required that it be implemented by 1975. Australian economists have found that "during the years when the relative wages of females increased most—1973 and 1974—the largest increase in the rate of unemployment for females in response to the relative wage change was 10 percent, or 0.2 of the labor force. Measured female unemployment appears to have been remarkably unresponsive to the equal pay decisions."[42]

The more limited data from the United States show similar trends, though the authors of these works stress the preliminary nature of their research. Looking at employment within jobs throughout the entire economy, Aldrich and Buchele estimate an average decline in employment of 1% as the result of their typical comparable worth wage adjustment of between 10% and 20% in female-dominated occupations. Examining 1980 census data for state and local public workers in 118 SMSAs (standard metropolitan statistical areas), Ehrenberg and Smith estimated that a 20% increase in wages for all female state and local government employees would produce "only a 2 to 3 percent decline in female employment."[43] In addition, Barbara Bergmann suggests that those who might face unemployment due to comparable worth adjustments would often be the same people who would benefit most from those adjustments when they find employment again. She estimates that even a rise in the unemployment *rate* of 10% would cause only a 2% reduction in yearly income for those affected. Further, that 2% reduction must be weighed against the 30% increases Bergmann suggests that comparable worth might bring those employees.[44]

Whether employment would actually drop in a particular jurisdiction or firm would depend, as was suggested above, on the employment policies of that employer and the role of competitive wages and prices in that industry. An example of the importance of policies and industrial structure can be seen on the one hand in the comments of Nina Rothchild, Commissioner of Employee Relations for the State of Minnesota, who has repeatedly remarked that no jobs were lost in state employment because of the comparable worth wage settlement. On the other hand, some local public officials in Minnesota do not rule out the possibility of cutting female-dominated jobs or the overall work force. Public employers are somewhat more cushioned against wage increases because they can consider employee wage rates as a public policy, and in that light comparable worth competes for public resources like any other policy option does. In addition to economizing or supplanting other types of policies, jurisdictions can also increase their taxes (or analogously businesses could increase their prices) to finance comparable worth. This option leads to the debate over whether comparable worth causes economic inefficiencies, a debate that returns to the questions about whether a comparable worth wage exceeds a worker's contribution to marginal revenue product or whether this wage policy corrects inequities in wage rates.

*Job Evaluation*

The generally unfavorable views about comparable worth held by neo-classical economists and the generally positive views held by institutional economists extend to their assessment of the role of job evaluation in setting wages. Neoclassical opponents of comparable worth decry the possibility of determining the value of a job. Some argue, incorrectly and mischievously, that proponents want to create a national ranking of the universal and immutable values of jobs. Instead, advocates argue that the wages of a job within a firm can be linked to the value system of that firm. Jobs can be evaluated by a firm according to the firm's values along those characteristics found in all jobs: skill, effort, responsibility, and working conditions.[45]

Although the attack on job evaluation has been a central part of the anti-comparable-worth effort, most opponents do not object to job evaluation per se, merely to its use in determining whether wages are inequitable in terms of gender, race, or ethnicity. For example, Herbert R. Northrup of the Wharton School, an ardent opponent of comparable worth, writes that job evaluation and wage classification systems are tools that "prevent the upward whipsawing of wages during the life of a collective bargaining agreement."[46] Designed to rationalize wages for employers and to workers, most job evaluation systems fall into one of two categories, policy-capturing methods or a priori methods. Both methods evaluate jobs (e.g., senior secretary, senior groundskeeper), not the incumbents of those jobs.

The policy-capturing method has traditionally been used to help set a firm's wages for those jobs for which it cannot determine or does not have the resources to determine a market wage, and to justify the wage structure to employees.[47] It is important to define what is meant by a market wage. A market wage is the "going wage" in a particular geographical region, often determined by formal or informal wage surveys that are commissioned by employers and whose results are shared between them. The market wage is really a range of wages for a specific type of job within a catchment area. In a policy-capturing job evaluation, a series of benchmark jobs are chosen from a firm's occupational structure. These jobs are usually chosen because it is possible to determine a range of market wages for them and because they can be viewed as "marker jobs" around which similar jobs can be slotted. The benchmark jobs are evaluated and given interim scores according to the firm's job evaluation system(s). Most private-sector firms that use job evaluation employ different systems for blue-collar, clerical, and professional and managerial jobs. The interim job scores are then analyzed in multiple regressions against the market wages for the appropriately related jobs. The resulting equations can then be used to set the wages for all other jobs within the firm because the regression coefficients have "captured" the relationship between job evaluation factors and market wages.[48] This technique assumes that jobs do not have intrinsic value to society or a firm and that wages should not be set mostly on the basis of job characteristics.[49]

The policy-capturing technique is used primarily by opponents of comparable worth because it brings market wages, with their history of wage distortions for women and minorities, into current wage-setting. It has been modified however, by supporters of comparable worth in the state of New York, to do a comparable worth analysis. In the adjusted policy-capturing study in New York, the current pay practices for jobs held primarily by white males are compared to jobs held primarily by women or minorities. New wages are proposed if female or minority jobs do not receive the same return on job characteristics, like skill or working conditions, as do white male jobs. No comparisons with market wages are made.[50] This approach has the potential of backfiring on proponents of comparable worth, however. What happens if certain job characteristics, like caring for people, are negatively associated with pay? Should all wages reflect this devaluation of an important job characteristic?

The a priori job evaluation method is the second major approach to analyzing job content, one that imposes pre-set views on what constitutes compensable factors in a workplace. In practice this means that a firm will design or purchase a job evaluation system that gives specific weights to skill, effort, responsibility, and working conditions (or whatever criteria the firm chooses). The firm will then describe the jobs, either by observation or by having workers fill out a form; perform quality control on the job description, usually through cross-checking done by supervisors or by worker-management committees; rate each job in terms of the specific evaluation factors; sum the scores (often in points) each job receives on all the evaluation factors; and then assign wages as a function of the overall job score. Many firms compare job scores with market-wage ranges in the final assignment of wages.

In a comparable worth wage-setting situation, a single a priori job evaluation would be used to assess the sum total of the compensable factors for all jobs within the firm. Next, several regressions are run where the salary-practices lines for male-dominated, female-dominated, and sometimes white and minority jobs are plotted. If, for example, a female-dominated job of 250 points were paid at $1,500 dollars a month and a male-dominated job of 250 points were paid at $1,750 a month, the wages in the female-dominated class would be raised. In a pure comparable

worth situation, the wage range in the female- or minority-dominated occupation would rise to equal the wage range in the male- or majority dominated occupation. In practice, some comparable worth policies enforce
pay for points, where low-wage occupations are brought up to the average
salary line and occasionally high-wage occupations are lowered.

Although the a priori job evaluation approach is favored by most comparable worth supporters, it has also posed a dilemma for them, beyond
the possible lowering of some wages. The commercially available job
evaluation systems used in this approach have been the object of serious
criticism. These systems come with fixed job traits that will be evaluated
and assigned weights that reflect the importance of skill, effort, responsibility, and working conditions. Both male and female workers have criticized these systems for not giving enough weight to working conditions,
and it is not unusual for working conditions to constitute less than 5% of
the total possible job evaluation score. In a moment of unanimity, police
officers, grounds keepers, and licensed practical nurses might agree that
bullets, pesticides, and human waste from sick people are conditions of
their work that they want more fully noted and more fairly compensated.
In addition, comparable worth advocates have kept up a steady critique of
the commercial systems' inattention to many of the skill, effort, and responsibility components of jobs traditionally held by women. In the job
evaluation process, jobs traditionally held by women tend to have shorter
descriptions, fewer strong adjectives or verbs, and often fail to include
those proficiencies related to women's traditional roles in child care, in-
struction, and mediation between conflicting points of view. These proficiencies are viewed as natural attributes rather than skills. In addition,
skills that are acquired in school, like good grammar and typing, tend to
be underrecognized in comparison with skills acquired on the job.[51]

Taken together, these criticisms have put activists in the strategically
awkward position of defending a priori job systems while also correcting
them. Opponents have taken supporters' criticisms of the subjective nature
of the construction and application of commercial a priori systems as a
point of departure for trying to undercut the use of job evaluation for
examining questions of wage equity. The criticism of opponents is that job
evaluation systems are too subjective or too biased. Legal policy analysts
David Kirp, Mark Yudof, and Marlene Strong Franks exemplify this position when they say that "though job evaluations promise an objective
assessment of the value of a job, using job evaluations unsullied by the
market to fix wages only builds in more biases. . . . Subjective preferences determine how jobs are described by the evaluator, the criteria
against which they are evaluated, and the weight attached to those crite-

ria."[52] In response, economists Ray Marshall and Beth Paulin reply that job evaluation "is not precise—it is inherently judgmental, but it is an established technique and comparable worth cases would involve no more judgment than ordinarily involved in wage and salary administration."[53]

In addition, the regression methodology based on a priori job evaluation systems has become the object of some discussion by both opponents and advocates. These discussions are well within the labor economics tradition, where scholars debate which functional form of the regression equation should be used (for example, linear least-squares regression versus one of several logarithmic forms), and the proper interpretation of the constant term, coefficients, and the error term. Again opponents see these debates as an indication of the difficulty and subjectivity of comparable worth wage-setting. Advocates note that the magnitude of wage changes proposed by most of the various forms or interpretations is roughly the same, indicating that the technical debate does not undercut the general findings about wage differences between jobs held by women and minorities and those held by men or whites.[54] The choice of the form of the regression line does have a significant effect on which specific occupations will receive comparable worth adjustments in a particular workplace, however. The choice of the form of the regression line has remained a management prerogative in most settings.

## *Wage Justice*

So far we have examined the stakes involved in comparable worth in the language and values of economics. This view of comparable worth is incomplete because it does not give sufficient attention to the political, historical, and cultural aspects of the controversy. We must also ask the integrative question of what constitutes wage justice for opponents and advocates. To answer this question we must investigate how each group views the role of individual choice versus the power of social structures, the obligations history places on current actions, and the place of government in changing personal and economic relations. Our examination of wage justice focuses on popular conceptions of fairness, the kinds of conceptions that create the consensus for or against a public policy.*

For most opponents and most advocates of comparable worth, espe-

---

*Political philosophers have just begun formally to consider comparable worth policies when examining concepts of justice. We hope that our discussion of the popular beliefs and actual practices associated with the issue will contribute that debate.

cially those involved in the policy debates, wage justice is centered in the conventionally available wage rates in an occupation and firm. For opponents, wage justice is by definition found in the market wage, which represents a worker's marginal revenue product. For advocates, wage justice comes through correcting a flaw in the market that has allowed systemic underpayment in women's and minority wages due to virtually universally held beliefs that women and minorities need not make or are not intrinsically worth the same wages as white men for either equal work or for equal contribution. Regardless of occasional polemics by a few virulent opponents of comparable worth, advocates do not favor a centrally administered economy.[55] Supporters do not want to do away with the market but to redeem it, a refrain that is frequently heard in American reform movements.

Some opponents of comparable worth have proposed that advocates hold other than market views defining wage justice. For example, June O'Neill writes that "by comparable worth I mean the view that employers should base compensation on the inherent value of a job rather than on strictly market considerations. It is not a new idea—since the time of St. Thomas Aquinas, the concept of the just price, or payment for value, has had considerable appeal."[56] O'Neill seems to confound the medieval concepts of the just wage and the just price in her remarks. But as economic history shows, the just wage, which is the relevant concept in medieval philosophy, was not thought to operate as O'Neill suggests, nor do comparable worth supporters claim that their policy is connected to this view of economic arrangements.

The confusion of the medieval term "just wage" and the current market-based approach of both proponents and opponents must be brought to the surface, if only to eliminate imprecise terminology. In the thirteenth century, the Thomistic notion of a just wage adopted by the Scholastics contained a variety of notions. As economic historian Karl Pribram has shown in great detail, Saint Thomas put forth that a "worker's livelihood was to be assured by the performance of his labor" and that wage rates were fixed "according to the *social position* and skill of the worker and the nature of his work."[57] In Scholastic reasoning, all goods and classes of people had intrinsic value. The just wage was as much connected to the worker and "his" product as it was to the occupation itself. Saint Thomas, influenced by Aristotle, believed that women's functions were both biologically defined and loathsome, and did not envision women as workers in any modern sense.[58] Thus it is a misreading of the Scholastics to say that they believed occupations alone had intrinsic worth, because the Scholastics did not separate occupations from the social origins of their regular incumbents as is usual in industrial societies. If anything, the Scholastic position binding wages to social position, skill, and type of work *reaffirms* the marginality of women (and, by extension, minorities) to the paid labor force, rather than argues for a universal ordering of occupations in the modern definition of the term. Moreover, and this is an important point, advocates of comparable worth do not argue for a universal ranking of jobs in society or between firms. Very much in the labor law tradition of the United States, supporters proposed to pay women and men, and minorities and whites, by the same standard of contribution to the firm as decided upon by the firm.

The idea of *a* just wage, even if it is not the Thomistic just wage, does capture the frustration that advocates of comparable worth feel with a powerful and impersonal capitalism that can deskill work and easily pay workers less than a living wage.[59] At a cultural level, supporters tap into widely held beliefs that the market does not always pay a fair wage. Public opinion polls repeatedly show that the general populace (in Indiana), state employees (in Minnesota), and employed persons (in a national survey) support paying nurses and electricians, secretaries and delivery van drivers, or nurses and pharmacists equivalently.[60] At the most general level these findings suggest that individuals see the market as paying wages that are not necessarily fair.

If the advocate's view is not a Thomistic notion of the just wage, neither is it that of the Marxist notion of the labor theory of value. The labor theory of value proposes that the value of a good is the sum of the labor embodied in it, both the current labor necessary to produce it and the past labor necessary to produce the nonlabor (i. e., goods) inputs to production.[61] Comparable worth advocates do not argue that the price of a good (the purpose for which the labor theory of value was promulgated) depends solely on the current or historical costs of labor, or that prices are not subject to fluctuation because of supply and demand, as Marx is commonly criticized for arguing. Advocates want a fair market wage and the recognition that the exchange of goods (i. e., the market) is not an automatically self-regulating process in a number of situations, some relating to production and some relating to reproductive and domestic labor.[62]

## Justice and Choice

It is in regard to the relationship between markets and families and the state where opponents and advocates differ and where many of the more hidden stakes of the comparable worth controversy lie. Opponents base their opposition to comparable worth on the ideology of free exchange of goods perhaps more than on the actual unencumbered functioning of exchange. In economic terms, the market is based on the selfish behavior of individuals ceaselessly seeking their preferences. In cultural terms, the linchpin of the market is individual choice.

Almost all of the economic and cultural differences between opponents and advocates rest on how they view choice. It is an old debate, between the power of individuals to shape their destinies and the limits imposed upon them by social and economic structures. For most opponents of comparable worth, free choices are real. People choose the amount of schooling they will pursue, the type of work in which they will engage, and the timing of marriage and pregnancy.[63] Normatively, nothing should impede these choices, and experientially only a few situations really do. The perspective of opponents on choice is one of extreme methodological individualism.[64] Individuals know what they want, can rank-order their preferences, and express their true rank-ordering in their behavior. This form of individualizing signals the erosion of community as well as the distrust of formal institutions.

These general views about choice are very recent inventions, especially in terms of occupational choice, for which they are less than a century old. For men, the transformation from an economy where sons learned their fathers' occupation to one where a father's occupation might well be useless or unwanted by a son caused a great transformation in work and social relations. In a study of middle-class homes in Chicago between 1872 and 1890, Richard Sennett found that with the exception of well-established entrepreneurs, a father's occupation was a poor predictor of a son's occupation. Sennett describes this situation as violating "normal" intragenerational authority patterns (between older and younger brothers and between husbands and wives) as well as fueling the realistic fears of a sudden fall into poverty which formed the darker side of the mythology of sudden riches also prevalent in this period.[65]

For women, notions of occupational choice are more problematic because opponents see women as being simultaneously totally free to traverse the worlds of reproductive, domestic, and productive labor while also constrained by their reproductive capacities. Opponents of comparable worth see women investing lightly in their education and training, a choice that is made in anticipation of a lifetime of childrearing and homemaking. In this view women choose marriage, choose sexual relations, choose pregnancy, choose children, and choose work located in the home. Women make these choices pretty much in this order (if they are smart) and each proceeds without a hitch. The economy responds by giving women the opportunity to move in and out of paid labor (the intermittency argument) but purports to enact a wage penalty on the type of jobs that allow this.[66]

The message of this view of occupational choice is that women choose to be unpaid domestic and reproductive workers having a customary claim on a husband's income, and by so choosing only get, on average, low wages for low-skilled work when they do enter the paid work force. Advocates see the women's customary claim on male income as a weak protection, one based on an unequal dependency in so monetized a society. They remind women that almost half of all marriages end in divorce, an indication that current ties of affection and the income they represent may not always be available to a women in the future.[67]

The tension between these two views of occupational choice have been central to employment-equity policy debates in the last decade. Perhaps the most striking example of it is found in the *Equal Employment Opportunity Commission v. Sears* case.[68] In this case the EEOC charged Sears with discriminatorily hindering women's hiring and promotion into commission sales for durable goods like washing machines. At the trial two noted historians, Rosalind Rosenberg and Alice Kessler-Harris, testified on the role of women's choices about family and work. Rosenberg testified that " 'men and women differ in their expectations concerning work, in their interests as to the types of jobs they prefer or the types of products they prefer to sell'." Kessler-Harris countered that " 'what appear to be women's choices, and what are characterized as women's "interests" are, in fact, heavily influenced by the opportunities for work made available to them'."[69] Sears won at the trial-court level where the judge commended Rosenberg's view that little constrains a woman's occupational choice except her own interests and desires. Comparable worth opponents rest their arguments on this reasoning.

The gender relations implied by this view of choice deserve more attention. The relations between men and women are understood to be unparadoxical. If women want marriage and children and the love and affection common to them, then low wages are to be expected; they even become the price for love. Indeed, women are presumed not to value affection if they agree to fight over the proper monetizing of the paid labor in which they have traditionally engaged. The result, in form if not necessarily in practice, is the patriarchal family. For opponents of comparable worth there is no exit from the dilemma of wage structure and family obligation unless a woman makes so much money that she can hire other women to take partial responsibility for her children.

Among the most culturally conservative opponents to comparable worth there is a direct expression of husband/father dominion in the family. A number, like Phyllis Schlafly of the Eagle Forum, Allan C. Carlson of the Rockford Institute, and author George Gilder, support some version of a family or manly wage, where a male head of family can support his wife and children without their working. Gilder expresses the concerns of cultural conservatives when he writes that "to the extent that we adopt programs of Comparable Worth which involve ever greater government involvement in society, and promote the steady usurpation of the man's role in the family, we will find increasingly erupting the same kinds of problems that government has already created so massively and tragically in America's inner cities." The not so subtle message of this text is that comparable worth will make middle class, perhaps white, families like inner city, perhaps Black, families.[70]

The preference for a family wage available to men implies that the cultural conservatives posit *need* as one basis for wage-setting. "Need," of course, is not within the economic tradition of market wages. But supporters can and do make an appeal on the basis of need as well. The use of these arguments based on need can be understood in the distinction between claims and appeals. Claims are made in reference to what is understood to be existing (i.e., real) circumstances, and appeals refer to a preferred normative order. In this way both opponents and advocates of comparable worth can remain within the market framework while criticizing it, a position that both feel is important for their credibility.

The advocates' appeal on the basis of need argues that women have economic needs regardless of their household structures. Citing Lester Thurow and others, supporters note that it was women's entry into the paid labor force that kept most middle-class families middle-class during the last thirty years. Without the economic contribution of working wives, middle-class families would have fallen from the second or third quintile of family incomes to the fourth or fifth.[71] Taking the logic of need further, mothers without access to male income are also in need of family wages, more so because of the low wages typical in many female-dominated occupations. Cultural conservatives are deeply uneasy about mothers without access to male income, whatever the reason; the women do not have a claim on a man's paycheck. The possibility of women's independence from men, whether the women choose it or bitterly oppose it, creates a world of diminished husband/father right and is opposed, often by the argument of how bad this situation is for women and children.[72]

Opponents' concerns about wages that support a family raise an important issue, however. Although the form of their concern is patriarchal, they acknowledge that childbearing and rearing is important work that is often undervalued, a position with which supporters of comparable worth agree, but for different reasons. The fear expressed by opponents that mothering will not be valued is a fear that the market and commodified exchanges will intrude more powerfully on women's traditional, if imperfectly realized, authority in families and on the affective spheres of life which encompass both men and women. Opponents of comparable worth want to solve the Freudian dilemma of "love and work" by enforcing separate spheres for women and men, and supporters want to make women and men more equal in both spheres. Opponents fear the necessity of two-wage-earner families and supporters say that the necessity already exists for the great majority of families. For supporters the question is whether families will have two incomes or one and two-thirds incomes.

Interestingly, opponents of comparable worth have been wholly unsuccessful in organizing local anti-comparable-worth groups among working or nonworking women. There have been no spontaneous anti-comparable-worth efforts at the grass roots. Comparable worth has not evoked the same counterorganization that the Equal Rights Amendment did or abortion does. Most likely, this situation exists because comparable worth does not pose the same cultural threat that either the ERA or abortion did to groups of women who believe their most valuable labor to be childbearing and child care.[73] Certainly, comparable worth poses less of an immediate threat to the values of women opposing the policy. But it may also be that when married women from religious backgrounds supporting traditional views of the primacy of women's responsibility for mothering do work, they often work at the kinds of jobs that would receive comparable worth raises if such a policy were implemented in their firms. The avowed reason why many of these women work is to help support their families. A program that raises the wages in their types of jobs might not arouse their opposition; or if it did, their reactions might be more complicated because comparable worth is so much more clearly an economic rather than ethical issue.

Opponents of comparable worth move from an implicit set of gender relations to a gendered set of class relations. Some opponents describe comparable worth as a movement to give middle-class women in fields like librarianship, nursing, and social work raises at the expense of blue-collar men. This assertion is occasionally refined to say that white, middle-class women will be advantaged at the expense of Black, blue-collar men.[74] While middle-class women and men in traditionally female professions have been important in organizing for comparable worth, clerical and service workers have been equally central to the movement and it is these clerical and service workers who have received the bulk of the raises. The message of opponents' claims is about the maintenance of male solidarity across class lines and the propriety of men providing the bulk of family income regardless of the work that men or women do. Opponents fear not only the possible decline in the rate of increase of men's wages, if comparable worth were imposed as part of a fixed-wage bill, but also the greater autonomy for women that higher female wages might mean in terms of family dynamics.

Advocates of comparable worth have a different view of choice and how choice is related both to types of labor (productive, reproductive, or domestic) and location of work (market or home.) Advocates do not see the market as floating on the family, where the family is understood to be separate and prior to productive exchanges. Neither is the family mostly the site of consumption, as it began to be for men after the industrial revolution. For women the family remains the location of a significant amount of their labor, although the reproductive and domestic work done there is not usually monetized. Similarly, the "law of supply and demand" is understood as a generalization about human behavior subject to social constraints, not as either a physical law akin to gravity, as it is sometimes construed by the press, or a prescription for action, as a legal statute would be. (When the judge in *Christiansen v. Iowa,* an early case comparing wages in different jobs, spoke about being unwilling to "repeal the law of supply and demand," he drew upon these last two misinterpretations of the relationship between supply and demand.)[75]

Advocates believe that women and men and minorities and whites have fundamentally different structures of choice, which are themselves the legacy of past and current actions and beliefs. For advocates there is no doubt that history is both important and leaves obligations for contemporary actions. The history of paid work for women and minorities is littered with structural barriers both to employment itself and to certain types of occupations. The legal, economic, political, and customary social arrangements found in slavery, tenant agriculture, migrant labor for commercial crops, protective legislation, and perhaps most universally, sexual activity between men and women all connect workers to sets of different and often profoundly unequal opportunities and realities of paid labor. Advocates of comparable worth do not believe that the legacies of these arrangements give individuals unfettered choices about employment or, for women, unfettered choices about pregnancy, having children, and raising them.

Advocates do not believe, however, that men and women are the pawns of social structure, borne down the river of class, gender, or race without any ability to affect their destinies. Neither do they hold that women and men are borne down the river of wholly "natural" gender relations. Rather, they assert that people's choices are located in the knotty intersection of human capacities for reproduction and individual choices about education and type of work preferred, both of which are located within deeply carved grooves of social arrangements. These social arrangements condition what is considered usual and what can be achieved by individuals under usual circumstances.[76]

Embedded in this difference between advocates and opponents is a different sense of the proper individuation of women and minorities. Advocates believe that increasing the value of traditional women's work starts a process that empowers individual women within their own families while also increasing the social recognition of occupations where women have predominated. Advocates believe that increased wages for working women increase women's power and autonomy within families, a situation which they believe strengthens families. So too advocates believe that increased power to minority workers means that they as individuals and their communities interact with the dominant white male culture on terms nearer to parity. This rhetoric of individuation in service of self, family, *and* group has parallels in much of the organizing activity of women and minorities. For example, historian Nancy Cott describes suffrage organizing in the 1910s as "a platform on which diverse people and organizations could comfortably, if temporarily, stand. The nineteenth-century view of the ballot as representing the self-possessed individual had been joined by the new emphasis on the ballot as the tool of group interest."[77] Using this type of approach, advocates of comparable worth have begun to make progress in redirecting these discussions away from a false debate between selfish female individualism and selfless female family love.

Advocates' and opponents' views of choice also play themselves out in views of comparable worth as a policy that enhances choices or requires specific solutions. The first view is seen as equality of opportunity and the second as equality of result. The preponderance of equity policy in the United States has consciously been designed as equality of opportunity predicated on removing barriers and thus enhancing choice. The Equal Pay Act of 1963 and the Civil Rights Act of 1964 are examples of this approach. For economic issues, the lesser-used equality-of-result approach has been the basis of public policy in a number of cases, most notably to establish a minimum wage, to determine occupational health and safety norms, and to develop clean air and water standards. Most opponents of comparable worth support equality of opportunity and decry comparable worth as an example of equality of result. June O'Neill makes this point when she writes that "in place of the goal of equality of opportunity [comparable worth] would substitute a demand for equality of results, and would do this essentially through regulation and legislation." She and others describe comparable worth as imposing wage rates based on uniform national rankings of jobs.

But comparable worth is clearly not what opponents like O'Neill portray it to be. Given its accurate description as a firm-level policy of paying women and men and minorities and nonminorities equivalently, on the basis of an evaluation of job content, is this policy even equality of result? It is hard to say. Advocates like Heidi Hartmann say no, arguing that comparable worth is a wage-setting process that gives all employees wages that reflect the choices available to the workers who have historically had the widest range of choices.

## Justice and Bureaucracy

For advocates, extending these choices to all workers makes the conditions of their labor more fair and just, and is a proper task of government. Opponents are very worried about the scale of bureaucracy that comparable worth might impose on employers, a worry that is magnified as opponents continue inaccurately to describe comparable worth as a policy designed to do a single job evaluation on a national scale.[78] Opponents see the bureaucratic threat of comparable worth in the classically conservative mode as the growth of publicly required rules enforced by ever-expanding public organizations. This concern mixes a fear about economic inefficiency with a long-standing mistrust of the power of large institutions, a mistrust found in many progressive American social movements as well as in conservative policy analysis.

Opponents bring up other large-scale, inter-organizational concerns, including the possibility that comparable worth cases would clog the courts, burden EEOC adjudication procedures, and strain the personnel capacities of businesses.[79] While the courts have shown reluctance to assess the adequacy of job evaluation systems, and the EEOC has been known for its backlog of cases at many times in its history, the concern about straining businesses needs to be specified.[80] Large employers, both public and private, already tend to use job classification and evaluation systems to assist in wage-setting. They have not until recently begun to use those systems to do a comparable worth analysis of their wage practices.[81]

Many private-sector job evaluation systems are not always adaptable to comparable worth analyses, however. Private sector employers tend to use several different job evaluation systems. But perhaps more important, large private employers have a history of using a tool they invented—job evaluation—to justify current wage arrangements.[82] It may be difficult to use the master's tools to dismantle the master's house.

As Chapters 5 and 6 will show, the paradoxes of using management tools and processes for fundamental social change have not previously been recognized in the discussions of this policy. Here, in the implementation process, new intra-organizational issues emerge. The first is the dilemma of changed wage rankings and the subjective losses and gains involved in changed rankings. Comparable worth redistributes status, even if the distribution of wages satisfies the Pareto optimal criterion of making at least one job classification better paid without changing the pay in all the others. By redistributing status and wage increases, comparable worth changes status and pay hierarchies. But most important, reform often comes in the dress of managerially determined technical analysis, mystified and controlled by people other than those who fought for the policy. The next chapter recounts the development of comparable worth policy around the country and more specifically in Minnesota. The Minnesota history shows how the structure of legislative decision-making renders considerations of implementation secondary to the maintenance of images and alliances necessary for passage.

# 4 Feminists, Union Leaders, and Democrats: The Passage of Comparable Worth Laws

Wages are a reflection of relative power
in our society.
*Nina Rothchild, Minnesota Commis-
sioner of Employee Relations*[1]

Minnesota was the first state to establish a comparable worth wage policy for state employees, fund it, and completely distribute the raises. From legislation to completed implementation took only five years, and during this time the state legislature also passed a law—the first in the nation—requiring that each local jurisdiction in Minnesota establish a comparable worth wage policy for its employees. In Minnesota the policy has always been called "pay equity" to emphasize its goal and encourage widespread support. "Other places may have comparable worth," said chief legislative author Senator Linda Berglin to the mostly skeptical members of the Association of Minnesota Counties, "but Minnesota has pay equity."[2] Passage of both pay equity laws was the product of fortuitous timing, skillful and committed legislators, an established women's policy community that had both a governmental and a grassroots base, and the vision of the state's largest public union, AFSCME. As is the case in most legislation, the problems of implementation were rarely considered, and when considered, were judged acceptable.

In this chapter we analyze the passage of both Minnesota pay equity laws and put Minnesota's efforts in national context. The experience in Minnesota is both typical and atypical of activism on this issue. Far more than has been currently recognized, Minnesota has been similar to most of the states that have moved quickly on comparable worth. Like them, Minnesota had legislation permitting collective bargaining in the public sector, had Democratic control of the House, Senate, and governorship during most of the period when the policy was adopted, and had an active Women's Commission to develop policy over the long run. But Minnesota was also one of the first states to act, enjoying the uncharacteristic luxury of considering comparable worth at a time when opposition forces were not as well organized as they would come to be. Likewise, Minnesota invented a new policy option: state legislation requiring local jurisdictions to implement a comparable worth wage policy. It is not clear whether state-mandated local implementation is just an interesting novelty or another, perhaps very powerful, tool for proponents to use in encouraging adoption on a wide scale. The importance of these infrequent or unique characteristics should not be lost. As Sidney Verba reminds us in his writings on comparative methodologies, "The 'unique historical event' cannot be ignored, but it must be considered as *one of a class of such events* even if it happened only once."[3]

## *Methodology*

The form of the case study presented here deserves special attention. The method used is what we call structured, highlighted comparison, after the structured, focused approach to comparative diplomatic history and politics suggested by Alexander George.* Like George and many other scholars of comparative social history, we hold that what one wants to understand in comparative history or policy is not so much the effects of variables on narrowly defined actions as the relationship of concepts, and the structures and processes they represent, to each other at certain histor-

---

*Alexander George's structured, focused comparison methodology presents a means of controlled comparison of a small number of richly developed cases. The purpose of the comparison is to develop the contingent generalizations that provide a basis of predictive theorizing. Organized in three phases, the structured, focused methodology begins with a design phase that specifies the problem, specifies the conditions and variables that will promote a controlled comparison, provides for the selection of appropriate cases that reflect the dimensions of controlled comparison, considers ways to increase the likelihood of discovering causal patterns, and formulates data requirements that need to be satisfied in the analysis of the cases. In the second phase, the case studies are explicated in detail and with adequate attention for the plausibility of alternative explanations. In phase three, the researchers refine the categorizations and relationships presented in phase one. Our methodology uses only one intensely detailed case study— Minnesota—but employs the rest of the methodology and provides summary information about every other state taking action on comparable worth. Hence, we have called our approach structured, highlighted comparison to show the emphasis on one contingently situated case study.

ical moments.[4] A structured, highlighted comparison is one that focuses on one case study (instead of several) but which has delineated the important relationships so that the focused comparisons that are made will advance the systematic investigation of the questions at hand.

In this chapter we use the experiences of the nineteen other states that have made some sort of comparable worth pay adjustments to highlight the passage of Minnesota's pay equity laws, especially Minnesota's state employees law. California, Connecticut, Florida, Illinois, Iowa, Massachusetts, Michigan, New Jersey, New Mexico, New York, Ohio, Oklahoma, Oregon, Pennsylvania, Rhode Island, South Dakota, Vermont, Washington, and Wisconsin join Minnesota as the states that provided some form of comparable worth pay adjustments as of August 1987. Six of these states (Minnesota, New Jersey, New Mexico, Oklahoma, South Dakota, and Wisconsin) primarily base their policies on enabling legislation, backed up by legislative appropriations.[5] In contrast, twelve states (California, Connecticut, Florida, Illinois, Iowa, Massachusetts, Michigan, New York, Ohio, Oregon, Vermont, and Washington) primarily based their policies on contract negotiations supported by legislative appropriations. Two states (Pennsylvania and Rhode Island) primarily depended on litigation to win comparable worth raises, although Washington state supporters used both negotiations and litigation. As a general rule, legislation provided comparable worth raises to the greatest number of workers in the largest number of job classifications, with negotiations covering a smaller pool of employees and litigation usually targeted to vary narrow job classifications and the smallest number of employees. Interestingly, the method of winning comparable worth had little or no effect on the conflicts that were faced. For these early-action states, the content of the policy, and the actors involved, were more important than the location of the activity.[6]

## State Efforts in National Perspective

The movement for comparable worth for public employees has progressed steadily since women's groups and unions in Washington began to press the policy in 1973. Considering the opposition of the Reagan administration, the record is quite impressive. By August 1987, forty-two states had engaged in research or data collection on comparable worth, thirty-six had appointed task forces or commissions, twenty-eight had participated in a job evaluation study, and twenty had provided some sort of comparable worth payments to at least a portion of state employees. (For the summary data on state comparable worth efforts, see Appendix B.)

The twenty states that have put money into some workers' paychecks form the basis of our comparisons with the Minnesota experience. Most of these states share both the structural conditions that promote progressive action and the specific political arrangements that act as the midwives to change. The cultural and economic structures these states share are frequently found in states that readily accept "liberal" economic policy. Thirteen of the active states have political cultures that at least partially support community-mindedness, a way of doing the state's business that has been described as moralistic in contrast to individualist or traditional.[7] In addition, the twenty most active states are more likely to have healthy, diversified economies; relatively high average personal incomes; more progressive (in the technical sense) taxation policies; and somewhat higher state and local tax burdens.

Specific political arrangements helped to translate the readiness for equity policy into equity action. Politicians and activists were most successful *when three political conditions coincided*: public sector collective bargaining, Democratic control of the state, and energetic Commissions on the Status of Women. Thirteen of the twenty most active states on this issue, Minnesota included, met all of these political conditions, and four of the most active states met at least two of them. The states that have met three of these conditions but have not implemented any portion of comparable worth pay raises (Alaska, Hawaii, Maine, Maryland, and Missouri) are the structurally most likely places for the next comparable worth successes. In fact, all five of these states have proceeded with comparable worth up to the point of making salary adjustments. But the next move is the most difficult and depends on very idiosyncratic combinations of political opportunity and political leadership. Missouri, a Phyllis Schlafly stronghold, offers the biggest challenge to organizers. One Missouri legislator who spoke with us reported that she had asked her priest if comparable worth was related to abortion, and only on hearing "no" had she settled into serious activism in favor of the issue. If these are the problems in states with supportive political conditions, states without at least two of the facilitative political characteristics are likely to be late adopters, if indeed they ever consider state-wide action for comparable worth. The intersection between state and national action will be very important for the states without the structural or political forces promoting change. Without the example of national legislation for federal workers, or the more remote but more effective option of mandated change though congressional legislation, many states will remain inhospitable to the theory and political activism of comparable worth.

Each of three political conditions supporting comparable worth deserves more attention because each elucidates a milieu conducive to success in policy innovation. Laws permitting collective bargaining in the public sector were perhaps the most important factors promoting comparable worth activism because they signalled the legitimacy and stability of worker organizations and facilitated the creation of coalitions of feminist and union activists typical of most early state action. There were exceptions, of course. Washington, the first state to embark on comparable worth, does not permit collective bargaining in the public sector, and neither does Oklahoma, though in Washington AFSCME was nevertheless a powerful actor in initiating comparable worth. But all of the other states making comparable worth adjustments to date allow public employees to unionize.

Comparable worth was more successful in states where Democrats exercised substantial (though by no means complete) control of the House, Senate, and governorship during the first four legislative biennia of the 1980s.[8] While many individual Republican politicians support comparable worth, the issue increasingly became associated with the Democrats and their constituencies, as the differences in the 1984 presidential platforms showed. Seventeen of twenty states giving comparable worth raises had substantial Democratic control during adoption or implementation. It is noteworthy that Democrats controlled forty-two states during this period. It was not Democratic control alone that promoted comparable worth, however, but Democratic control in conjunction with supportive labor laws and successful women's commissions. The existence of Democratic political power clearly supported public union activity even when the location of activity was the negotiation table and not the floor of the legislature.

The activism of commissions or task forces on the status of women provided the arena where policy was developed and where interest could be maintained as the political seasons changed. Public commissions on the status of women existed in sixteen of the states providing comparable worth raises, but in some other states more informal arrangements provided the continuity to act over a long period of time. In Minnesota, Oregon, California, and Connecticut, for example, the policy development efforts for comparable worth came from institutionalized women's groups like commissions on the status of women, which were in turn aided and supported by grass-roots feminist organizations, public unions (most frequently AFSCME or SEIU), and interested legislators.

These official women's groups were especially important because the states that acted most extensively on comparable worth tended to have highly professionalized legislatures, with relatively weaker interest-group power over the lawmaking process.[9] The structure of legislative decision-making made internal staff allies, like the legislatively housed Minnesota Commission on the Economic Status of Women, very important. The advantages that accrued to issues with inside support tended to make state legislative efforts for comparable worth more elite than grass-roots-dominated. Local efforts outside of Minnesota showed much greater variation of grass-roots and elite predominance in the issue.

As always, some successful states with highly professionalized legislatures did not have the advantage of help from official women's organizations. In Washington, the state women's council was abolished in 1978, midway through the comparable worth effort, but its advocacy role was picked up by Washington Women United, an umbrella organization for Washington feminist groups. In New York, the Center on Women and Government at the State University at Albany functioned in the agenda-setting process like a quasi-official women's commission. Somewhat unusually, support for the New York effort was completely dominated by elite advocates, with no grass-roots women's groups active in the effort to pass or implement a comparable worth policy. The New York Center's role was especially important because it, alone of most commissions or grass-roots groups at the time, had the capacity to undertake sophisticated job-content analyses, and it became one of the grantees providing job evaluation information to the state.[10] The Center's unique position demonstrates that although most feminist organizations were important in mobilizing interest for early state action, they could not contribute substantively to the technical debates on implementation, which became a struggle between labor and management, and occasionally among labor groups as well.

The content of comparable worth policies differs notably from state to state. Indeed, state variability of similarly labelled policies is one of the least-discussed aspects of the diffusion of innovation literature. The National Committee on Pay Equity reports a variety of approaches to the equal value question as comparable worth policy. Some states such as Washington, Minnesota, and New York base their policies on job evaluation and the comparison of equally valued jobs. Other states such as New Jersey and New Mexico have raised wages for the lowest-paid state workers before doing a job evaluation, which may or may not ever be completed.[11] The states in this second group have established what in Europe, especially Sweden, would be called a wage solidarity policy, although the policymakers using this approach in the United States do not use that language.[12] With wage solidarity, the lower-paid workers in a firm or sector (depending on the level at which bargaining is conducted) routinely get a higher-percentage raise than better-paid workers do. In this way, lower-paid and lower-skilled workers continue to make a living wage and the wage-spread between the lowest- and highest-paid workers is kept in check. This policy also allows more productive sectors to have higher wages. In this country, states that adopted an implicit wage-solidarity approach to comparable worth did so mostly for political reasons, either wanting to get raises to low-paid, mostly female and minority workers before a job evaluation could be done, or not wanting to undertake a job evaluation and be bound by the findings about job values.

In practice there are three operational definitions of achieving equal pay for equal value, two associated with the job evaluation approach and a third associated with the wage solidarity approach. Among those states with a comparable worth policy based on job evaluation, only Minnesota currently uses the pay in male-dominated jobs as the standard against which jobs with a preponderance of women are compared. (New York began its analysis by using the values of white and male jobs as the standard against which other jobs would be compared, but technical and political actions by the state altered this approach.)[13] In most other states, comparable worth means pay for points, where each increase in job evaluation points added a specified sum to wages. In practice, however, many states modified pay for points, bringing each job classification below the all-jobs pay practices line up to, or near, it. In wage solidarity states a certain percentage-raise or dollar increase in base pay, usually implemented as a one-time permanent change in wage rates, constitutes a pay equity policy.

The conflicts surrounding agenda setting for comparable worth were remarkably similar in most of the active states, in large part because the issue came to be understood in similar ways by the policymakers and the publics in those states. With the exception of Wisconsin, where the Association of Manufacturers and Commerce waged a vitriolic campaign against comparable worth based on accusations of employee inefficiency and high wages in the public sector,[14] the politics of comparable worth were conducted in the language of increased wages for historically underpaid female- and minority-dominated jobs. Within this setting two types of conflicts arose. The first concerned job evaluation. Did the state already use job evaluation and, if so, did it use one or more than one system? A 1986 report by the U.S. Government Accounting Office showed that 46 of 48 states responding to a GAO survey used job evaluation, and 34 of the 46 used a single system.[15] But many states redid their job evaluation systems when they decided to initiate comparable worth. In that case other questions arose. To what extent did management control job evaluation? Did the interest of management in job evaluation go beyond examining jobs for equal value to encompass a possible reclassification of the personnel system or redefinition of existing job classifications? The extent to which management controlled evaluation and classification was defined by each state's labor laws and practices and the policies developed to implement comparable worth. In Oregon the attempt to reconfigure the entire classification system contributed to the failure of the pay equity efforts of 1985–86.[16] The prior existence of a job evaluation system used in Minnesota's comparable worth implementation greatly facilitated the process.

The second conflict concerned financing. Would comparable worth primarily be an add-on to the wage bill, or would it redistribute existing wages or wage increases? If the political choice was to make comparable worth an add-on, many of the conflicts that arose focused around financing. If the choice was to emphasize restraining the pressure on the wage bill, many of the conflicts were over sharing the pain of slower wage growth or possible wage freezes, as well as sharing the gain in higher salaries for undervalued and underpaid classes. The first situation, in which Minnesota and Iowa fell, meant that advocates had to win the support of the people who controlled the state's revenue and appropriation politics.[17] The second situation, in which Oregon fell, meant that advocates had to win the support of the other labor groups, many of which saw comparable worth as a loss.[18] The real world can of course pose both types of problems for advocates, although the tendency so far has been for one or the other type of financial, and thus political, situation to dominate.

### *State Employees Pay Equity Act*

Structurally and politically, Minnesota was well positioned to take the lead in comparable worth. In particular, the political culture of Minnesota created an atmosphere supportive of this issue. In his classic study *Cities of the Prairie,* Daniel J. Elazar describes the moralistic political culture of Minnesota with emphasis on its traditions of community-mindedness:

"[T]he political order is conceived to be a commonwealth—a state in which the whole people have an undivided interest."[19] These traditions are part of the territorial legacy of Minnesota, a product first of English settlers of Puritan stock and then of German and Scandinavian settlers who brought their traditions of community participation. Political arrangements helped as well. Minnesota had a long and successful populist tradition and sustained its socialist experiments longer than did most states and cities on the eastern seaboard.

The political institutions and processes in Minnesota continue to reflect this legacy. Traditionally, the two major political parties define themselves as more liberal than their national counterparts. The Democratic-Farmer-Labor (DFL) party was formed in 1944 as a merger of the then-dominant Farmer-Labor party and the struggling Democratic party.[20] Until quite recently the Independent Republican (IR) party, a name adopted in 1975 in response to national trends away from partisanship, had traditionally portrayed itself as more sympathetic with the reform climate of Minnesota than with the increasingly powerful conservative wing of the national Republican party. The progressive nature of both parties on women's issues can be seen by the fact that both have feminist (not women's) caucuses. Partisanship was eschewed in the legislature, however, where elections were nonpartisan between 1913 and 1973.

Both the public and the private sectors are highly unionized in Minnesota. In 1981, 43.5% of public-sector workers and 20.7% of private-sector workers belonged to unions or professional associations that bargained for them. The labor history of the state was not without violence, however. In 1934 the famous teamsters' strike in Minneapolis pitted hundreds of workers against police and armed guards hired by the business owners. Four people died in the strike, and the union was finally recognized by employers. Modern labor relations have generally been calmer.[21] Public-sector employees were given the right to unionize in 1971, and the existing labor organizations of public workers, some which had been in existence since the 1930s, quickly took on their new roles.

AFSCME first raised the issue of comparable worth in 1974. Council 6 of AFSCME (which represents state employees) wanted the state to investigate possible discrimination in the pay practices and promotions of women. This move paralleled the efforts that AFSCME had underway in Washington State at that time. Paul Goldberg, the executive director of Council 6, expressed the union's concern when he told the press that "Salary rates for experienced, responsible clerical positions often requiring post high school business education are $10 to $150 less than the pay for inexperienced janitors, whose duties may be extremely limited."[22] The next year Council 6 successfully bargained for the study, but it was never funded or conducted.

By the late 1970s, however, a key set of state leaders capable of pursuing comparable worth coalesced around the Council on the Economic Status of Women. The legislature established the Council in 1976 with a budget of $95,000 and a requirement to report back by the end of 1977 on the "laws and practices constituting barriers to the full participation of women in the economy."[23] DFL Representative Linda Berglin, who chaired the Council, hired Nina Rothchild, a suburban school-board member and political activist, to serve as the Council's senior staff. Together they stood at the center of a network that reached out into grass-roots women's organizations, AFSCME, and the Coalition of Labor Union Women (CLUW), feminist caucuses in both major political parties, and members of the Minnesota legislature sympathetic to women's issues.

Two powerful women with complementary talents, Berglin and Rothchild oversaw a stream of research and publications on women in the Minnesota economy. Defining "economic status" broadly, the Council examined and made legislative recommendations on issues such as sex discrimination in insurance, inheritance taxes, and housing; minimum wage and tip credits; tax credits for child care; age discrimination; and family planning. In avoiding divisive issues like abortion (which the Council declined to define as an economic issue) and by lobbying only *for* its own bills and not *against* bills of which it disapproved, the Council compiled a remarkably successful record in its first two and a half years, winning passage of 21 of 32 recommended bills. Legislators who agreed to sponsor Council legislation received copies of suggested wording for the bill, background information packets, and suggestions for persons who could be called upon to testify.[24]

The Council maintained a special interest in the status of women who worked for the state, holding hearings in 1976 on women as state employees and publishing a report on the same topic in 1977. The analysis noted the low wages of women and their concentration in jobs held primarily by women. By documenting wage disparities and the gender segregation of the state's labor forces, the Council contributed to a growing recognition that the 1963 Equal Pay Act and Title VII of the 1964 Civil Rights Act did not raise women's wages because women and men so rarely held the same jobs.

In 1978 and 1979, in moves distinct from the research of the Council, the state undertook an examination of its personnel system that would later

have profound ramifications on the course of comparable worth policy
making. Faithful to its traditions, Minnesota was a national leader in civil
service reform. Its interest in personnel reform and rationalization pre-
dated similar actions on the part of the federal government. The Minnesota Legislative Audit Commission completed an evaluation of the state's
personnel system in 1978, and in 1979 the Department of Finance published its "Public Employment Study" which included the findings of a
Hay Associates study of salary and benefit policies. These reports provided the data necessary to compare equally valued jobs. The crucial information was contained in the job evaluation Hay undertook of 762
multi-incumbent job classes. Hay Associates did not plan for its data to
be used in a comparable worth analysis. In fact it reported that " 'in general there appears to be a slight tendency to pay male-dominated occupations at a higher level than female-dominated classes. However . . . this
includes an extremely small percentage of positions.' "[25]

In the fall of 1981, the Council on the Economic Status of Women
appointed a Pay Equity Task Force to reanalyze the Hay Associates data
by comparing male- and female-dominated job classes having the same
point values. The Council had undergone a good many changes in the
two-year period between the publication of the Hay Associates report and
the formation of the Task Force. In 1981 the DFL-controlled legislature
granted permanent status to the Council with an amendment that prohibited it from advocating abortion in any way. Newly elected IR Governor
Al Quie appointed several conservatives to be public members of the
Council, including some who had worked to abolish it.[26] During the summer, AFSCME, the Council's long-time ally in economic issues concerning women, was involved in a strike against the state.

With the AFSCME strike resolved and interest in comparable worth
growing everywhere, the Council astutely appointed the members of the
Pay Equity Task Force with an eye for future legislation. The Council
called on the services of six legislators representing both parties who were
sensitive to women's issues and well-placed in the legislature. The Task
Force also included representatives of important constituencies, most notably AFSCME. In using the term "pay equity" to name the Task Force,
the Council chose to emphasize the issue of fairness and build its political
constituency.

Council staff member Bonnie Watkins compiled the list of comparable
jobs after the Council pried the Hay data out of a reluctant Department of
Employee Relations. Her first task was to sort out male- and female-
dominated job classes, defining these as jobs which were 80% or more

male and 70% or more female. Her second task was to compare the pay scales of equally valued positions for gender differences.[27]

The results were striking; it was found that women's jobs routinely paid around 20% less than men's jobs at the same Hay-point level (see table 1.1). In 1981, the highest monthly pay of the Delivery Van Driver position, a male-dominated class receiving 117 Hay points, was $1,382. The highest monthly salary for the Clerk Typist 2 position, a female-dominated class with 117 Hay points, was $1,115. At the highest end of the pay range, the Delivery Van Driver position made $267 (23.9%) more per month than the Clerk Typist position. The findings repeated themselves at every level of Hay points. Grain Inspector 2, at 173 Hay points, earned a monthly maximum of $1,693 while Human Services Specialist, at 177 Hay points, earned a monthly maximum of $1,343, a 26.1% difference. The highest salary for the Pharmacist position, 353 Hay points, was $2,297, which compared to $1,911 (or 20.2% less) for the Registered Nurse 3 position having the same number of points.[28]

Once the tabular analysis was completed, Watkins plotted each class on a graph whose axes were Hay points and income (highest point of the pay range for that job.) The resulting now-familiar scattergram, figure 1.1, demonstrated the dramatic differences in pay between comparable male and female jobs. Not a single female-dominated job class reached the pay line established by the male classes.

The Task Force report based on Watkins' analysis was released in January 1982. It made public the disparities between male- and female-dominated job classes receiving equal points under the Hay system. The report formed the basis of the State Employees Pay Equity Act introduced by Council Chair Linda Berglin, who had moved to the state Senate in 1980. The bill was shepherded through the legislature by Berglin and DFL Representative Wayne Simoneau with a minimum of fanfare. The bill established the principle of pay equity as the *primary* basis of remuneration in state employment, spelled out a process by which it could be achieved, but did not carry an appropriation. The state was in the midst of a deep recession in 1982 and the specter of a possible budget deficit made a new personnel appropriation a difficult if not impossible option. In hearings, scattergrams like figure 1.1 graphically depicted the Task Force's findings while lobbyists quietly assured legislators that funding for the bill could wait another year. Rick Scott, the chief lobbyist for AFSCME, later indicated that the decision to separate the law and the appropriation was the most critical step in establishing the policy.[29] The final vote on the measure was 63 for and 0 against in the Senate, and 82 for and 3 against in the House. Governor Al Quie signed the bill with no delay.

The press remained silent, in large part because the bill's sponsors chose a low-keyed approach to passage, and there was no opposition from the business community. In March the *Minneapolis Star and Tribune* barely noted passage of the bill. Buried in a longer article on the sixth page of the second section were a series of photographs under "Other bills signed by the Governor were. . . ." The second of five read: "Establish a state policy of comparable worth in state employment, aimed at ensuring that so-called 'women's' jobs carry salaries equal to comparable jobs usually reserved for men."[30]

The purpose of the State Employees Pay Equity Act was to "attempt to establish equitable compensation relationships between female-dominated, male-dominated, and balanced classes of employees in the executive branch."[31] The law placed this wage innovation within existing labor legislation regarding pay practices for public employees. Like many laws governing state employees, Minnesota's public employment statute required "reasonable relationships" between the compensation of classified and unclassified positions, between similar jobs inside and outside state employment, between management and subordinate classes in collective bargaining units, and among related job classes. Indeed, achieving parity for state jobs with positions in the private work force was a hard-fought battle for public employee organizations.[32] Recognizing the importance of these relationships, the State Employees Pay Equity Act elevated comparable worth to "*the primary* consideration" in compensation policy.[33] The law left unchanged the presumption that the choice of a job evaluation system remained a management prerogative, subject only to "meet and confer" requirements with unions (i.e., unions must be informed and their opinions solicited, but the choice is not a matter for negotiation). At the same time the legislation reaffirmed the centrality of collective bargaining as the mechanism for establishing the terms and conditions of employment for unionized employees. In particular, unions could negotiate the timing and schedule of pay equity raises, although the amount necessary to achieve pay equity for each job class was determined by the Department of Employee Relations' analysis and the amount available in any biennium to move toward that correction was determined by the legislative appropriation process.

In the fall of 1982 Minnesotans elected DFL Governor Rudy Perpich, bringing the control of the governor's mansion as well as the state house into the hands of the DFL. Perpich appointed Nina Rothchild, senior staff member of the Council on the Economic Status of Women, to serve as Commissioner of Employee Relations. Rothchild's office, refining CESW figures, estimated that the full cost of implementing pay equity would be approximately $26 million or about 4% of personnel costs. Perpich was unwilling to absorb the full cost in one biennium, a politically astute judgment shared by most but not all of the law's backers. In consultation with others, Perpich chose a four-year implementation period. He included an appropriation for more than half of the pay equity raises in his 1983–1985 biennial budget. The full implementation period paralleled the governor's term in office, thereby insuring as much as possible that the dispersal would not depend on the vagaries of the next gubernatorial election. As it turned out, the legislative elections of 1984 gave the House of Representatives to the IRs, an electoral surprise that endangered the last year of the pay equity implementation.

## *The Local Law*

The passage and initial funding of the Minnesota State Employees Pay Equity Act brought comparable worth to the attention of Minnesotans and Minnesota to the attention of the nation. The increasing local and national attention to the issue, in part brought about by successes in Minnesota and elsewhere, meant that comparable worth was no longer an issue well-known only to its supporters and closely controlled by them. Minnesota legislation for local employees was passed in this new atmosphere of greater awareness. Its success depended on the same constellation of political forces, aided by a state constitution that gives the legislature rather significant power over the internal workings of local governments.

In Minnesota, newspaper coverage of pay equity increased noticeably after the state law had passed, with reporters and editors praising the new wage policy. Minnesota labor and feminist activists took heart as well from the increased national visibility of comparable worth. National unions like AFSCME and the Service Employees International Union (SEIU), District 925, made comparable worth more prominent on their organizing agendas, while the National Committee on Pay Equity expanded its operations and the number of organizations affiliated with its work. The NCPE made a concerted effort to publicize the importance of race and ethnicity in comparable worth analyses. All over the country local unions and women's groups, from NOW chapters to business and professional women's associations, were initiating comparable worth efforts.[34]

But the Minnesota success also coincided with a new and more vociferous phase of activity by opponents. Nationally, business interests were fearful that comparable worth would be forced on the private sector. A number of business associations supported anti-comparable-worth efforts. For example, the associate director of human resources and equal opportunity for the National Association of Manufacturers was quoted in an article in *Business Week* in 1985, referring to comparable worth, "What employers don't want is some court or government agency playing God,"[35] The Association, like many other business organizations, has always been opposed to any government intervention on behalf of employees in business activities. It had, for example, opposed various laws limiting child labor with the same argumentation it marshalled against comparable worth. In 1924 it adopted a resolution that read, "Resolved that we, the members of the N.A.M. in convention assembled, pledge ourselves to the protection and betterment of child life in our respective communities, disapprove of this revolutionary grant of power to the Congress as repugnant to our traditional conception of local responsibility and self-government, tending to stimulate growth of enlarged and extravagant bureaucracy and serving to defeat the very humanitarian purpose which its disguise suggests."[36]

The Minnesota business community played only a small role in the politics of comparable worth. The Minnesota Association of Commerce and Industry (MACI, now the Minnesota Chamber of Commerce and Industry, MCCI), was mostly inactive in regard to the passage of the Local Government Pay Equity Act, although several years later, emboldened by the changing national climate against pay equity and the success of its Wisconsin counterpart in recasting that state's comparable worth lawmaking, the Minnesota group took an anti-comparable-worth stand in its briefings of state legislative candidates. In the early 1980s, however, no business opposition hindered local unions in their push for local pay-equity legislation. This push presumed the legality of state control over the pay policies of local jurisdictions. The legality of such action, in turn, rested on specific constitutional and statutory arrangements. These state and local power arrangements form the basis for understanding the implementation of the local comparable worth law in Minnesota and its implications for other states.

Localities, states, and the federal government were not created equally powerful in the American political system. Through the ratification of the

U.S. Constitution the states created a permanent federal government of expressly delineated powers, with the states retaining their independent existence and residual power.[37] Relations between the states and the localities within their borders do not parallel federal-state relations. Whereas the states created the federal government, localities did not create the states. The relation between localities and states is just the opposite. Localities are for the most part the subordinate creations of the states, and "in the absence of express [state] constitutional provisions to the contrary, the power of the state legislature over local government units is plenary and supreme."[38] The principle that guides state hegemony over local power is called "Dillon's rule" of statutory construction, which articulates that local governments "can exercise only powers granted in [a] state statute or those necessarily or fairly implied or incident to the powers expressly granted."[39]

In practice, states do not wholly determine the policies of localities. By charter, statute, or provisions of state constitutions, localities may formally acquire explicit "home rule" (i.e., independent) powers, and tradition defines other home-rule practices. One constant tension in state and local relations is the resolution of which laws will prevail—state or local. States and localities often have separate and competing interests. In a recent review of home-rule issues, C. Dallas Sands and Michael E. Libonati show that, in the main, state concerns continue to hold sway over local considerations in the resolution of such differences. Using the example of wage disputes in which local entities may define their interests in terms of maintaining low wage-rates for local employees while the state legislature presumes that a higher quality of public service can be attained "if the pay is higher and uniform for similar kinds of work," the authors conclude that, in general, statutory or constitutional home-rule provisions do not "limit the plenary power of the state legislature . . . within the sphere of state affairs."[40]

The powers acquired under home-rule provisions vary from location to location, and the general character of home-rule power does not perfectly predict whether specific action, like state legislation requiring local comparable worth, is possible. California grants to municipalities perhaps the widest array of home-rule powers, permitting a municipality with a home-rule charter to make and enforce virtually all laws and regulations concerning municipal affairs.[41] The New York Constitution explicitly delineates the "rights" of local governments, including the control of the "compensation, hours of work, protection, welfare and safety of its [local government's] officers and employees."[42] Minnesota does not have a history of strong home rule. While the Minnesota Constitution permits "any local government when authorized by law" to adopt a home-rule charter, it also leaves to the state legislature the power to legislate on the "creation, organization, administration, consolidation, division or dissolution of local government units and their functions."[43]

Senator Linda Berglin, who understood the constitutional arrangements of Minnesota very well, never thought twice about whether the state could impose a comparable worth law on local governments. She knew it was possible and legislatively proper.[44] The interest in comparable worth at the local government level was very evident. In the summer of 1983, Minnesota Working Women, an organization of clerical workers, reported that the salaries of men in Minneapolis city employment averaged more than $20,000 per year, but women's average earnings were much less. In a separate action, three employees of Hennepin County (greater Minneapolis) who were members of AFSCME undertook a pay equity study matching county jobs to the state's Hay-point system and job descriptions. This study, done on the employees' own time, showed that women employees earned less than men in comparable county jobs. From this study AFSCME learned about pay inequities and the commitment of a group of county employees to extend pay equity to the local level. Some union activists wanted to win local pay equity by negotiations and others wanted to achieve it through legislation, but all knew management would not be as supportive locally as it had been at the state level. When the results of the Hennepin County job-match study were announced, county personnel administrators were unenthusiastic. Most elected county officials were no more supportive than were professional personnel staff. At that time, Hennepin County Commissioner Mark Andrew, a Democrat, indicated that he was probably the only one on his board willing to adopt pay equity.[45]

Elected officials in Minneapolis and St. Paul were more supportive. Minneapolis Mayor Don Fraser and St. Paul Mayor George Latimer, both Democrats, favored the policy and many city council members expressed their support as well. Both mayors were the object of grass-roots comparable worth pressures in the summer of 1983. Minnesota Working Women pressured the Minneapolis administration to adopt pay equity. They were joined in their efforts by AFSCME, which had also initiated a pay equity study in St. Paul.

All efforts to encourage local pay equity were buoyed by the reports in September 1983 of the decision of the U.S. District Court Judge Jack Tanner in *AFSCME v. State of Washington.*[46] Tanner's ruling that comparable worth was a valid form of redress for sex discrimination under Title

VII of the 1964 Civil Rights Act made real the threat of suits and motivated advocates and opponents alike. In the same month, representatives of local clerical workers, including Minnesota Working Women and AFSCME, approached the newly fashioned Commission on the Economic Status of Women to propose pay equity on the local level. Their demands came a mere seven weeks after the well-publicized first round of pay equity raises for state employees. A newspaper's response to the distribution of state pay equity raises acknowledged that the policy was more complicated than equal pay for equal work but concluded that "If justice is to be attained without chaos or governmental interference, Minnesota has shown the way to go about it: from workplace to workplace, with decisions based on reasoned comparisons that can command general acceptance."[47]

The Council on the Economic Status of Women had had political troubles earlier that year. In the spring of 1983 Republican citizen-appointees to the Council had joined with its single Republican legislator to oust the Council's chair, Senator Berglin, and to elect a new chair.[48] In response, the DFL-dominated legislature voted to transform the council into a legislative commission whose members would all be drawn from the legislature itself. This conflict did not detract from the consideration of local pay equity which occurred several months later.

In the midst of all this ferment for a law covering local jurisdictions, Senator Berglin began to canvass the professional associations representing public managers and officials, including the Association of Minnesota Counties (AMC), the League of Minnesota Cities (LMC), and the Minnesota School Boards Association (MSBA), about the feasibility of a local pay equity law. The importance of state action was heightened when, in October 1983, the Minnesota School Employees Association filed an EEOC complaint on behalf of clerical workers in the Anoka-Hennepin School District because the board (like the Hennepin County board) refused to accept the principle of comparable worth. In neighboring suburban St. Louis Park, clerical workers were deadlocked in bargaining with the school board over the same issue.[49] By this time, AFSCME had read the cards and decided to place state-mandated local pay equity at the top of its legislative agenda.

Legislative efforts began in earnest when the session opened in January 1984. Although the Local Government Pay Equity Act passed in both houses by overwhelming margins, its legislative history was more conflictual than that of the state law. Early in the 1984 session, IR Representative

David Bishop proposed a bill to make pay equity a voluntary rather than state-mandated local government wage policy. In contrast, Senator Berglin, DFL Representative Phillip Riveness, CESW Executive Director Aviva Breen, the Department of Employee Relations, and AFSCME formulated the successful local bill.

This bill *required* all political subdivisions of the state to adopt a pay equity wage policy. Specifically, the law required jurisdictions to conduct job evaluation studies, to examine the results of the studies for differences in the pay of equivalent male, female, and balanced classes, to estimate the cost of remedying the differences in equivalently valued male- and female-dominated and balanced classes, and to provide a plan for implementing the necessary pay changes. Jurisdictions were given a great deal of freedom in choosing the methodology for accomplishing these goals. Most important, the choice of job evaluation methodology was left solely to localities, whose only requirement was to "meet and confer" with unions (if any), not to negotiate with them, on the choice of job evaluation system. The only requirement imposed on localities was to report the results of their studies and plans to the Department of Employee Relations by October 1985, but even this stricture was not backed up with a penalty for noncompliance. The Department in turn was required to make a summary report of local activities to the legislature early in 1986. In the shadow of *AFSCME v. State of Washington,* Minnesota lawmakers included a provision in the local government pay equity law that protected local jurisdictions from actions in state courts or by the State Human Rights Department until August 1987. Such protections did not extend to protection from suit in federal court under Title VII of the Civil Rights Act, however. In practice, many local jurisdictions took the deadline for protection from suit in state courts, not the reporting requirements to the Department of Employee Relations, as the clock they had to beat.

Backers of the Local Government Pay Equity Act saw the freedom they gave to public managers, including their control of the choice of job evaluation system, as an unbreachable defense against the inevitable charges that the state was "out to control" local governments. The philosophical positions of advocates underpinning this stance were complicated. From philosophical and tactical perspectives, proponents believed that local control of efforts like this was a good idea. Regarding the substance of the policy, they were not really worried about what different job evaluation systems would show in Minnesota because all the previous research on comparable worth had demonstrated that every job evaluation system found disparities between equally valued male and female jobs. They were unaware, as was the rest of the policy community nationwide, of what the different evaluations of similar jobs from jurisdiction to jurisdiction would mean to the public perception of the issue. Similarly, they judged the varying capacities of localities to undertake job evaluation as an acceptable cost of implementation. Their source for considering the implementation capacities of local governments was a memo written by legislative analyst David Lutes. The memo reported that large cities had well-developed personnel capacities but that smaller jurisdictions had old classification and pay schemes, if any at all. Supporters assumed that large governments with existing classification systems would *not* refashion these systems, and that small governments would match their job definitions with the state's job definitions. The widespread use of consultants was not predicted.

Few of these concerns were voiced in hearings on the local bill. Instead, the legislative conflict was over voluntary or mandated change. For example, the League of Minnesota Cities and the Minnesota School Boards Association testified in favor of the principle of pay equity but preferred a voluntary bill over a state mandate. Voluntary compliance did not seem adequate in the wake of the Tanner decision, especially with a public perception of a gender gap in voting in a presidential election year. The House passed the bill requiring local pay equity in a vote of 104 to 20, and the Senate gave its assent 60 to 0.[50] Governor Perpich readily signed it.

In final form, the local bill was not as strong as the state bill. Two changes, each sparked by the concerns of professional groups representing localities, would come to have serious effects on how local managers implemented the law. Unlike the state bill, the local bill did not give comparable worth considerations primacy over all other factors affecting the compensation of local public employees. Instead of using the language of the state law designating "equitable compensation relations" as *"the primary"* wage-setting consideration, the local law made equitable compensation *"a primary"* consideration. Thus the statements in the law establishing relations between pay within and outside local government service came to play an important role in implementation, especially the section requiring that "compensation for positions bear reasonable relationship to similar positions outside of that particular subdivision's employment."[51] As we shall see in Chapter 6, this section has been interpreted by many managers as requiring that jurisdictions connect pay levels to market wages as well as to comparable worth considerations, a position advocates believe weakens the comparable worth provision, and violates comparable worth theory.*

A second change in the law reflected a compromise with the Association of Minnesota Counties, which had worked actively against the law. The AMC was the most vigorous group lobbying for the changes in the policy statement making equitable compensation relationships "a primary" rather than "the primary" determinant of pay policy. In addition to their war on the definite article, the AMC successfully lobbied for the inclusion of the phrase "and other relevant work related criteria" to the section designating that positions be paid in proportion to skill, effort, responsibility, and working conditions. The major use of this phrase has been internal to the job evaluation and wage-setting process, where managers have been encouraged to give job evaluation points to managerial and professional employees who are not eligible for overtime under the Fair Labor Standards Act. This practice is used to justify the vertical wage distance between salaried and hourly employees.

### Attempts to Change the Laws

The local law was weaker than the state law, a weakness that opponents tried to exploit through two attempts to undercut the local legislation, as well as one related, but unsuccessful, attempt to cut short the implementation of the state pay equity raises. Two bills designed to weaken the local legislation were introduced in 1985 legislative session. In the first, police and firefighters tried to have their positions removed from the job evaluation studies. In the second, opponents, led by the AMC, attempted to have the reporting deadlines and legal protections extended by two years. Police and firefighters, often important actors in state and local politics, have unusual clout in Minnesota politics. They argued that, because they were essential employees who could not strike and whose intractable labor disputes routinely went to interest arbitration, they should not be included in

---

*This highly complex argument proceeds on very different levels. Managers and their legal counsels have generally viewed the law as specifying the factors that should influence local pay rates, namely, "equitable compensation relationships" and "reasonable relationship to similar positions outside of that particular political subdivision's employment." The former requires an internal pay equity analysis; the latter presumes a market survey of some kind. Pay equity advocates point out that the central purpose of pay equity is to rectify historic discrimination perpetuated by the market. To allow the market a strong influence over wage rates for female- or minority-dominated job classes, then, runs counter to the purpose of pay equity.

the job evaluation system. Using another tack, representatives of the county association argued that the job evaluation studies were too difficult to complete in the time allocated and that a two-year extension was necessary.

These changes were successfully avoided by the coordinated efforts of the League of Women Voters, AFSCME, and the Department of Employee Relations. Independent Republicans had gained control of the House in 1984, so advocates concentrated their efforts on the Senate, where DFL friends of the legislation retained control of the relevant committees. The extension bill was scotched. Lieutenant Governor Marlene Johnson actively worked against the extension, and Governor Perpich threatened to veto any changes in the law. In a closed meeting, with AFSCME protesting, the firefighters and the police won a change in the language of the law dealing with interest arbitration. Arbitrators were directed to "consider" rather than "follow" equitable compensation standards as part of the broader standards they employed in making compensation decisions.[52]

In the 1986 legislative session, pay equity legislation faced its third challenge, this one directed at the state law. By this time three years of the planned four-year implementation of the wage increases had been completed. Minnesota state government suffered a revenue shortfall, however, due in large part to a politically motivated tax cut the year before. Independent Republicans in the House of Representatives suggested that the last segment of the pay equity raises be "unallocated."

All the attacks on pay equity had taken the women's community somewhat by surprise. At each juncture where the laws were attacked, legislators supporting pay equity contacted the Minnesota Women's Consortium, an organization of 154 women's organizations, which then mobilized its member groups to counter the threat to the legislation. There were no women's groups which could afford a full-time paid legislative liaison, although the League of Women Voters had an excellent representative in unpaid part-time lobbyist Carolyn Hendrixson. In addition to a lack of resources for tracking legislation, the women's community had a crowded agenda which encouraged activists to move from one pressing issue to the next. Once a bill became a law little attention would or could be paid to it. Each time the pay equity laws were assailed, something of a crisis atmosphere developed, especially during the attempt to "unallocate" the last pay equity raise for state employees.

Local women's groups saw the move to stop the implementation of the state law as part of a three-pronged attack against women's issues that included not only pay equity cuts but also significant reductions in AFDC payments and the serious underbudgeting of the Commission on the Economic Status of Women (in an attempt to end its role in policy initiation). All three efforts were checked. The last state pay equity raises were allocated and the CESW was saved. The most difficult victory was the restoration of most of the AFDC budget, which took the combined efforts of all the major religious leaders in the Twin Cities plus labor, women's, and civil rights groups.

Proponents of pay equity were glad when the DFL retook the House of Representatives in November 1986, extending Democratic control of the legislature and governor's mansion through 1988. This situation protected the local implementation process through that period. Legislative supporters used this Democratic control to solidify the implementation process and redress some of the weaknesses in the local legislation. In a barely noticed move, DFL Senator Ember Reichgott added some bite to the local implementation process. In the 1987 legislative session, she tied school appropriations to the timely completion of a school district's pay equity study, a move that caused all school boards to meet an October 1, 1987, deadline for developing policy. In the 1988 session, supporters passed legislation imposing penalties on cities and counties with more than ten employees that do not comply with the pay equity reporting requirements by October 1, 1988. Furthermore, they required local implementation of pay equity by December 31, 1991 (unless another date is established by the legislature) and provided a 5% reduction in local government aid for failure to implement. Not surprisingly, localities expressed mixed reactions. While most would have implemented some part of comparable worth by the legislative deadline, many chafed at the specificity of the new law. The scale of local implementation, and its control by managers wary of its equity premises, led to great variations in the local patterns of adoption and thus to this new requirement. The state, on the other hand, enjoyed an unusually easy implementation process, as the next chapter shows.

# 5 Textbook Implementation: Comparable Worth for State Employees

> Study says state women live longer,
> know more, earn less.
> *Headline,*Minneapolis Star and
> Tribune, *September 26, 1984*[1]

Implementation of comparable worth for Minnesota state employees went very smoothly, and the effects on the state government apparatus, the unions, and employees were mostly positive. The important actors were different in this phase of the policy process than in the legislative struggle, however. In particular, women's groups, so crucial to passing and sustaining the legislation, were absent from implementation because implementation was an internal state government process. Indeed, the absence of women's groups is the first lesson of implementation politics for this issue: one of the major social supporters of comparable worth was not a regular participant in its implementation.

In this chapter we analyze how the Department of Employee Relations and the unions completed the legislative mandate set forth in the State Employees Pay Equity Act. We discuss where this case fits into the literature on implementation, analyze the bargaining and administrative processes that made the policy a reality, and show the consequences of implementing pay equity for the groups and individuals supporting and opposing it.

## Implementation and the State of Minnesota Case

In many ways, the state of Minnesota's experience is a model of easy implementation. Daniel Mazmanian and Paul Sabatier argue that the fulfillment of legislative directives requires a clearly written statute that structures the implementation of a tractable problem supported by committed leaders.[2] This fortuitous situation does not occur very often, but the implementation of pay equity at the state level in Minnesota was almost a textbook example of implementation made easy. Viewed in the light of Mazmanian and Sabatier's general guidelines, implementation went smoothly because the state enjoyed a statute that unambiguously required that pay equity become *the* principle for establishing wage policy. The legislature made the appropriation for pay equity raises separate and distinct from general pay raises, thus forestalling any financial games that might have been played with the money earmarked for pay equity raises.[3] In the Department of Employee Relations, no new administrative routines in salary dispersal were necessary. Collective bargaining activities required only slight and temporary alterations. And the leaders most directly responsible for carrying out the policy were committed to it and capable.

Beyond these guidelines, however, there existed a series of specific conditions and decisions that allowed this policy to be adopted without great fuss. One condition was wholly accidental, but it proved crucial. The state had completed its job evaluation several years before it established its pay equity policy and distributed the first pay equity raises. Because of this, pay equity was not tied to the often painful and disruptive process of establishing job hierarchies. A second important condition was the fact that all the important leaders in the implementation process understood in great detail the arguments supporters made about the structural origins of women's low wages. For the most part, leaders in AFSCME and the Department of Employee Relations wholeheartedly believed that the jobs held primarily by women had low wages in part because women usually held those jobs. Their commitment to the underlying rationale of equal pay for jobs of equal value led them to decide to use the male pay practices line as the standard against which female-dominated jobs would be compared. Commissioner of Employee Relations Nina Rothchild was often asked why the state did not merely compute the pay practice line for all jobs and compare salaries in female-dominated jobs with it. She responded with humor and firmness that "I was a math major at Smith College. I know enough not to include the salaries of women's jobs, which have been held down by discrimination, in my standard for nondiscriminatory wages."[4]

The use of the male pay practices line as the standard for all wages and the existence of a separate allocation for comparable worth raises alert us to an important quality of implementation at the state level: in theory and practice supporters of pay equity at the state level designed a distributive program, that is, a program that increased not only the wages of female-dominated jobs but the overall wage bill. In innovative research about implementation patterns, Randall Ripley and Grace Franklin propose that different types of policies—distributive, competitive regulatory, protective regulatory, and redistributive—have different types of implementation patterns.[5] Because they provide "add-ons" or inducements, distributive policies, like grants to localities to build airports or cash payments to purchase agricultural products and support their prices, are fairly easy to implement if existing management systems are running smoothly.[6] This was certainly the case for state implementation of comparable worth. But designing a distributive policy and persuading people that the resources are actually supplementary are separate political problems. The whole political success of implementing state-level comparable worth rested on retaining the sense that comparable worth raises were an addition to rather than a competitor with general salary increases, and that no job classification would have its salary lowered.

The distributive quality of implementation at the state level differs from the redistributive quality of comparable worth at the local level.[7] As the analysis of local implementation will show, the lack of commitment to the male pay practices line, the uncertainty that supplementary funds would be allocated by localities for comparable worth raises, and the concomitant possibility that some wages might be frozen or lowered, made the implicit theory and practice of local implementation more redistributive. Redistributive policies are harder to implement than distributive ones because they are more unpopular and require continuous bargaining between bureaucrats and beneficiaries. The stress of redistributive politics, where one group's win is another group's loss, often leads to efforts to make such policies more distributive. Indeed, most localities chose to make a redistributive situation more distributive by giving raises to male and balanced classes below the all-jobs line.

## *Bargaining for and Administering Equity*

### *History of Public Unionism*

The distributive politics of state implementation were a product of the labor relations in state employment, themselves an example of new labor relations in the public sector. The relationship between public employers and their employees has changed dramatically over the last several decades. In 1959, for example, only one state permitted public employees to unionize.[8] This situation was a legacy of the Wagner Act of 1935, the legislation that fully legalized and protected many aspects of collective bargaining but which did not cover public employees. Both the public norms and the case law during the first sixty years of this century argued that public employment was a privilege and that public bodies did not have the right to share power with their employees.[9]

In the early 1960s this tradition began to change, aided in part by John F. Kennedy's Executive Order 10988, promulgated in 1962, which gave limited collective bargaining rights to federal employees. Using the federal example, many states, mostly outside the South, passed laws allowing state and sometimes local employees to engage in certain collective activities including bargaining and occasionally striking. During the so-called "first generation" of public sector bargaining, roughly from 1960 to 1975, public employment grew at an average yearly rate of approximately 5%, more than twice as fast as private employment.[10] Public sector unionization grew markedly as well, with 12.8% of the public labor force covered by unions and professional associations in 1960 and 39.4% covered in 1976.[11] The comparable worth movement had its roots in this period, when AFSCME, one of its prime union sponsors, enjoyed a great deal of success in state and local organizing. By 1978, AFSCME had over a million members nationwide, and represented just under one in four unionized workers at the state and local level.[12] The period after 1975 has often been considered the "second generation" of public sector bargaining. In the years between 1975 and 1983 public employment grew by roughly 1% annually, while private employment grew at a yearly rate of approximately 4%.[13] In the first three years of the 1980s, public employment declined by approximately 400,000 people, with most of the cuts seen in local government, which accounts for about 60% of public employment. This decline has been interpreted both as a reflection of politicians' and citizens' attack on government size and a response to a greatly altered economic situation in the country as a whole.[14]

The State Employees Pay Equity Act was a result of the power of public unions in Minnesota. In 1971, both collective bargaining in the public sector and the right of "nonessential" public personnel to strike became the law with the passage of the Public Employees Labor Relations Act (PELRA). There was a long tradition of public labor organizations in Minnesota dating to the 1930s and 40s. But these organizations could not represent workers in contract negotiations. All that was changed by PELRA, which greatly strengthened all the existing labor groups, but especially AFSCME Council 6.

In the early days of public unionism, the state bargained with as many as 118 bargaining units. In 1980, in a move to rationalize the bargaining process, PELRA was amended to create sixteen functionally defined bargaining units. The legislature authorized the director of the state Bureau of Mediation Services to certify unions that could show they represented a majority of workers in the new units. In that year a group of approximately 5,000 professional employees broke away from AFSCME and were recertified as the Minnesota Association of Professional Employees (MAPE). Around the country, AFSCME was having trouble retaining its professional employees. The creation of MAPE out of AFSCME members resulted in prickly relations between the two unions.

In 1981, AFSCME employees struck the state of Minnesota over the salary settlement in its contracts and higher health insurance costs. This action, the first under the 1980 PELRA law, became the largest public employee strike in state history, lasting twenty-two days. When the strike ended, the state claimed to have saved over $7.2 million in reduced payroll, enough to meet the union's wage demands. The union debated that interpretation, pointing to the new higher wage-base. As Chapter 4 showed, the strike had no effect on the passage of the state pay equity statute in April 1982.

By the time the first round of negotiations for pay equity raises occurred in the summer of 1983, MAPE represented professional employees and AFSCME represented a more traditional union constituency of craft, service, technical, correctional, nonprofessional health care, and clerical workers. MAPE's constituency comprised 20.1% of the work force covered by the pay equity law, and 29.4% of its membership was female. AFSCME's constituency comprised 61.9% of the work force covered by the law, and 49.9% of its members were women. But it is important to note that AFSCME represented 75.0% of the women employed by the state.[15]

Disagreements between unions representing state employees did not diminish the good unionism had done for state employees. Approximately 86% of the work force was covered by contracts from eleven unions. These unions had helped to make state of Minnesota employees among the best-paid public workers in the country.[16] The mean salary in 1984–85 (two years into the comparable worth pay raises) was approximately $22,500. Almost 60% of the work force earned more than $20,000 per year. But even with the first half of pay equity implemented, there were significant gender differences in who earned $20,000 or less. Just over a quarter (26.8%) of male employees earned $20,000 or less, compared to just over half (54.8%) of female employees.

*Distribution Mechanisms*

The implementation process began when, in January 1983, the Commissioner of Employee Relations gave the Legislative Commission on Employee Relations (LCER—the body that oversees labor relations between state employees and state government) a list of the job classes for which comparable worth inequities existed. In addition to providing the list of job classifications, Commissioner Rothchild also estimated the total cost of implementing comparable worth to be $26 million. Later in the legislative session, the LCER submitted its request for a pay equity allocation, separate from the general allocation for regular raises.

There has been considerable speculation about the extent to which the pay equity allocation really added new wage dollars to the state's personnel costs, and thus, the extent to which state implementation was a distributive policy. It is not possible to know for certain what the wage increases would have been without pay equity. Nor are the data available that disaggregate the pay equity component of wages from regular wage increases. The data that do exist present a mixed pattern as to whether the pay equity raises were a pure add-on to the total wage bill. Pay equity was implemented after a period when average annual wage increases of state employees were running barely half of the inflation rate. In fact, in 1980, the average hourly wage of state of Minnesota employees declined 1 percent from the previous year. All unions were eager for wage increases that would begin to make up for losses in real buying power. One basic measure of success in union bargaining is how unions individually and collectively do against the inflation rate. The 6.1% average increase in overall hourly wages of state employees during the first and most expensive year of pay equity implementation was almost twice the inflation rate of 3.2%. In the last year of implementation, with more than 75% of the pay equity raises already a part of base wages, the average wage increase was 5.2% and the inflation rate was 4.4%. If comparable worth had been redistributing a completely fixed wage-pie, one might have found wage increases declining significantly toward the inflation rate. A number of people close to the financial negotiations remarked that it would have been much more difficult to implement comparable worth in high-inflation years.

The individual wage increases of specific groups of workers, also difficult to disaggregate, are more complicated to interpret. In the year before pay equity was implemented, AFSCME and MAPE received virtually equal percentage increases in average hourly wages. In the first year of pay equity raises, AFSCME's total average wage *including pay equity adjustments* calculated across all six AFSCME bargaining units (both mostly female and mostly male bargaining units) increased 53¢ (6.5%) to $8.71. MAPE's average wage increased 30¢ (2.7%) to $11.62. In the four years of implementation, the ratio of MAPE's average hourly wage to AFSCME's average hourly declined from 1.38 to 1.31, or 5.0%. This average hourly wage-ratio difference measures the narrowing of the wage differences between the blue- and pink-collar workers represented by AFSCME and the white-collar workers represented by MAPE. Not surprisingly, AFSCME liked this situation a good deal better than MAPE did. To MAPE it seemed like a loss of expected future wages.[17]

The legislature allocated $21.7 million for comparable worth during the first biennium of a four-year implementation process. About $7 million was appropriated for the first year, and an additional $14 million for the second year. Of the second year's allocation, $7 million maintained the raises implemented the first year, and $7 million closed further the pay equity wage gap. In 1985, when the second pay equity allocation was made, the previous costs for pay equity became part of the state's salary base and only the amount necessary to finish the pay equity process had to be allocated through the procedure of a Department of Employee Relations report to the LCER and then a special allocation. For the 1985–87 biennium, $11.7 million was allocated and distributed in the same manner as the first biennium's allocation.

When implementation was complete on June 30, 1987, the full cost of pay equity totaled 3.7% of the 1983 base payroll, a bit under the initial estimate. As reported by the Commission on the Economic Status of Women, approximately 8,500 employees in 200 female-dominated job classifications received pay equity raises. Most of the people receiving pay equity raises worked at clerical or health care jobs; about 10% of the recipients were men. The estimated average increase from over four years for pay equity raises was $2,200.[18]

For the "average" employee who received $2,200 over four years, the raises may not have been very noticeable in any specific paycheck. In the first two years of implementation, the average pay equity raise was $1,600, and the pay equity raises in the second biennium averaged $600. The $800 available in the first year would have been divided into twenty-four biweekly increments of $33.33, before taxes. In the second year, the employee would have received another pay equity raise of $33.33 per pay period, followed by $12.50 per pay period in year three and again in year four. By the end of the four-year implementation period, the employee's biweekly salary had increased $91.66 over the 1983–84 base. Employees would not have been able to distinguish their pay equity raises from their general raises in the documentation that accompanied their checks.

Although the pay equity raises may not have been dramatically notice-able to employees, the effect on salary levels was very important. A con-crete example shows how significantly pay equity improved salaries in female-dominated positions. If pay equity had not been implemented, the base pay of an entry level Clerk 1 in contract year 1983–84 would have been $11,922. If, over the next four years, the position had received the general salary increases of $1,753 but no pay equity raises, the base pay of an entry level Clerk 1 would have increased to $13,675. With pay equity, entry level base pay for the Clerk 1 position was $15,931 in con-tract year 1986–87. Of the $4,009 increase in base salary, $1,753 came from regularly negotiated raises and $2,256 came from pay equity raises.

Another perspective on these raises can be seen by comparing salaries available to entry Clerk 1s to the poverty line for a family of four. The poverty line was developed in the mid-1960s as a way to determine by a uniform measure the income poverty in the country. In a classic article in the *Social Security Bulletin* of January 1965, Mollie Orshansky suggested that a family or household was poor if its money income was less than three times the cost of the Department of Agriculture's economy food plan. The Department of Agriculture had estimated food costs for families of different compositions since the 1930s. Not long before Orshansky did her analysis, the Department had issued "an economy food plan, costing only 75–80 percent as much as the basic low cost plan for 'temporary or emergency use when funds are low.'" Household expenditure surveys had shown that food constituted approximately one-third of all household ex-penditures, although the precise proportions depended on family size and location. It is this formula, approximately three times the cost of the econ-omy food plan for families of different sizes, that constitutes the set of poverty lines. Each year since they were developed the poverty line for each family size has been increased by the cost of living, but the basic structure remains the same.[19] Orshansky herself and a host of social policy analysts have remarked on the stinginess of the measure. But it does pro-vide a consistent set of measures of one aspect of income insufficiency.[20]

The poverty line for a family of four, the most reported of the poverty measures, has come to symbolize the minimum income necessary for family survival.

In 1983, the poverty line for a family of four was $10,178 and the base salary for an entry level Clerk 1 was $11,922, or 117% of the poverty line. If over the next four years this position had received only the pay raises negotiated between the union and the state, the base salary of $13,675 would have been 122% of the poverty line (which was $11,203). The actual salary of $15,931—the salary with four years of pay equity raises as well as general salary increments—was 142% of the poverty line. Of course, not every Clerk 1 supported a family of four, but the salary change indicated the change in the capacity of people working as Clerk 1s to support or help to support families.

*Bargaining*

To implement these raises over four years, the state and the unions bargained twice, first in 1983 and again in 1985. AFSCME members received 85% of the pay equity raises, a figure that is not surprising given the fact that AFSCME represents most of the employees in underpaid female-dominated classes.[21] In 1983, the AFSCME bargaining team headed by executive director Peter Benner and the state team headed by chief labor negotiator Lance Teachworth undertook the pay equity negotiations at the end of a thirty-six-hour general negotiating session. Both men characterized these general negotiations as respectful and straightforward.[22] (This situation may have been aided by the fact that the negotiators who had participated in the strike were gone.) Nonetheless, members of the negotiating team from the various AFSCME bargaining units wanted the bargaining for pay equity to take place after the regular negotiations, to make certain that pay equity raises were an add-on to the general pay raises. Likewise, Teachworth wanted separate pay equity negotiations to follow the general bargaining because he too believed they would demonstrate the "add-on" nature of these raises to other unions that did not represent classes receiving pay equity raises. Unknowingly, the state and AFSCME chose a bargaining strategy typical of distributive issues. Indeed, bargaining the pay equity raises in this manner reinforced their add-on character. The pay equity bargaining went quickly and easily, conducted in the celebratory atmosphere that marked the conclusion of the successful general negotiations. The 1985 negotiations were, if anything, more easily accomplished.

Benner used two implicit rules in negotiating the distribution of pay equity money in the AFSCME-represented classes in the first round. AFSCME wanted all clerical classes to receive raises, and to target those classes farthest from their new wage rates for larger initial pay equity raises. In most cases, implementing pay equity meant that a job classification moved to a higher step or range on the salary grid. In one instance, for Human Services Technicians, Senior (the people who work as patient aides in state facilities) the negotiators decided to extend the salary range, allowing long-term employees to make higher salaries, but not raising the entry salaries of these workers. The state felt that the entry-level pay for these positions were already compensated above the market, but did not oppose higher salaries for the long-term incumbents of this job. The state also agreed to raise the base pay of a few classifications so that no "leap-frogging" due to pay equity would occur. Leapfrogging is the condition when the pay scale of one class of workers in a ranked set of classes, say Licensed Practical Nurse 1, jumps over the pay scale of a higher-ranked job within this set, say, Licensed Practical Nurse 2. This could have occurred if the former were a female-dominated class and the latter were male-dominated. As the person responsible for the whole range of the state's bargaining, Teachworth was particularly concerned that leapfrogging not occur. Together Benner and Teachworth crafted a settlement committed to pay equity but also sensitive to the wide range of salary relationships that labor and management need to consider.

MAPE's stance in the pay equity bargaining was understandably different than AFSCME's. MAPE did publicly support pay equity. But President Mike Haney, a former official with AFSCME Council 6, felt that the decision not to move the balanced classes up to the male pay practices line was a misinterpretation of the state law, whose purpose was "to establish equitable compensation relationships between female-dominated, male-dominated, and balanced classes of employees in the executive branch."[23] Even more firmly, he believed that the compression of wages caused by pay equity would send the message to employees that professionalism was not highly valued. Compression is the situation where the pay differences between nonprofessional positions and professional positions in a field, or specific positions in a ranked class of positions, narrow markedly. Haney reported the case where after pay equity accounting clerks senior made "pennies less than the first accounting officer."[24] One accounting officer wrote to Nina Rothchild specifying this problem: "When first hired, the Accounting Officer earns 22 cents an hour more than the Account Technician. After six months, this difference is a negative one cent. It never again reaches a 22 cent an hour difference in favor of the Accounting Officer."[25] Rothchild responded, saying that "during the negotiations that resulted in the current contract with the Minnesota Association of Professional Employees, the negotiator representing the State discussed equity adjustments with Mike Haney, the negotiator for the Association. Inherent in the negotiating process is the realization that neither party will prevail on all issues because the parties come to the table as equals. Now that an agreement has been reached, we are committed to abide by that agreement until the end of this biennium."[26]

Although the tension from whether to file a lawsuit over the issue of balanced classes became part of a power struggle in MAPE, the union eventually chose to use collective bargaining both to raise the salaries of individuals in its balanced classes and to fight salary compression. In the 1985–86 contract, entry-level Account Officers began at 14 cents more per hour than Account Technicians. After six months, Account Officers lose their initial advantage, a measure of MAPE's difficulty in achieving this aim through collective bargaining in a short period of time.

Regardless of bargaining unit, employees received no official notification of pay equity from unions or the state. Employees covered by collective bargaining could determine both their eligibility and the amount of their comparable worth raises by carefully examining their contracts during ratification. For instance, while voting for the contracts that implemented pay equity, AFSCME members could check the contract to see how many compensation codes their job classification had risen due to pay equity. In the contract this information was given solely in compensation code abbreviations and had to be cross-checked by the employee in another portion of the contract to determine the salary assigned to that compensation code. The Department of Employee Relations did not notify employees of pay equity raises, an action the unions would have opposed because it would have highlighted the state's role in a wage settlement won through collective bargaining.

Those unions that were interested in pay equity did most of their employee education about pay equity during the agenda-setting and decision-making phases of the policy process and not during implementation. At several state conventions prior to implementation, AFSCME had held sessions on pay equity, at the request of women members. The Minnesota union distributed materials developed by AFSCME at the national level. Throughout the legislative and implementation processes, AFSCME's approach was actively to promote pay equity in the mostly female bargaining units (health care nonprofessionals and clerical) and quietly to respond to worker unease that pay equity would come out of the general salary increment in the mostly male bargaining units (craft, service, technical, and correctional guards). The Minnesota Nurses Association (MNA), which bargains for state-employed nurses, also did most of its member education before the implementation process. Geraldine Wedel, assistant executive director of the Association, reported that the MNA is "a very democratic union. All discussions about pay equity were held before [deciding to] support the policy."[27] One consequence of this approach was that members of unions like MNA and AFSCME had a much better sense of the policy than of its application.

## Consequences for Groups and Individuals

### The Unions and the Department of Employee Relations

Neither the unions nor the Department of Employee Relations received many complaints (or much praise) about the implementation of comparable worth. Some professional employees expressed concern for salary compression. A number of clerical workers who had confidential jobs and were thus not represented by AFSCME were apprehensive about whether they would get raises equivalent to those given to represented employees in the same job classifications. (They did.) Apart from these instances, the implementation evoked very little sustained response from employees.

In the absence of complaints, the major short-term outcome of comparable worth was that winners liked the policy, and their power was both demonstrated and solidified by it. The big winners were AFSCME and the Department of Employee Relations. Certainly the unions representing large numbers of balanced classes would have much preferred pay equity raises for those groups too, but they did not describe themselves as big losers. In their objections about salary compression unions like MAPE expressed not only their resistance to salary changes but also to status changes, a theme that would resonate throughout the implementation process at the local level. But among state unions upset about comparable worth there was no deeply etched sense of loss. All the participants in the implementation were seasoned veterans of labor politics. They had a keen sense that bargaining in the public sector is not like bargaining in the private sector. The tradition of many unions within any one jurisdiction meant that unions were used to fighting with each other while also fighting with management. The conflict that existed between unions on this issue was universally interpreted as business as usual.

For AFSCME the most immediate outcome of implementing pay equity was being able to deliver on a fundamental issue of higher return for women's labor in a way that did not especially disturb its male members and did not ration labor. The biggest consequence of pay equity was that "We worked it," as Pete Benner said. In four years the union put $21.7 million in the hands of 8,500 workers, and almost 85% of those workers belonged to AFSCME.

The state saw itself as a big winner too. The success of the implementation demonstrates how important committed feminist leadership was to the policy's success. Nina Rothchild received national attention and awards for her work, but she was also backed up by policy staff who were committed to the work, and a supportive technical and managerial staff who wanted to do it right. In fact, part of the reason the state was a big winner is that it did not have to make very many changes in routines. Able negotiators on both sides easily invented the "add-on" approach to bargaining. The state's negotiators were backed up by well-running, automated compensation systems. Jim Lee, compensation manager, who was fondly referred to by his colleagues as the "compensation king," devised a sophisticated system for estimating total comparable worth costs. Most of the people who worked on comparable worth for state employees at the Department of Employee Relations thought it was important, challenging, even fun.

The long-term consequences of implementing pay equity for state workers were less tangible but equally important. One long-term consequence was to make all the participants realize that the job evaluation process had become a central part of compensation management and labor relations. Many unions saw the necessity of doing the job evaluation again at some point, although no urgency was expressed. Both MAPE and AFSCME had complaints about the Hay system, MAPE because Hay undervalues technical skills and AFSCME because Hay undervalues working conditions. Systems like Hay were not originally designed to be used to evaluate blue-collar or technical jobs. Hay's emphasis on managerial, administrative, and clerical tasks demonstrates that it values white-collar, directive, and financial responsibilities above other job traits. In contrast to MAPE and AFSCME, the Minnesota Nurses Association recognized that jobs can change over time. In an era of rapid changes in the delivery of health care, the evaluation done in 1979 might no longer adequately describe nursing classifications in the state.

A second long-term consequence of pay equity is the changed set of norms and procedures within the Department of Employee Relations, which constitutes a reconfiguration of organizational culture. High-ranking policy makers and managers rethought the history of salary-setting for state employees. There was an acknowledgment, for example, that the Stores Clerk position had been created in the 1950s specifically to pay male clerical workers more than female clerical workers. Lance Teachworth, the state's chief labor negotiator, demonstrated the change in work culture when he said that "the state had made a long-term commitment to defining compensation in a new way" and that "pay equity meant a commitment not only to policy but to the process."[28]

*Employee Reactions to Pay Equity*

The changes in rules and activities of salary-setting certainly could not have occurred or been maintained without the support of the committed leaders. But what were the results of comparable worth for individual workers?[29] Part of the answer has already been discussed: 8,500 employees got raises averaging a total of $2,200 over four years. The change visible in any one paycheck may have been small, but the cumulative effect could be dramatic, especially for the lowest-paid workers. But we also need to know how individual employees interpreted this change in wage policy.[30] In particular we need to know the answers to three sets of questions: *Support and knowledge questions* (Who supported the concept of comparable worth or pay equity? Who had heard of the policy? How detailed was the knowledge?); *experience questions* (Who believed they received and who actually received pay equity raises?); and *impact questions* (What long-term consequences did employees see arising from the adoption of pay equity? How did pay equity affect job satisfaction?).

No other comparable worth research has yet focused on these questions. Neither the monetary nor the labor relations consequences for employees of adopting a pay equity wage policy has received much attention, perhaps because so few workplaces have adopted the policy. A few commentators have ventured their speculations, views that depend on their overall support for or resistance to comparable worth. Advocates suggest that pay equity will contribute to employee self-esteem, encourage job satisfaction, and reduce friction in the workplace.[31] Opponents suggest that pay equity will disrupt the workplace with jealousy and decrease the job satisfaction of women workers by encouraging men (through higher wages) to enter traditionally female occupations.[32]

To determine the accuracy of these assumptions and to answer the specific support, knowledge, experience, and impact questions the University of Minnesota's Comparable Worth Research Project designed a Public Employee Survey of 493 state of Minnesota employees that was fielded by the Minnesota Center for Social Research in June 1985, half-way through the implementation process. Conducted over the telephone, the survey asked 176 questions on work history, attitudes toward public employment, employee experiences in the workplace, worker satisfaction, information and attitudes about pay equity and experience with Minnesota's pay equity policy, political beliefs, use of social programs, and socioeconomic and demographic variables.[33] Appendix C describes the survey methodology in detail.

The support and knowledge questions are especially important because they contribute to the debate within the economics literature about whether and when individuals attempt to maximize their salaries or wages. At the most removed level of generalization, much of economic analysis is predicated on the belief that workers are wage maximizers within the limits of their knowledge, willingness, and ability to change jobs and locations. Such assumptions rest on the belief that employees know a good deal about monetary and nonmonetary rewards of their labor. Interestingly, very little research exists on this topic. The few available research reports suggest that, while employees have a general knowledge of their wages or salaries, they know very little about their fringe benefits or raises at any given time.[34]

We suggest that employees who are better off materially, in terms of salary and education, and employees who are more powerful organizationally, especially managers and professionals, will have greater and more accurate knowledge about comparable worth policy and practices. In addition, we expected that those most likely to benefit from the raises would be more knowledgeable. But we must also caution against "over-determining" employees' responses to comparable worth. Comparable worth was only one part of the financial situation of employees, and remuneration only one part of the work environment. Even those who might be advantaged most by the policy change could reasonably have had a limited interest in it, especially when information was provided sporadically and selectively, as it was by the state's unions.

The question "If studies showed the work of delivery van drivers and clerk typists required the same level of skill, training, responsibility, and so forth, should an employer pay these types of positions the same?" determined whether employees supported the concept of pay equity. The survey showed that employees gave the concept of equal pay for jobs of equal value overwhelming support (tables 5.1, 5.2, 5.3). Overall, 81.2%

TABLE 5.1
## Knowledge about Pay Equity by Material Variables

| | Total Popu-lation | Sex | | Age | | | Education | | | | Salary | | |
|---|---|---|---|---|---|---|---|---|---|---|---|---|---|
| | | Male | Female | ≤30 | 31–45 | ≥46 | ≤12 | 13–15 | 16 | ≥17 | ≤20K | 20K<X ≤30K | >30K |
| Drivers and typists paid equivalently (% agreed)[a] | 81.2 (484) | 75.8 (248) | 86.9 (236) | 81.9 (94) | 83.5 (218) | 77.9c (172) | 77.8 (153) | 87.4 (151) | 81.9 (72) | 76.9 (108) | 81.6 (196) | 84.3 (217) | 70.4b (71) |
| Ever heard of pay equity (% yes) | 81.5 (493) | 81.2 (239) | 81.9c (254) | 76.8 (95) | 85.8 (218) | 78.8c (179) | 67.7 (155) | 78.6 (154) | 91.8 (73) | 98.2 (111) | 72.9 (198) | 84.9 (220) | 95.9 (74) |
| Source of information[d,e] (% newspapers) | 29.9 (402) | 36.5 (208) | 22.7 (194) | 17.8 (73) | 32.6 (187) | 32.6c (141) | 19.0 (105) | 20.7 (121) | 44.8 (67) | 41.3 (109) | 19.3 (118) | 30.6 (204) | 49.3 (80) |
| (% unions) | 25.6 (402) | 21.6 (208) | 29.9 (194) | 24.7 (73) | 24.7 (187) | 28.4 (141) | 32.4 (105) | 33.1 (121) | 14.9 (67) | 18.4 (109) | 30.3 (118) | 28.0 (204) | 9.9 (80) |
| Pay equity only for women[d] (% disagreed) | 94.4 (395) | 92.1 (202) | 96.9c (193) | 97.3 (74) | 94.5 (183) | 92.8c (138) | 96.1 (103) | 95.8 (119) | 89.4 (66) | 94.4c (107) | 95.8 (144) | 95.6 (181) | 88.6c (70) |
| Pay equity means better pensions[d] (% agreed) | 82.7 (370) | 83.4 (193) | 81.9c (177) | 65.2 (66) | 82.0 (172) | 92.4 (132) | 80.8 (99) | 84.8 (112) | 83.6 (61) | 81.6c (98) | 72.9 (133) | 87.2 (172) | 90.8 (65) |

[a] The X² statistic for each distribution is significant at the .01 level unless marked with a "b" or "c."
[b] X² is significant at the .05 level.
[c] X² is not significant at the .05 level.
[d] Only asked of those who had heard of pay equity.
[e] Other sources of information on pay equity include television, supervisors, co-workers, friends and unspecified sources. These sources are not reported here.

TABLE 5.2
**Knowledge About Pay Equity by Organizational Variables**

| | Total Population | Years Employed by the State | | | Occupation | | | | | | | | | Full- or Part-Time Work | |
|---|---|---|---|---|---|---|---|---|---|---|---|---|---|---|---|
| | | 0–7 | 8–16 | 17+ | Manag. | Prof. | Tech. | Cler. | Protect. Serv. | Other Serv. | Farm, Fish, Forestry | Precis. Prod. | Opera-tives | Full | Part |
| Drivers and typists paid equivalently (% agreed)[a] | 81.2 (484) | 83.2 (196) | 79.2 (178) | 80.9[c] (110) | 79.9 (76) | 77.4 (93) | 89.2 (37) | 81.5 (130) | 94.1 (17) | 74.0 (50) | 93.8 (16) | 80.8 (52) | 100.0[c] (10) | 80.8 (447) | 85.7[c] (35) |
| Ever heard of pay equity (% yes) | 81.5 (493) | 78.8 (198) | 84.4 (180) | 81.7[c] (115) | 97.4[c] (77) | 88.4 (95) | 79.5 (39) | 84.0 (131) | 100.0 (17) | 49.1 (53) | 87.5 (16) | 65.4 (52) | 80.0 (10) | 83.3 (456) | 57.1 (35) |
| Source of information[d,e] (% newspapers) | 29.9 (402) | 30.1 (156) | 25.0 (152) | 32.2[c] (94) | 46.7 (75) | 38.1 (84) | 16.1 (31) | 19.1 (110) | 35.3 (17) | 26.9 (26) | 14.3 (14) | 29.4 (34) | 25.0 (8) | 29.7 (380) | 35.0[c] (20) |
| (% unions) | 25.6 | 23.7 | 30.3 | 21.3 | 18.7 | 17.9 | 35.5 | 30.0 | 17.6 | 38.5 | 28.6 | 32.4 | 25.0 | 26.1 | 20.0 |
| Pay equity only for women[d] (% disagreed) | 94.4 (395) | 98.1 (156) | 93.9 (148) | 89.0[b] (91) | 93.3 (75) | 89.2 (83) | 93.1 (29) | 96.3 (108) | 93.8 (16) | 100.0 (26) | 92.9 (14) | 100.0 (33) | 100.0[c] (8) | 94.4 (373) | 95.0[c] (20) |
| Pay equity means better pensions[d] (% agreed) | 82.7 (370) | 73.4 (139) | 85.4 (144) | 93.1 (87) | 86.8 (68) | 80.8 (73) | 82.1 (28) | 82.5 (103) | 86.7 (15) | 73.1 (26) | 71.4 (14) | 90.9 (33) | 87.5[c] (8) | 94.4 (373) | 95.0[c] (20) |

[a]The X² statistic for each distribution is significant at the .01 level unless marked with a "b" or "c."
[b]X² is significant at the .05 level.
[c]X² is not significant at the .05 level.
[d]Only asked of those who had heard of pay equity.
[e]Other sources of information on pay equity include television, supervisors, co-workers, friends and unspecified sources. These sources are not reported here.

TABLE 5.3
**Knowledge About Pay Equity by Ideological Variables**

| | Total Popu-lation | Ideology | | Party Identification | | | Support for Women's Movement | | |
|---|---|---|---|---|---|---|---|---|---|
| | | Liberal | Conservative | Democrat | Independent | Republican | Not Far Enough | As Far as Should | Gone Too Far |
| Drivers and typists paid equivalently (% agreed) | 81.2 (484) | 86.4 (213) | 78.1[b] (256) | 84.6 (201) | 77.8 (189) | 83.5[c] (79) | 87.3 (228) | 81.0 (163) | 66.2 (77) |
| Ever heard of pay equity (% yes) | 81.5 (493) | 89.4 (216) | 76.5 (260) | 79.6 (201) | 84.5 (194) | 82.3[c] (79) | 88.7 (230) | 73.9 (165) | 76.3 (60) |
| Source of information[d,e] (% newspapers) | 29.9 (402) | 33.2 (193) | 27.1[c] (199) | 23.8 (160) | 38.4 (164) | 24.6[b] (65) | 33.3 (204) | 26.2 (122) | 26.2[c] (66) |
| (% unions) | 25.6 | 20.2 | 30.7 | 31.3 | 20.7 | 24.7 | 26.5 | 29.5 | 16.4 |
| Pay equity only for women[d] (% disagreed) | 94.4 (395) | 96.8 (189) | 91.9[c] (197) | 97.5 (159) | 92.5 (161) | 92.1[c] (63) | 98.5 (202) | 91.7 (121) | 87.9 (58) |
| Pay equity means better pensions[d] (% agreed) | 82.7 (370) | 78.3 (175) | 86.7[b] (188) | 76.0 (146) | 87.5 (152) | 86.9[b] (61) | 84.2 (190) | 78.1 (114) | 85.1[c] (55) |

[a]The $X^2$ statistic for each distribution is significant at the .01 level unless marked with a "b" or "c."
[b]$X^2$ is significant at the .05 level.
[c]$X^2$ is not significant at the .05 level.
[d]Only asked of those who had heard of pay equity.
[e]Other sources of information on pay equity include television, supervisors, co-workers, friends and unspecified sources. These sources are not reported here.

reported that if studies found these two positions similar they should be paid the same. Even those who might be thought to oppose the policy actually supported it. For example, among Minnesota employees, 78.9% of managers supported equal pay for drivers and typists, as did 78.1% of self-defined conservatives. More liberals support pay equity than conservatives, but the high level of conservative support for the policy is the most striking feature of the ideological comparison.

Women and strong supporters of the women's movement (both men and women) gave the concept of pay equity the most support: 86.9% of women supported equal pay for drivers and typists, compared with 75.8% of men. Likewise, 87.3% of the respondents who reported that the women's movement had not gone far enough supported paying drivers and typists equally, compared to 66.2% of those who felt that the women's movement had gone too far. This is a particularly noteworthy finding because men and women gave equal support to the women's movement.

Just as the concept of pay equity was well supported, the actual policy was well known. The survey asked "Have you heard anything about pay equity or comparable worth?" to which 81.5% of the respondents answered yes. As with all the questions of fact in this survey, respondents with more organizational power and greater informational and economic resources were more knowledgeable. In this instance, higher-salary and higher-status employees, e.g., managers and professionals, were more knowledgeable. In contrast, service workers were notably lacking in information about the policy: only 49.1% had heard of pay equity or comparable worth. For our interests, those who had not heard of pay equity are particularly important to define. Of those who had not heard of the policy, 59.3% earned $20,000 or less per year (compared to 40.4% of the sample), 29.7% were service workers (compared to 10.8% of the sample), and 16.5% were part-time employees (compared to 7.1% of the sample).

Having heard of pay equity or comparable worth does not indicate what, specifically, employees knew about it. Respondents who replied that they had heard about the policy were asked whether they agreed or disagreed with two statements about policy content. The first statement, "Only women can get pay equity raises," inquired about the prevalent misconception that pay equity raises were available only to women, rather than being available to all the incumbents of female-dominated occupations. Almost everyone (94.4%) understood that pay equity raises went to men as well as women.

The second statement, "Pay equity will increase the state retirement benefits of people getting these raises," determined whether respondents knew that the state's pay equity policy did in fact increase retirement income. Here too, employees were quite knowledgeable, with 82.7% knowing that pay equity raises would also raise pension benefits. Employees with salaries greater than $30,000, over age 45, or with more than 17 years' tenure in state employment were especially knowledgeable about the pension effects of pay equity.[35] In fact, virtually all employees with 17 years' or more tenure with the state, regardless of age or income, correctly understood that pay equity would improve pensions. This suggests that state employees who are beginning to think about retirement know at least the rudiments of the formulas that determine retirement benefits.[36]

Responses to the question "Which of the following was your *most important* source of information about pay equity or comparable worth . . . newspaper, television, your supervisor, co-workers, conversation with friends, or a union?" showed that newspapers and unions provided employees with the most of their information. Overall, 29.9% of those who knew about pay equity reported that newspapers were their major source of information and 25.6% reported that unions were their major source of information. As education and salary increased, reliance on newspapers increased but reliance on unions decreased, especially for those earning more than $30,000.

AFSCME's strategy of emphasizing pay equity primarily in its female-dominated bargaining units is amply demonstrated by comparing the information sources of female- and male-dominated bargaining units. In the mostly female clerical and nonprofessional health care bargaining units, 45.5% of the respondents learned about pay equity from unions, compared with 26.5% of the respondents in the mostly male craft, service, technical, and correctional guard units.

It is clear from the discussion of support for and knowledge about comparable worth that state of Minnesota employees knew the basics of the policy. But did they know enough to be certain of whether they received comparable worth raises, and if so, how much? These questions are crucial because they get at the heart of the social movement potential of the comparable worth issue. Can comparable worth be a transformational strategy if it is not well known? Can increased salaries alone, without the knowledge of how the raises were achieved, give people (mostly women) in traditionally low-paid female-dominated jobs increased social and familial autonomy?

To help determine the answers to these questions, interviewers asked respondents "Did you receive a pay equity or comparable worth raise in 1984?"; the information elicited was then cross-checked against the official list of job classifications eligible for pay equity raises. Respondents also gave information on the size of their pay equity raises for that year, information that was also cross-checked against the state's salary schedule.[37]

When asked about receiving a pay equity raise, 23.5% of respondents reported receiving one, 58.0% reported not receiving this raise, and 18.6% never heard of the policy and so were not asked.[38] The results of the cross-tabulation of reported and actual raises reveal very important findings (table 5.4). On the one hand, 75.7% of those who reported receiving pay equity raises and 88.0% of those who reported not receiving raises were accurate in their reports. On the other hand, if we examine those who actually received a pay equity raise, we find that only 56.9% knew they received it. Another 21.6% reported not receiving a raise although they received one, and 21.6% never heard of the policy even though they received a raise. The social movement potential of comparable worth is certainly unfulfilled if 43.2% of the people who benefit from the policy are unaware of their benefits.

The information from table 5.4 can be displayed and analyzed in another form. Respondents can be divided into six groups representing their subjective and objective pay equity raise situation.

1. Yes reported raise, no raise received        5.8%   ( 28)
2. No reported raise, no raise received        50.5%   (242)
3. Never heard of pay equity, no raise received  11.7%   ( 56)
4. Yes reported raise, yes raise received        18.2%   ( 87)
5. No reported, yes raise received               6.9%   ( 33)
6. Never heard of pay equity, yes raise received 6.9%   ( 33)

Groups 2 and 4 were accurate in their reports; groups 1 and 5 were inaccurate; and groups 3 and 6 were unknowledgeable. Accuracy increased markedly with each increase in salary and educational level.[39]

The composition of each of the pay equity raise groups tells us a great deal about the organization of the state's labor force (tables 5.5, 5.6, and 5.7). Looking first at the accurate groups, we find that group 2 (no reported raise, no raise received) was made up mostly of men in high-prestige, male-dominated occupations that were not eligible for pay equity raises. Group 4 (yes reported raise, yes raise received) was mainly made up of longer-tenured women in clerical occupations. If we turn to the inaccurate groups, group 1 (yes reported raise, no raise received) was not particularly distinctive, its only notable feature being that most of the men who reported inaccurately were located in this group. Group 5 (no reported raise, yes raise received) was similar to group 4 (yes reported raise,

TABLE 5.4
**Experience with Pay Equity: Reported Versus Actual Pay Equity Raises**

|  | Received Raise | No Raise Received | Row Total |
|---|---|---|---|
| Raise | 75.7 | 24.3 | 100.0 |
| Reported[a] | [56.9] | [8.6] | |
| n = | (87) | (28) | (115) |
| No Raise | 12.0 | 88.0 | 100.0 |
| Reported | [21.6] | [74.2] | |
| n = | (33) | (242) | (275) |
| Never Heard | 37.1 | 62.9 | 100.0 |
| of Pay Equity | [21.6] | [17.2] | |
| n = | (33) | (56) | (89) |
| Column Total | [100.1] | [100.0] | |
| n = | (153) | (326) | (479) |

*Note:* Both row and column percentages presented; column percentages are in brackets.
[a]$X^2$ is significant at the .01 level.

yes raise received) in that it was composed of more than 90% women, but group 5 had more technical and service workers, and fewer clericals. Group 6 (never heard of pay equity, yes raise received), also predominantly female, was made up of the least well-educated and well-paid of those getting raises. In many ways, these were the most marginal female employees in state employment. Just over 30% were service workers, 39.4% were part-time employees. In terms of social and organizational positions, those who had no knowledge of pay equity but received pay equity raises were the hardest to reach. In contrast, group 3 (never heard of pay equity, no raise received) was made up mostly of men in blue-collar occupations not eligible for pay equity raises.

Accurate knowledge of the amount of one's pay equity raise was understandably rarer than accurate knowledge of receiving the raise. Of those who reported receiving a raise (n = 115), more than a third did not know the amount of the raise. Of those reporting receiving a raise and attaching an amount to it (n = 73), 71.2% (n = 52) actually received a raise. Of those correctly reporting a raise and volunteering its size, 17.6% (n = 9) were correct within ± 15% of the real pay equity raise.

Monetary information pertaining to individuals was much less evident than policy information pertaining to groups. The fact that almost half of the recipients of pay equity raises did not know that they received them and even fewer could correctly name the amount is one consequence of the implementation process in the state of Minnesota.

It was very important to know what employees thought would be the

TABLE 5.5
**Experience with Pay Equity Raises by Material Variables (in Percentages)**

| Experience Group | % of Population in Each Group (n=479) | Sex (n=479) | | Age (n=478) | | | Education (n=479) | | | | Salary (n=479) | | |
|---|---|---|---|---|---|---|---|---|---|---|---|---|---|
| | | Male | Female | ≤30 | 31–45 | ≥46 | ≤12 | 13–15 | 16 | ≥17 | ≤20K | 20K<X ≤30K | >30K |
| Group 1: Yes reported, no raise[a] | 5.8 (28) | 46.4 | 53.6 | 21.4 | 35.7 | 42.9[b] | 39.3 | 32.1 | 14.3 | 14.3 | 50.0 | 42.9 | 7.1 |
| Group 2: No reported, no raise | 50.5 (242) | 75.2 | 24.8 | 12.9 | 51.5 | 35.7 | 20.2 | 19.8 | 21.1 | 38.8 | 18.2 | 57.4 | 24.4 |
| Group 3: Never heard, no raise | 11.7 (56) | 76.8 | 23.2 | 17.9 | 37.5 | 44.6 | 50.0 | 37.5 | 8.9 | 3.6 | 48.2 | 50.0 | 1.8 |
| Group 4: Yes reported, yes raise | 18.2 (87) | 6.9 | 93.1 | 28.7 | 40.2 | 31.0 | 39.1 | 46.0 | 10.3 | 4.6 | 67.8 | 32.2 | 0 |
| Group 5: No reported, yes raise | 6.9 (33) | 9.1 | 90.9 | 24.2 | 45.5 | 30.3 | 27.3 | 57.6 | 3.0 | 12.1 | 75.8 | 21.2 | 3.0 |
| Group 6: Never heard, yes raise | 6.9 (33) | 6.1 | 93.9 | 33.3 | 30.3 | 36.4 | 60.6 | 36.4 | 3.0 | 0 | 81.8 | 18.2 | 0 |

[a]The $X^2$ statistic for each distribution is significant at the .01 level unless marked "b."
[b]$X^2$ is significant at the .05 level.

TABLE 5.6
**Experience with Pay Equity Raises by Organizational Variables (in percentages)**

| Group | % of Population in Each Experience Group (n=479) | Years Employed by the State (n=479) | | | Occupation (n=477) | | | | | | | | | Full- or Part-Time Work (n=475) | |
|---|---|---|---|---|---|---|---|---|---|---|---|---|---|---|---|
| | | 0–7 | 8–16 | 17+ | Manag. | Prof. | Tech. | Cler. | Protect. Serv. | Other Serv. | Farm, Fish, Forestry | Precis. Prod. | Opera-tives | Full | Part |
| Group 1: Yes reported, no raise[a] | 5.8 (28) | 49.9 | 25.0 | 32.1 | 10.7 | 25.0 | 7.1 | 14.3 | 7.1 | 14.3 | 7.1 | 7.1 | 7.1 | 92.9 | 7.1 |
| Group 2: No reported, no raise | 50.5 (242) | 31.8 | 40.9 | 27.3 | 27.8 | 26.6 | 7.5 | 9.1 | 6.2 | 2.9 | 5.0 | 12.4 | 2.5 | 96.3 | 3.7 |
| Group 3: Never heard, no raise | 11.7 (56) | 41.1 | 30.4 | 28.6 | 3.6 | 16.1 | 1.8 | 8.9 | 0 | 30.4 | 3.6 | 32.1 | 3.6 | 96.4 | 3.6 |
| Group 4: Yes reported, yes raise | 18.2 (87) | 49.4 | 37.9 | 12.6 | 3.5 | 4.7 | 9.3 | 75.6 | 0 | 7.0 | 0 | 0 | 0 | 95.4 | 4.6 |
| Group 5: No reported, yes raise | 6.9 (33) | 57.6 | 33.3 | 9.1 | 0 | 18.2 | 6.1 | 51.5 | 0 | 24.2 | 0 | 0 | 0 | 84.4 | 15.6 |
| Group 6: Never heard, yes raise | 6.9 (33) | 57.6 | 30.3 | 12.1 | 0 | 6.1 | 18.2 | 45.5 | 0 | 30.3 | 0 | 0 | 0 | 60.6 | 39.4 |

[a]The X$^2$ statistic for each distribution is significant at the .01 level.

TABLE 5.7
**Experience with Pay Equity Raises by Ideological Variables (in percentages)**

| | % of Population in Each Experience Group (n = 479) | Ideology (n = 464) | | Party Identification (n = 461) | | | Support for Women's Movement (n = 462) | | |
|---|---|---|---|---|---|---|---|---|---|
| | | Liberal | Conservative | Democrat | Independent | Republican | Not Far Enough | As Far as Should | Gone Too Far |
| Group 1: Yes reported, no raise[a] | 5.8 (28) | 44.4 | 55.6[b] | 57.1 | 35.7 | 7.1[c] | 52.0 | 28.0 | 20.0 |
| Group 2: No reported, no raise | 50.4 (242) | 51.3 | 48.7 | 35.2 | 48.5 | 16.3 | 53.0 | 30.1 | 16.9 |
| Group 3: Never heard, no raise | 11.7 (56) | 27.5 | 72.5 | 44.0 | 38.0 | 18.0 | 37.0 | 46.3 | 16.7 |
| Group 4: Yes reported, yes raise | 18.2 (87) | 46.4 | 53.6 | 43.5 | 36.5 | 20.0 | 49.4 | 38.6 | 12.0 |
| Group 5: No reported, yes raise | 6.9 (33) | 42.4 | 57.6 | 53.1 | 28.1 | 18.8 | 56.3 | 28.1 | 15.6 |
| Group 6: Never heard, yes raise | 6.9 (33) | 25.8 | 74.2 | 51.5 | 33.3 | 15.2 | 12.5 | 56.3 | 31.3 |

[a]The X² statistic for each distribution is significant at the .01 level unless marked with a "b" or "c".
[b]X² is significant at the .05 level.
[c]X² is not significant at the .05 level.

long-term impact of this policy. To determine these perceived consequences, we asked respondents who had heard of pay equity whether they
agreed or disagreed with two worst-case scenarios posited by opponents
of pay equity. The first statement read "Pay equity causes many problems
in the workplace," with which 35.9% of those queried agreed and 64.1%
disagreed. Men and women were similar in their views, with two-thirds
of both groups believing that pay equity did *not* cause many problems.
Most socioeconomic, demographic, and organizational variables were
poor predictors of employees' beliefs about pay equity causing problems.
Of these variables, only tenure with the state differentiated beliefs. Almost
46% of those with 17 or more years' tenure thought that pay equity caused
problems. Many of these respondents did not support the women's movement in general or pay equity in particular (tables 5.8, 5.9, and 5.10).

Indeed, ideological variables were the most consistent predictors of beliefs about pay equity causing problems. Those who were comfortable
with the pace of the women's movement or who wanted the women's
movement to move faster did *not* think pay equity caused problems in the
workplace. In contrast, those who thought that the women's movement
had gone too far believed that pay equity caused many problems in the
workplace. Similar patterns were found for the question on equal pay for
drivers and typists, with those supporting equal pay responding that pay
equity did not cause problems and those opposing equal pay responding
that the policy did cause problems. While it is possible that the reactions
to problems in the workplace question might be a result of experiences
with the implementation of pay equity, it is unlikely that views on the
women's movements are a result of pay equity policies. In the absence of
serious or widespread complaints about the consequences of pay equity, it
appears that respondents fitted their expectations (and perhaps experiences) about the policy to their prior beliefs.

The second negative question elicited a different pattern of responses.
Individuals were asked whether they agreed or disagreed that "Pay equity
would result in some salaries being frozen." As previously discussed, this
did not occur. No salaries were frozen or lowered due to pay equity. Nonetheless, 59.2% of respondents believed that pay equity would result in
some frozen salaries. Roughly 60% of *every* socioeconomic, demographic, organizational, and ideological group harbored this fear. What is
particularly noteworthy about these salary-related fears is that the question
asked about salary cuts, the worst possible response to pay equity, not
about salary slowdowns, and still six out of ten employees worried about
this outcome.

TABLE 5.8
Impact of Pay Equity by Material Variables

| | Total Popu- lation | Sex | | Age | | | Education | | | | Salary | | |
|---|---|---|---|---|---|---|---|---|---|---|---|---|---|
| | | Male | Female | ≤30 | 31–45 | ≥46 | ≤12 | 13–15 | 16 | ≥17 | ≤20K | 20K<X ≤30K | >30K |
| Pay equity causes many problems[d] (% agreed) | 35.9 (395) | 38.2 (204) | 33.5[c] (191) | 37.5 (72) | 34.1 (185) | 37.7[c] (138) | 44.7 (103) | 39.8 (118) | 34.8 (66) | 24.1[b] (108) | 35.7 (143) | 35.2 (182) | 38.6[c] (70) |
| Pay equity means some frozen salaries[d] (% agreed) | 59.2 (390) | 60.6 (203) | 57.8[c] (187) | 64.4 (73) | 58.8 (182) | 57.0[c] (135) | 54.0 (100) | 61.9 (118) | 56.1 (66) | 63.2[c] (106) | 62.0 (142) | 56.7 (178) | 60.0[c] (70) |
| Job satisfaction (% very satisfied) | 57.4 (493) | 55.9 (254) | 59.0[c] (239) | 46.3 (95) | 60.1 (218) | 59.8[c] (179) | 52.9 (155) | 60.4 (154) | 61.6 (73) | 58.8[c] (111) | 55.8 (283) | 57.7 (167) | 60.8[c] (43) |

[a]The X² statistic for each distribution is significant at the .01 level unless marked with a "b" or "c".
[b]X² is significant at the .05 level.
[c]X² is not significant at the .05 level.
[d]Only asked of those who had heard of pay equity.

TABLE 5.9
**Impact of Pay Equity by Organizational Variables**

| | Total Popu-lation | Years Employed by the State | | | Occupation | | | | | | | | | Full- or Part-Time Work | |
|---|---|---|---|---|---|---|---|---|---|---|---|---|---|---|---|
| | | 0–7 | 8–16 | 17+ | Manag. | Prof. | Tech. | Cler. | Protect. Serv. | Other Serv. | Farm, Fish, Forestry | Precis. Prod. | Opera-tives | Full | Part |
| Pay equity causes many problems (% agreed) | 35.9 (395) | 28.8 (153) | 37.3 (150) | 45.7[b] (92) | 29.3 (75) | 38.6 (83) | 37.9 (29) | 35.5 (107) | 35.3 (17) | 30.8 (26) | 38.5 (13) | 41.2 (34) | 62.5[c] (8) | 35.9 (373) | 35.0[c] (20) |
| Pay equity means some frozen salaries (% agreed) | 59.2 (390) | 62.3 (154) | 58.2 (146) | 55.6[c] (90) | 58.9 (73) | 61.4 (83) | 50.0 (28) | 56.6 (106) | 66.7 (15) | 69.2 (26) | 57.1 (14) | 64.7 (34) | 37.5[c] (8) | 58.8 (369) | 63.2[c] (19) |
| Job satisfaction (% very satisfied) | 57.4 (493) | 55.6 (198) | 58.9 (180) | 58.3[c] (115) | 58.4 (77) | 60.0 (95) | 61.5 (39) | 62.6 (131) | 64.7 (17) | 41.5 (53) | 50.0 (16) | 51.9 (52) | 60.0[c] (10) | 57.5 (456) | 60.0[c] (35) |

[a]The $X^2$ statistic for each distribution is significant at the .01 level unless marked with a "b" or "c".
[b]$X^2$ is significant at the .05 level.
[c]$X^2$ is not significant at the .05 level.
[d]Only asked of those who had heard of pay equity.

TABLE 5.10
**Impact of Pay Equity Raises by Ideological Variables**

| | Total Popu-lation | Ideology | | Party Identification | | | Support for Women's Movement | | |
|---|---|---|---|---|---|---|---|---|---|
| | | Liberal | Conservative | Democrat | Independent | Republican | Not Far Enough | As Far as Should | Gone Too Far |
| Pay equity causes man,, problems[d] (% agreed)[a] | 35.9 (395) | 28.8 (190) | 42.6 (197) | 25.9 (158) | 40.1 (162) | 46.9 (64) | 30.0 (200) | 34.7 (121) | 57.4 (61) |
| Pay equity means some frozen salaries[d] (% agreed) | 59.2 (390) | 61.0 (187) | 57.9c (195) | 56.1 (155) | 62.1 (161) | 63.5c (63) | 60.0 (200) | 56.3 (119) | 64.4c (59) |
| Job satisfaction (% very satisfied) | 57.4 (493) | 54.6 (216) | 60.0 (260) | 54.2 (201) | 58.2 (194) | 63.3c (79) | 55.7 (230) | 60.0 (165) | 53.7c (80) |

[a]The X² statistic for each distribution is significant at the .01 level unless marked with a "b" or "c".
[b]X² is significant at the .05 level (none on this table).
[c]X² is not significant at the .05 level.
[d]Only asked of those who had heard of pay equity.

A number of factors may have contributed to the widespread concern that salaries would be frozen. Employees may not have known about the separate salary appropriation for pay equity. Or employees may not have believed that the state would fully absorb higher overall salary costs in the name of equity. Or they may have viewed the state pay equity process as equivalent to the local pay equity process. Newspaper accounts of local pay equity often contained the dire predictions of wage freezes made by local managers unsympathetic to comparable worth. Whatever the reasons, a large majority of state employees thought that pay equity would have negative effects on some employees, but not necessarily on their own wages.

Salaries may be the most immediate comparable-worth-related concern of employees, but certainly not their only one. The introduction of comparable worth in a workplace can affect the way employees experience their work. Job satisfaction is one measure of the work experience. Job satisfaction is the product of several related qualities of work life: the intrinsic nature of the work; the "convenience" aspects of the work, including working conditions in the broadest sense; financial rewards, including salary, fringe benefits, and security; relations with coworkers; ability to develop a career; and adequate resources to do the job.[40] Overall, people with higher salaries and more intrinsically interesting work (which often involves a good deal of independent judgment) are more satisfied with their jobs. This finding might be taken to imply that job satisfaction increases linearly as pay increases, work becomes more engaging, and jobs offer greater autonomy. The process by which individuals determine job satisfaction is somewhat more complicated, however. Individuals determine job satisfaction by comparing the job traits they value to the job traits that are rewarded in their firm. Expectations about rewards and type of occupation, firm, and sector influence this determination. Gender-based socialization to work roles is especially important in understanding expectations of work satisfaction. Most studies show that women are at least equally as satisfied with their work as are men, but women's satisfaction is believed partly to be a function of low expectations and low rewards, especially for women in nonprofessional, female-dominated occupations.[41] In terms of location in the economy, workers employed in highly capitalized firms or sectors, and workers with greater control over their individual work or joint production process are more satisfied with their jobs.[42]

One of the problems with the job satisfaction research is that it stops short of proposing how changes *in the workplace* affect satisfaction. The direction of much of the current research suggests, somewhat unreasonably, that a change in monetary expectations and an "equivalent" change in monetary rewards results in no change in the total amount of job satisfaction, thus denying the effects of *experiencing* changes in expectations and rewards. The introduction of a comparable worth wage policy in the state of Minnesota offers the opportunity to rethink and test, in a preliminary way, the consequences of wage changes on employees' job satisfaction. As a policy, pay equity says that the work traditionally done by women is more valuable than the pay available for it has reflected. To the extent that individuals know about pay equity and believe its premises, the policy has the power to change expectations, where expectations reflect both altered perceptions of deserving higher salaries and wanting them.[43] If individuals know about the policy and also receive the raises, it is possible that they will have increased their expectations and increased their rewards. We suggest that when comparable worth is not tied to divisive issues, in particular to an organizationally divisive struggle to establish job hierarchies through a contested job evaluation, the *process* of increased expectations and rewards will increase overall satisfaction with work.

It is very difficult to assess changes in job satisfaction in a one-time survey. Cross-sectional data provide a current snapshot of job satisfaction without explicit reference to past levels of satisfaction. In addition, this survey used a general question assessing overall job satisfaction, rather than a question specifically aimed at determining satisfaction with salary.[44] Mindful of these characteristics of the measure and the data, the survey found that state of Minnesota employees are quite satisfied with their jobs. In the year prior to the interview, 57.4% found their jobs satisfying very often, 33.9% occasionally found their jobs satisfying, and 8.7% rarely found their jobs satisfying. This pattern remained the same for men and women, high- and low-salary employees, average- and well-educated workers, and people of every organizational experience and ideological persuasion.

The only distinctive pattern of job satisfaction was associated with the accuracy of reporting and receiving pay equity raises (table 5.11). The most satisfied employees were those who had accurately known about their pay equity raises (Group 4), 67.8% of whom found work satisfying very often. Those who knew about the pay equity policy but not about their own raises were among the least satisfied employees. Only 39.4% of those who did not report a raise but received one (Group 5) expressed satisfaction with their jobs very often. In fact, Group 5 had *lower* job satisfaction than those in Group 6 (never heard of pay equity, yes received

TABLE 5.11
**Impact of Experience with Pay Equity Raises on Job Satisfaction (in percentages)**

|  | Very Satisfied | Occasionally Satisfied | Rarely Satisfied | n |
|---|---|---|---|---|
| Group 1: Yes reported, no raise[a] | 53.6 | 42.9 | 3.2 | (28) |
| Group 2: No reported, no raise | 57.9 | 30.2 | 12.0 | (242) |
| Group 3: Never heard, no raise | 60.7 | 37.5 | 1.8 | (56) |
| Group 4: Yes reported, yes raise | 67.8 | 25.3 | 6.9 | (87) |
| Group 5: No reported, yes raise | 39.4 | 48.5 | 12.1 | (33) |
| Group 6: Never heard, yes raise | 54.5 | 42.4 | 3.0 | (33) |

[a]$X^2$ significant at the .05 level.

raise), 54.5% of whom reported being very satisfied with their jobs.[45] In a modest way, these results suggest that increasing expectations (in the form of knowledge about a new wage policy) and increasing rewards related to those expectations (through pay equity raises known to individuals) increase job satisfaction. Similarly, increasing expectations and not communicating rewards decrease job satisfaction.

## Paradoxes of State Implementation

The results of the survey of state of Minnesota employees indicate that pay equity was very well known, very well supported, and, among those who could accurately report receiving a pay equity raise, a source of job satisfaction. Most employees did *not* believe that pay equity would cause problems in the workplace, but a substantial majority feared that salaries would be frozen because of this change in wage policy.

These mostly supportive results were the consequences of a lot of hard work by many people, but they also reflect the paradoxes of this particular implementation process. The first paradox is that elite control of information and limited participation on the part of employees made implementation work smoothly. It is a perfect example of the dilemma of technocratic reform and democratic values. Employees had very little input in the job evaluation done several years before the comparable worth analysis was undertaken. But even more important in understanding the tension between technocracy and democracy is AFSCME's strategic decision to promote comparable worth in mostly female bargaining units and to respond quietly to the worries of employees in the mostly male bargaining units. From AFSCME's perspective, too much publicity would have raised more concern over whether the pay equity raises targeted for women came from what might otherwise have been a larger general salary settlement.

The second paradox of AFSCME's strategy is that in order to dampen opposition the union implicitly chose to dampen support. Such a strategy maintained the distributive rather than redistributive quality of the reform, and kept male AFSCME employees from disrupting the implementation. The survey results suggest that employees who knew about the pay equity policy and accurately reported receiving pay equity raises were more satisfied with their jobs than any other group, and especially more satisfied than those who knew about the policy but not about their own raises. More information about pay equity might have increased job satisfaction for the eligible women workers who had never heard of the policy, but it might also have increased dissatisfaction among the men not eligible for raises. Thus in the state of Minnesota case, the long-term transformational potential of pay equity rests awkwardly on those individuals who knew about their pay equity raises as well as spent them, and on those who only spent them but did not know the reasons for the increases. This situation is surely present in many reforms, with the most notable parallels being with the institution of the minimum wage. The paradoxes of state implementation alert us to the challenges of maintaining a popular component in the drive for comparable worth, a component that links wage gains and improved autonomy for women with the increased possibility of opposition of male workers and family members.

*Paradoxes and Unintended Consequences: Implementation of Comparable Worth in Local Jurisdictions*

> You want to know how to understand lo-
> cal implementation of comparable
> worth? Just remember: The police hate
> women and firefighters hate the police.
> *Minnesota Union Official*

The three most important characteristics of the successful implementation of the State Employees Pay Equity Act were the separation of job evaluation from comparable worth adjustments, union and management agreement on the importance of the policy and the technology used (the Hay system and the male wage line), and the relatively easy process of funding the increases. None of these facilitating conditions existed in quite the same way in the implementation of the Local Government Pay Equity Act. Most local jurisdictions throughout the state had no job evaluation systems. Thus implementing comparable worth required simultaneously combining job evaluation and the determination of pay inequities. Local governments were less likely to be unionized, and if unionized, it was rare for any one union to have the power that AFSCME had in state government. Under the local law, as with the state law, managers controlled the choice of job evaluation systems. But local managers were less familiar with job evaluation methodology, and both unionized and nonunionized employees were often confused and sometimes angry about technical decisions.

Everyone had discovered that the people who controlled job evaluation won the comparable worth sweepstakes. It was clear that the initial technical definitions—of compensable factors, weights allocated to each factor, and job-class descriptions—would determine the new wage structure and status hierarchy. With so much riding on job evaluation, blue-collar, clerical, and professional employees alike worried that key aspects of their jobs would be overlooked or allocated insufficient weight. Public managers worried about money. Local jurisdictions, still reeling from the antitax backlash of the late 1970s and early 1980s, had few sources of extra revenue. Their heavy reliance on a property tax capped by a state-imposed levy limit fueled financial fears throughout the implementation process.

## *Methodology*

Four months after the passage of the Local Government Pay Equity Act, the University of Minnesota's Comparable Worth Research Project began collecting data and following the implementation process in twenty-four local jurisdictions. The aim was to conduct a large-scale natural experiment on the hitherto unstudied questions of implementation of comparable worth in local jurisdictions.[1] We employed a two-tier research design, with the first tier focusing on the policy direction given by professional organizations of jurisdictions and the second tier focusing on activities in individual jurisdictions. The two-tier research strategy proved especially effective in that it linked the legislative process to local implementation efforts through the actions of the professional associations that were active in both arenas. Data for both tiers of research consisted of interviews with leaders of professional organizations, public managers, union representatives, and elected officials; media reports; and public and private documents.

In the first tier of the research, we chronicled the role of the jurisdictional professional organizations: the Association of Minnesota Counties (AMC), the League of Minnesota Cities (LMC), the Metropolitan Area Management Association (MAMA), the Minnesota School Boards Association (MSBA), and local and statewide employee groups. These groups worked with, and against, the Department of Employee Relations, which was mandated by the local law to give technical assistance to localities. Together these leaders were the most influential pacesetters in the policy development process, occasionally joined by the managers and elected officials of the large jurisdictions in the Twin Cities area. Their recommendations and activities shaped to a marked degree interpretations of the law, perceptions of choices, and actions taken.

In the second tier we chose jurisdictions to analyze in detail. The jurisdictions were chosen to vary across five dimensions: type of jurisdiction (cities, counties, and school boards), size (large, medium, or small, with the numbers varying by type of jurisdiction), location (urban and rural), timing of implementation (before or after the local law was introduced), and level of unionization (70% or greater, 35% to 69%, and less than 35%).[2] As is the case in any natural experiment, the dimensions of comparison were often related to one another. The patterns of implementation varied primarily by type and size of jurisdiction. Not surprisingly, size served as a rough proxy for unionization, as small jurisdictions tended to be rural and less unionized. Size is a better proxy for unionization among cities and counties. School employees tend to have high levels of unionization across the state. The timing of initial implementation had no demonstrable effect.

The importance of type of jurisdiction and size to our findings deserves close attention. Five patterns of implementation emerged, one each associated with large, medium, and small cities; a fourth associated with counties of all sizes; and a fifth with all school boards. These patterns go beyond size and type of jurisdiction. Embedded within these characteristics are five constellations of leadership and power of women in decision-making, and organizational—especially personnel—capacities. It is not surprising that jurisdictions with strong, politically committed leaders, supported by women who were incorporated into local power structures, and able to draw on established personnel systems, more easily implemented comparable worth.

Tables 6.1 through 6.3 list the jurisdictions analyzed in this study and give information on their population, number of employees, type of government, number of unions and bargaining units, percentage of employees in unions, consultants and consultant fees (where available), type of job evaluation system, type of salary line used, existence of a wage corridor around the salary line, budgetary implications of comparable worth findings, and timetable for implementation. Minneapolis and St. Paul are the large cities; Columbia Heights, Golden Valley, Maple Grove, Rochester, and St. Cloud the medium-sized cities; and Granite Falls, Hutchinson, and Princeton the small cities. The sample of counties included one large county (Hennepin—Greater Minneapolis), three medium-sized counties (Anoka, Olmsted, and Washington), and one small county (Beltrami). Anoka-Hennepin, Minneapolis, and St. Paul are the large school districts; Rochester and Stillwater are the medium-sized school districts; and Blue Earth, Chaska, Eden Prairie, and Little Falls are the small school districts. Map 6.1 shows where these jurisdictions are found within Minnesota.

TABLE 6.1
Characteristics of Cities in the Minnesota Comparable Worth Study (1987)

| Population | No. of Employees | Type of Government | No. of Unions | Total Bargain. Units | % of Employees in Unions | Consultant and Fee | Job Evaluation System | Salary Line | Corridor | Budgetary Implications | Timetable for Implementation |
|---|---|---|---|---|---|---|---|---|---|---|---|
| *Large* (over 60,000) | | | | | | | (Civil Service System) | | | | |
| Minneapolis (364,160) | 4,000 | Mayor City Coord. City Council | 16 | 20 | 95 | $94,000 thus far Mercer-Meidinger (are not using now) | Point-factor | To be decided | To be decided | Unknown | Possibly begin: 8/1/87 Complete: 8/1/89 Retro to: 7/1/85 |
| St. Paul (268,750) | 4,000 | Mayor City Manager City Council | 33 | 43 | 90 | Hallcrest-Craver $185,000 | Point-factor | Balanced job classes | 7½ +/- | $5–6 mil. 10% of payroll | Begin: 10/1/87 Complete: Unknown |
| *Medium* (18,000–60,000) | | | | | | | | | | | |
| Columbia Heights (19,560) | 120 | Mayor City Manager City Council | 6 | 6 | 75–80 | Hay Mgmt. Cons. $18,000 + Exp. | Point-factor | All class | Undecided as of 9/10/87 | Unknown as of 9/10/87 | Begin: 1/1/88 Complete: 1/1/91 |
| Golden Valley (22,380) | 110 | Mayor City Manager City Council | 2 | 4 | 55–60 | Control Data $7,000 | Point-factor | All class | +/– 10% | 2½% of payroll | Begin: 1/1/87 Complete: 7/1/87 |
| Maple Grove (33,449) | 112 | Mayor City Admin. City Council | 2 | 3 | 33 | Control Data | Point-factor | [Council decided not to implement—would not give out information—council will reconsider study in 6 months as of 9/10/87] | | | |
| Rochester (59,307) | 650 | Mayor City Admin. City Council | 10 | 15 | 85 | Arthur Young $60,000 | Decision-band method | Male trend | +/– 7% | $34,300 2.34% of payroll | Begin: 7/1/87 Complete: 12/31/91 |

| St. Cloud (43,311) | 315 | Mayor City Admin. City Council | 3 | 3 | 75–80 | Control Data $12,000, also used state job match | Point-factor | Combined | +/− 10% | Unknown | Unknown |
| *Small* (under 20,000) | | | | | | | | | | | |
| Granite Falls (3,326) | 25–30 | Mayor City Manager City Council | 1 | 3 | 52 | None | State job match | None | None | $0 No inequities found | None |
| Hutchinson (9,490) | 75 | Mayor City Admin. City Council | 0 | 0 | 0 | Hutchinson staff and human rels. cons., $1,500 | State job match | Combined | +/− 15% | $3,369/mo 2.8% of payroll | Begin: 1/1/85 Complete: 1/1/85 |
| Princeton (3,193) | 40–45 | Mayor City Admin. City Council | 1 | 2 | 60 | Princeton system | Point-factor | Male | None | $0 No inequities found | Had already implemented pay equity before state law |

TABLE 6.2
**Characteristics of Counties in the Minnesota Comparable Worth Study (1987)**

| Population | No. of Employees | Type of Government | No. of Unions | Total Bargain. Units | % of Employees in Unions | Consultant and Fee | Job Evaluation System | Salary Line | Corridor | Budgetary Implications | Timetable for Implementation |
|---|---|---|---|---|---|---|---|---|---|---|---|
| *Large* (over 300,000) | | | | | | | | | | | |
| Hennepin (945,970) | 8,700 | Council and Administrator | 14 | 19 | 55 | Arthur Young $218,000 | Point-factor | Balanced trend | +/- 10% | $1.6 million .08% of payroll | Begin: 6/15/87 Complete: 6/15/89 |
| Ramsey (457,123) | 3,100 | Council and Administrator | 4 | 14 | 60 | Peat, Marwick, and Mitchell $100,000 | Point-factor | All class | +/- 8% | $3–4 million .05% of payroll | Begin: 6/30/8? Complete: 6/30/91 |
| *Medium* (80,000–300,000) | | | | | | | | | | | |
| Anoka (207,355) | 850 | Council and Administrator | 2 | 2 | 25 | Hay Mgmt. Cons. $79,500 | Point-factor | Male | *None* (used midpt of male line to determine) | $153,000 1.6% of payroll | Begin: 3/1/87 Complete: 3/1/8? |
| Olmsted (95,791) | 750 | Council and County Administrator | 4 (also 2 assns.) | 5 | 45 | Arthur Young $46,000 | Decision method | Male | *None* (used midpt of male line) | $70,256 5.19% of payroll | Begin: 1/1/87 Complete: 12/31/81 |

| | | | | | Staff-consultant | Decision method | Class | | Cost | Dates |
|---|---|---|---|---|---|---|---|---|---|---|
| Washington (120,502) | 570 | 3 Council and Administrator | 5 | 80 | Staff-Wash. Cty. $62,653 Arthur Young $58,304 | Decision band method | All class | 7% | $29,952/mo. 2.57% of payroll | Begin: 1/11/87 Complete: 12/31/91 |
| *Small* (under 80,000) | | | | | | | | | | |
| Beltrami (32,903) | 340 | 4 Council and Commission | 5 | 66 | Steffen, Munstenteiger, Beens, Parta and Peterson law firm | Point-factor | Combined | +/-4% | $14,000 3.5% of payroll | Begin: 1/1/86 Complete: Unknown |

TABLE 6.3
**Characteristics of School Districts in the Minnesota Comparable Worth Study (1987)**

| Population | No. of Employees | Type of Government | No. of Unions | Total Bargain. Units | % of Employees in Unions | Consultant and Fee | Job Evaluation System | Salary Line | Corridor | Budgetary Implications | Timetable for Implementation |
|---|---|---|---|---|---|---|---|---|---|---|---|
| *Large* (over 30,000) | | | | | | | | | | | |
| Anoka-Hennepin (32,000) | 3,154 | School Board Superintendent | 11 | 14 | 95 | Arthur Young $30,000 | Decision band method | Male | None | $2.5 million (over 2 yrs) 3.4% of payroll | Begin: 7/1/85 Complete: 7/1/89 |
| Minneapolis (38,200) | 6,000 | School Board Superintendent | 14 | 18 | 98 | Lee Anderson Associates $60,000 | Point-factor | Combined | +/- 7½% | $80,315 .65% of payroll | Begin: 7/1/87 Complete: 7/1/90 |
| St. Paul (30,000) | 4,379 | School Board Superintendent | 22 | 28 | 45 | Hallcrest-Craver w/ city:$60,356 own: $61,922 Total: 122,278 Lee Anderson Associates $4,700 | Point-factor | All class | +/- 7½% | $2.079 million over 5 yrs., 1.9% of payroll | Begin: 7/1/87 Complete: 7/1/91 |
| *Medium* (7,500–30,000) | | | | | | | | | | | |
| Rochester (11,900) | 550 | School Board Superintendent | 5 | 5 | 70–75 | Arthur Young $20,000 | Decision band method | Combined | +/- 7½% | $300,000 over 2 yrs. 5–6% of payroll | Begin: 9/1/86 Complete: 9/1/88 |
| Stillwater | 740 | School Board | 9 | 9 | 90–95 | Arthur Young | Decision | Male | None | $510,528 | Begin: 1/1/86 |

| District | | Authority | | | | Consultant (cost) | Method | Gender | Range | Cost | Dates |
|---|---|---|---|---|---|---|---|---|---|---|---|
| (7,600) | | Superintendent | | | | $16,500 (MSBA paid other half) | band method | | | 2.8% of payroll | Complete: 6/30/90 |
| *Small* (under 7,500) | | | | | | | | | | | |
| Blue Earth (1,100) | 130 | School Board Superintendent | 1 | 1 | 50 | Arthur Young $5,000 | Decision band method | Combined | +/− 15% | $348.00 .10% of payroll | Begin: 7/1/86 Complete: 7/1/86 |
| Chaska (3,000) | 362 | School Board Superintendent | 3 | 3 | 95 | Arthur Young $7,500 | Decision band | Male | +/− 6% | 2.39% of payroll | Begin: 7/1/86 Complete: 7/1/89 |
| Eden Prairie (3,900) | 575 | School Board Superintendent | 6 | 8 | 95 | Towers, Perrin, Forster, and Crosby $20,000 | Point-factor | Male | +/− 15% | $48,766 4.54% of payroll | Begin: 7/1/84 Complete: 7/1/87 |
| Little Falls (3,200) | 300 | School Board Superintendent | 4 | 7 | 85 | None | State job match | Male | None | $17,840 2.74% of payroll | Begin: 11/1/85 Complete: 11/1/89 |

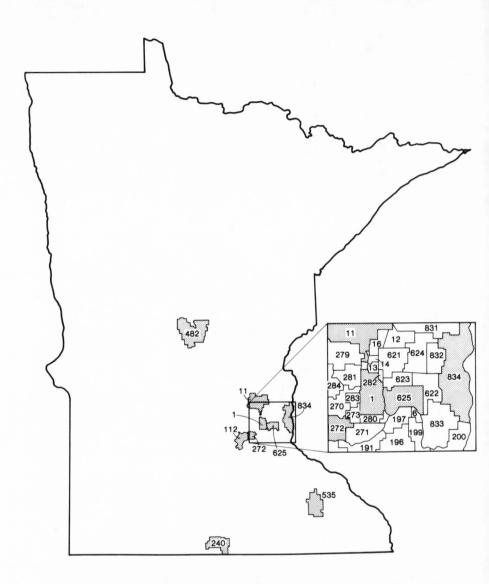

**Map 6.1 Minnesota School Districts Studied.**     Key: District

    1 = Minneapolis
    2 = Anoka-Hennepin
  112 = Chaska
  240 = Blue Earth
  272 = Eden Prairie
  482 = Little Falls
  535 = Rochester
  625 = St. Paul
  834 = Stillwater

**MINNESOTA**

0 10 20 30 40 50     75     100
Scale of Miles

KITTSON

ROSEAU

LAKE
OF THE WOODS

MARSHALL

BELTRAMI

KOOCHICHING

PENNINGTON

RED LAKE

COOK

POLK

CLEAR
WATER

ITASCA

ST. LOUIS

LAKE

NORMAN

MAHNOMEN

HUBBARD

CLAY

BECKER

CASS

WILKIN

OTTER TAIL

WADENA

CROW
WING

AITKIN

CARLTON

PINE

GRANT

DOUGLAS

TODD

MORRISON

MILLE
LACS

KANA-
BEC

BENTON

ANOKA

TRAVERSE

BIG
STONE

STEVENS

POPE

STEARNS

Princeton

St. Cloud

SHERBURNE

ISANTI

CHISAGO

Maple Grove

WASHINGTON

SWIFT

KANDIYOHI

WRIGHT

Columbia
Heights

RAMSEY

Stillwater

LAC QUI
PARLE

CHIPPEWA

MEEKER

HENNEPIN

RAM-
SEY

Golden
Valley

Minneapolis

St. Paul

Granite Falls

McLEOD

Hutchinson

CARVER

WASHINGTON

HENNEPIN

YELLOW MEDECINE

RENVILLE

SCOTT

DAKOTA

SIBLEY

LINCOLN

LYON

REDWOOD

NICOLLET

RICE

GOODHUE

LESUEUR

WABASHA

BROWN

PIPE-
STONE

MURRAY

WATONWAN

BLUE
EARTH

STEELE

OLMSTED

COTTONWOOD

WASECA

DODGE

Rochester

WINONA

ROCK

NOBLES

JACKSON

MARTIN

FARIBAULT

FREEBORN

MOWER

FILLMORE

HOUSTON

**Map 6.2 Minnesota Counties and Cities in Which Study Was Carried Out (counties in capital letters, cities in capital and lowercase letters)**

## Local Readiness to Respond

The configuration of local governments in Minnesota forms the backdrop for understanding the implementation of the Local Government Pay Equity Act. Minnesota has only two large cities, Minneapolis with a population of 364,000 and St. Paul, the capital, with a population of 269,000. In addition there are approximately 1,500,000 suburban residents, and these more than two million inhabitants of the greater metropolitan area constitute more than half the population of the state. Three other metropolitan areas with populations of one to two hundred thousand exist in other parts of the state. The state's eighty-seven counties, however, are dotted with hundreds of smaller cities and townships. All together, Minnesota has 855 cities and townships covered by the comparable worth legislation. These communities support 435 school districts.

All of these localities plus 230 special-purpose governments, 1,607 jurisdictions in all, were required to implement comparable worth according to the legislation's timetable. The legislation was passed in April 1984 and gave localities until October 1, 1985, to present a report to the Department of Employee Relations that evaluated jobs, investigated the possibility of gender-based wage bias, estimated the costs for remedying the bias if any existed, and developed a plan for changing the wage structure. The Department was required by the statute to report the results of the local government studies to the legislature by January 1986.

The choice of the type of job evaluation system was left completely up to each jurisdiction. Localities could invent their own system, borrow a system used by another locality, purchase a commercially developed system, or match their job classifications to the state's job classifications and use the state's Hay points. The Department of Employee Relations anticipated that, with the exception of the largest localities, most jurisdictions would find it easy and cheap to use the state's "job match" by examining state job descriptions to find equivalents to their own positions and then applying the state's Hay-point system. This did not prove to be the case.

What constituted a jurisdiction for the purpose of the Act caused something of a problem, because taxing, administrative, and personnel capacities of a local jurisdiction were not always identical. In Minneapolis, for example, a single civil service system served the city council, the park and recreation board, the library board, the school district, and the community development agency, but each of these entities traditionally bargained separately and set its own wage policies. Libraries, hospitals, and utilities were frequently in ambiguous positions, operating as employers but owned by or receiving funds from a city or county. The guideline the state finally used was the definition of employers established under the Public Employees Labor Relations Act (PELRA). If a jurisdiction acted as an employer under the terms of PELRA it would be considered an employer for the purposes of meeting the requirements of the Local Government Pay Equity Act. As we shall see, in a few instances, this decision undid long-standing salary practices.

When the Local Government Pay Equity Act was passed, the big cities were already deeply involved in examining comparable worth policies for their employees. For them, the legislation merely set a timeline, but did not set policy. Initial reactions from public officials in other jurisdictions ranged from measured acceptance to suspicious hostility. Even those who followed the legislature closely registered surprise, having expected a voluntary law rather than a mandate. Many responded defensively, wary of required change, suspicious of the theory behind comparable worth, and fearful of the cost. Bill Joynes, the well-respected and influential city manager in Golden Valley (a suburb of Minneapolis), remarked that "comparable worth is one of those issues that is hard to argue [against] on its face" but concluded that "we will try to do it right and try to do it slowly. . . . This bill is going to raise a lot of controversy. People are saying it is unworkable in its present form."[3] Counties, being more conservative than cities and school districts, and perhaps encouraged by their lobbyists in the Association of Minnesota Counties, generally gave less support to the concept of comparable worth than did other types of jurisdictions. In Otter Tail County, located in west-central Minnesota, one county commissioner called the pay equity law "the most asinine thing I've ever heard of."[4]

### *Help from the Specialists: Jurisdictional Associations and the Department of Employee Relations*

Local governments faced a series of decisions at the outset that would establish the broad patterns of compliance. The first decision was simply whether to comply. There was no penalty for noncompliance prescribed in the law aside from the possibility of lawsuit. The second choice, once they had decided to comply, concerned methods of job evaluation. The magnitude of the task depended on the size of the jurisdiction's labor force, whether it had an existing job classification system, whether managers were satisfied with the existing job classification system, and whether managers felt existing systems could successfully sustain a court challenge.*

The Department of Employee Relations quickly geared up to provide the technical assistance it had promised the legislature would be forthcoming with passage of the local government law. Commissioner Nina Rothchild created a "Pay Equity Team" within the Department, drawing on the expertise developed in the state among activists inside and outside state government. The team was headed by Bonnie Watkins, who had been the primary author of the original Pay Equity Task Force Report, and included David Lutes, a computer specialist who as a researcher for the legislature had fashioned the scattergrams in the original report, and Carol Flynn, a former staff member of AFSCME who had lobbied extensively for pay equity.

Commissioner Rothchild and the pay equity team undertook a heavy round of speaking engagements to explain the law and urge rapid compliance modeled on the state's approach. In most instances the Department of Employee Relations advocated the use of a job match with the state's Hay-point system. They argued that a job match was simple, cheap, and avoided the disruptive effects of instituting a new job evaluation and reclassification system. In a letter to personnel administrators, Commissioner Rothchild emphasized the fact that the local law was modeled on the State Employees Pay Equity Act of 1982: "The law does not require you to replace an existing job evaluation system, if you have one. It does not require you to revise your entire personnel system, and it will not change normal collective bargaining relationships."[5]

Members of the pay equity team made over seventy presentations from June to December 1984, including speeches and workshops at the professional meetings of cities, counties and school boards. The team produced five technical assistance publications by the fall of 1984. *A Guide to Implementing Pay Equity in Local Government*—with supplements for school districts, cities, small cities, and counties—defined pay equity, the requirements of the local law, and the process of determining comparable work value. The Department also offered free pay equity software packages for IBM-compatible personal computers, which could produce scattergrams demonstrating pay patterns and estimating the cost of imple-

---

*The law defined a job class as "one or more positions that have similar duties, responsibilities, and general qualifications" and required that comparability in skill, effort, responsibility, and working conditions be a primary factor in determining the pay of male-dominated, female-dominated, and balanced classes. Minnesota Statutes Annotated, Section 471.992, Subdivision 1 (West, 1988).

menting comparable worth. Active use of the Department of Employee Relations as a resource is perhaps best reflected in the extensive consultations conducted over the phone. The pay equity team estimated an average twenty calls per day from October through December 1984.[6]

While larger jurisdictions for the most part declined to follow Department of Employee Relations advice and often regarded its suggestions with some suspicion, the energy, accessibility, and optimism of the pay equity team encouraged compliance. Members of the team even received calls from management consultants hired by local jurisdictions and suspect that their free software found its way into many places where the Department continued publicly to be regarded with disdain.[7] The Department's emphasis on simplifying the technical aspects of comparable worth, however, failed to recognize the political realities that pushed many local jurisdictions into more expensive and time-consuming options.

In the first few months after the local law was passed, interpretations of the legislation were most powerfully shaped by the professional associations to which jurisdictions turned for advice. Outside Minnesota, comparable worth has been implemented in individual jurisdictions rather than across the board. As a result, the role of professional associations has not been visible. The across-the-board nature of change in Minnesota, however, brought associations immediately into play, because they serve as a primary information network (for all but the largest jurisdictions) about the state bureaucracy, political currents (these associations regularly lobby in the interests of their respective jurisdictions), and professional expertise. The relationships between associations and local jurisdictions range from extremely close links with the Minnesota School Boards Association, which offers collective bargaining services and assistance in job searches, to much looser ties with the Association of Minnesota Counties. In each case, however, the flow of information and advice has proved critical.

Initially the associations, principally the League of Minnesota Cities, the Minnesota School Boards Association, the Association of Minnesota Counties, and the Metropolitan Area Management Association, turned to their own internal experts for advice on the legal ramifications of the law and the technical requirements of job evaluation. These early discussions within the associations shaped the long-term propensity of jurisdictions to comply. As the representatives of local jurisdictions' views before the legislature, these groups also served as trusted sources of explanation about the meaning and the requirements of the law. The very different recommendations of these four key associations both shaped and reflected the structure, scale, and leadership characteristics of the jurisdictions they represented. We shall outline their decision-making processes, which created a framework for the patterns of compliance we observed, and then explore the outcomes for different types and sizes of jurisdictions.

*Association of Minnesota Counties*

The AMC from the beginning assumed a stance of begrudging compliance that reflected the strong resistance to state mandates on the part of its constituent units as well as a philosophical opposition to comparable worth. Leaders simultaneously argued strenuously that comparable worth was not justifiable, either on the grounds of equity or of good management practice, and that they would assist counties in complying with the terms of the law.[8] AMC Attorney Dick Cox, for example, suggested that "the Legislature is handing us the gun [job evaluation] and allowing us to shoot ourselves in both feet [by becoming vulnerable to lawsuits modelled on *AFSCME v. State of Washington*]."[9] But he also told resistant counties that "non-compliance with the law is not an available option."[10] Before any other association had developed recommendations, the AMC contracted with Arthur Young and Company in the summer of 1984 to offer evaluation services "because of the . . . felt need for consistency among counties to provide a more defendable legal position."[11] At the same time, relations with the Department of Employee Relations were consistently hostile. Earl Larson, AMC president, criticized the department's compliance plans as creating "the potential for a statewide, state-run personnel system."[12]

While advocating timely compliance, the AMC also continued to test the legislative waters regarding repeal or extension of the time limits. The perception that the law might change in the 1985 legislative session may have led many counties to suspend compliance efforts for four or five months.[13] In effect, the philosophical stance of staff attorney Dick Cox, who travelled around the state to debate Nina Rothchild, and of outspoken leaders in Minnesota's largest county (Hennepin), meshed with widespread resistance on the part of many county commissioners to undermine AMC's simultaneous efforts to encourage compliance. Indeed, many advocates of comparable worth believed that, beyond its rhetoric, the AMC actually did little to encourage movement toward implementation.

*Minnesota School Boards Association*

The MSBA has traditionally provided extensive services to local school boards, including bargaining, superintendent searches, board evaluations, policy training, and lobbying.[14] As a result, school superintendents immediately looked to this trusted source for guidance on the meaning of pay equity and the requirements for compliance. Recently elected MSBA President Jean Olson, a strong supporter of comparable worth, guided a special advisory committee away from debates over whether comparable worth was a good idea, as in the counties, and toward the practical steps of implementation. Rejecting the state job-match approach as inappropriate for school districts, many of whose jobs could not be duplicated at the state level, the advisory committee recommended that the MSBA develop its own job match by employing a consultant to develop a prototype plan and a training program so that local districts could adapt it to their specific needs.[15]

In rapid order the advisory committee selected Arthur Young and Company as a consultant, chose two school districts—one suburban and one rural—for the pilot studies, held a statewide meeting to explain the process (500 attended), and prepared a series of training workshops to be held in February and March 1985.[16] More than 600 representatives from 400 of the 435 school districts in the state eventually attended these workshops.[17] Thus the MSBA set in motion a process that encouraged and facilitated rapid compliance, with a fairly high level of employee participation.

The prominent role of the Arthur Young company, recommended by both the MSBA and the AMC, was largely due to the fact that the company had close connections with staff at AMC and through them "saw it coming." As soon as the law passed, Young approached city, county, and school associations with detailed proposals. The fact that the firm had some prior experience with pay equity in the public sector in Iowa and Michigan gave it additional credibility. For school districts in particular, the Decision Band Method (DBM), a relatively new technique acquired by Young in 1980–81, seemed to meet the need for a method that would reflect the underlying values they believed set them apart from other types of jurisdictions.[18] DBM relies primarily on a single factor, decision-making, to sort jobs into "bands" and "grades." For this reason many unions were opposed to its use.*

## League of Minnesota Cities

The LMC represents a very wide variety of constituencies, ranging from the large cities of Minneapolis and St. Paul to hundreds of tiny com-

---

*AFSCME opposed DBM as did many blue-collar unions, the latter because it did not evaluate working conditions. Two unions, the Minnesota School Employees Association and the International Union of Operating Engineers, sought a Hennepin County district court injunction against the use of DMB. The suit was dismissed in March 1985 on the grounds that the law protected jurisdictions against suits prior to August 1, 1987.

munities in rural Minnesota. As an association it exercised very different forms of influence on small cities, through its cooperation with the Department of Employee Relations, and on medium-sized cities, through the Metropolitan Area Managers Association (MAMA, discussed below); it had little or no effect on the two large cities. Through a series of annual regional meetings held each fall the league provided small communities with their primary source of information about current state policies, new legislation, and future political agendas of the league. In 1984, its newly elected president, Mayor Mary Anderson of Golden Valley (a Minneapolis suburb), invited the Department of Employee Relations to hold a workshop on pay equity at the regional meetings. These regional workshops, led by members of the Department of Employee Relations' pay equity team and by Faith Zwemke, former mayor of Princeton, Minnesota, were extremely well received, to the surprise of both LMC staff and department representatives. Though many local officials were unhappy about having a new, potentially expensive requirement, they appreciated the unusual level of technical assistance from the state.[19] The goodwill generated in these meetings made small cities the primary group to follow the model of compliance urged by the Department of Employee Relations.

### *Metropolitan Area Managers Association*

MAMA, an affiliate of the League of Minnesota Cities consisting of about fifty-five suburban cities, had, even more than the School Boards Association, a history of close involvement in the labor relations of its members. For more than two decades they had conducted joint labor negotiations with unions representing police, firefighters, and public utilities workers. From the outset, leaders like Bill Joynes, Golden Valley City Manager and chair of the MAMA Labor Relations Committee, worried that "if thirty or forty cities do their own [pay equity] plans, the unions would come back and hold up the highest one as the standard."[20] By June 1984 MAMA had decided to explore the possibility of a joint study. As one headline put it: "MAMA Will Mother Suburbs in Comparable Worth Labor."[21]

The decision to pursue a professional job evaluation study rested on grounds similar to those used by the AMC and the MSBA. Local jurisdictions of any substantial size argued that their labor forces had unique characteristics not captured by state-level job classes. Police and fire-fighters in cities, like teachers and school secretaries in school districts, were employees central to the jurisdiction's mission. But analogous employees of the state had somewhat different duties and responsibilities as well as significantly different relationships to the central mission of the governmental body in question. In addition, jurisdictions whose employees were organized into a variety of unions faced pressures from male-dominated unions.[22] These localities wanted a system that would be credible with all employees and doubted that a job match would serve the purpose. They hoped that a professional reclassification based on employee input would encourage employees to "buy in" and see the process as fair; this hope acted as a strong incentive to hire outside consultants, especially where preexisting job evaluation or job classification systems were outdated or nonexistent. Indeed, consultants frequently insisted on employee participation, making the commercial job evaluation systems more participatory in process than the job match option. Finally, legal anxieties drove lawyers for associations and large jurisdictions to express considerable concern about future litigation, using the Washington State case to warn officials and managers of a variety of legal dangers.

More than most, MAMA added to the above a strong desire to rationalize personnel and wage policies. Labor consultants Cyrus Smythe and Karen Olson, whose firm, Labor Relations Associates, regularly negotiated for MAMA, devoted their column in *Minnesota Cities* throughout 1984 to discussions of comparable worth, job evaluation, and the ramifications of the local law, placing the stamp of their professional concerns on the broader discussion. Smythe argued, for example, that "the Minnesota Comparable Worth Act provides an incentive for Minnesota's political subdivisions to bring their employee compensation plans more closely into line with those of well-managed private sector companies."[23] The MAMA decision to request a multi-employer study was made with the advice of Labor Relations Associates, who pointed out the dangers of having the same job valued differently in different cities, especially essential employees (police and fire) whose wages frequently are set through arbitration. Karen Olson drew up the request for proposals specifying the desire for state-of-the-art methodology and employee participation.[24]

After interviewing six applicants, the Labor Relations Committee of MAMA recommended the selection of Control Data Corporation's task analysis system. The grounds for this choice included Control Data's willingness to evaluate every job, not just benchmarks (a process they felt was more defensible legally); the highly participative process proposed, which would involve thousands of employees (something Joynes believed would make it more difficult for people to question later); legal defensibility of the method itself; the capacity for easy local updating in the future as jobs change; and Control Data's grasp of the size of the proposed project.[25]

The proposed methodology, Control Data's Human Resource Focus System, represented one of the most recent innovations in job analysis, highly computerized and centered on the valuing of tasks rather than of whole jobs. A consortium of medium-sized cities outside the metropolitan area sent representatives to every stage of this decision-making process, and most of them eventually joined the MAMA/Control Data study. By the end, a total of 134 jurisdictions joined this massive study.[26]

Together, professional associations tried to provide to local jurisdictions technical and political information and advice analogous to what state and national unions provide their locals. Though they had to begin from scratch, they conveyed to local jurisdictions an understanding of the implications of comparable worth which emphasized, especially in large and medium-sized jurisdictions, the importance of management-controlled, professional job evaluation. The collective experience thus generated will no doubt also flow back through these state associations and into the national networks of which they are a part.*

## *Patterns of Compliance*

While the first tier of research revealed distinctive patterns of implementation shaped by jurisdictional associations, the second tier made possible a more finely tuned analysis of the leadership patterns associated with implementation in different types and sizes of jurisdictions. It is the whole pattern of political and organizational arrangements, the textured cloth of governmental interactions in each type of locality, that makes understanding local implementation possible. A comparison of jurisdiction and size (among cities, where it is more relevant than among counties and school boards) demonstrates that it is the political characteristics of jurisdictions, especially the existence of a strong, politically committed

---

*For example, in response to passage of a bill imposing financial penalties for noncompliance on school districts, the AMC, LOC, and MSBA planned a symposium on comparable worth for September 1988 "to share information on the status of pay equity implementation in state and local government." Though concerned primarily with avoiding future political and legal tangles on the issue, the organizers of the conference (including former leading opponents of the *concept* of comparable worth), had changed their stance considerably in four years. They presumed that comparable worth was a fact of life (as an "equity issue," not a "women's issue"), and were rather proud of the systems they had instituted. On the other hand, they remained embattled with the Department of Employee Relations around specific issues of interpretation. (Meeting with Merry Beckman, Association of Minnesota Counties, and Raleigh Toenges, Hennepin County, 22 June 1988).

executive and the presence of women in the administrative processes, that do the most to structure the implementation process. There are five patterns of implementation, one each associated with large, medium, and small cities, another associated with all counties, and a fifth with all school boards. Most notable are the differences associated with city size and ultimately city political arrangements, including employment policies. Large, medium, and small cities differed significantly in how they implemented comparable worth.

## Large Cities

Large cities had popular, partisan mayors, as well as active councils. The Democratic mayors of Minneapolis and St. Paul understood the growing feminist demands for policies more responsive to women's social position, an understanding that was consistent both with their programmatic goals and with their electoral calculations. Both were willing to act as "fixers" in the implementation process, and neither shied away from political solutions when technical solutions devised by personnel managers were unsatisfactory.[27] They also had the benefits of existing, if not exactly state-of-the-art, personnel systems.

Big cities also had a relatively large proportion of women on their councils. In 1984, six of the thirteen Minneapolis city council members were women. In both Minneapolis and St. Paul women were fully incorporated into the power structure, being important members of voting and policy coalitions and holding major offices, such as city council president in Minneapolis.[28] In both the representation of women on city councils and their incorporation into the power structure, the two large cities in the state (and in our sample) were unusual. Overall, in 1983, only 13.8% of city council members throughout the state were women, and nowhere did they have political clout as they did in Minneapolis and St. Paul.[29] Given the political culture of the Twin Cities, which has been the seedbed for feminist caucuses in both political parties, and the strong presence of women in city government, the political power of feminist agendas should not be surprising. The high level of public-sector unionization in both cities (95% in Minneapolis, 90% in St. Paul) served both to increase the political appeal of comparable worth and to complicate its implementation. In each city, AFSCME provided a powerful ally pressing for comparable worth. But other, equally powerful male-dominated unions resisted or opposed specific aspects of the implementation process, forcing negotiation and compromise.

As a result, both major cities initiated comparable worth policies prior

to the passage of the state mandate, but difficulties arose in the clash between political pressures, fiscal restraints, and technological complexities.
Managerial pressures led each city to embark on a major reclassification
process as part of its pay equity plan, and in each case both the process
and the results of the study provoked conflict and consumed inordinate
amounts of time and effort. In both cases initial results were technically
(and politically) unsatisfactory and the studies had to be revised or redone.
Ultimately each city also reverted to a traditional mix of politics and collective bargaining. In the midst of the turmoil, in late 1985, St. Paul
Mayor George Latimer expressed his own doubts with a quote from Oliver
Cromwell to Parliament, " 'Think ye in the bowels of Christ that ye may
be wrong?' I'm not sure that this agony, time and cost is necessary to
achieve justice. Why not just address the fact that some people are not
making a living wage?"[30] Ultimately St. Paul instituted a new system that
reduced the number of job classes from 850 to 500, but the consultant's
proposed uniform pay scale for 33 separate bargaining units was impossible to implement and has become an ongoing bone of contention in collective bargaining. Minneapolis, on the other hand, tabled its unsatisfactory study and used the previous point system to calculate pay equity
increases, a solution proposed by AFSCME from the outset.[31]

### Medium-sized Cities

In contrast with large cities, many medium-sized cities did not have
strong, unambiguously political executives. The medium-sized cities were
the heirs of the Progressive era urban reforms towards technical government and diffuse power arrangements. For example, in Rochester the
mayor was a part-time official, the council president was the top vote-
getter (and the person who presided over the council), and a city administrator managed the city. In all medium-sized cities, city managers exercised a great deal of power and brought with them a technocratic outlook
to the governance of their cities. Not elected, they were somewhat insu-
lated from the changing mood of the electorate. And their electorates,
often suburban, were frequently more conservative than those in big cities,
in any event. One example of the relative power of managers in setting
policy in medium-sized cities can be found in Golden Valley. City Manager Bill Joynes was much more influential in the implementation process
in his city than was Mayor Mary Anderson, who, also politically active
and recognized, was then President of the Minnesota League of Cities.
While women in managerial positions were more likely to accept the
underlying rationale for pay equity as a remedy for past discrimination,

they, like their male counterparts, were circumscribed by their professional orientation and tended to emphasize technique and cost-containment. In 1988 there were fifteen women serving as city managers or administrators in Minnesota.

While the leadership on comparable worth came from managers, organized through MAMA, the personnel capacities of medium-sized cities were often underdeveloped or nonexistent. Unionization of public employees varied (from 55% to 85%), but in general was substantially less than in the large cities, and nowhere did representatives of clerical workers wield substantial clout. In most cases, police, firefighters, and engineers or maintenance workers bargained collectively while other workers did not. The historic evolution of pay practices, based on a mixture of bargaining for some groups and not for others and classification systems (if any) that had little internal logic, meant that the pay practices of many jurisdictions were based, in the words of Bill Joynes, on "tradition, favoritism, political clout, and whim."[32] Women exerted important leadership in specific instances, as mayors or city managers, but neither feminist political activists nor female public employees significantly shaped the political agenda.

The leadership pattern and political environment of medium-sized cities proved conducive to one of the more striking unanticipated consequences of the local pay equity law: comparable worth became the catalyst for a kind of managerial revolution which revised, rationalized, and streamlined personnel and pay practices.* The most dramatic stories of this change come from the MAMA/Control Data study. For some it was two years of "pain and agony," with at least two dimensions. First was simply the difficulty of applying a relatively new technology on a massive scale. Second was the discontent of employees when the job values and job hierarchies were finally published.

Control Data's technology, a highly computerized method that valued tasks, not whole jobs, arrived at job values through "time spent profiles" that estimated the time devoted to each task within a specific job. This approach had never been applied in the public sector nor on such a large scale, and each step took longer than expected. Consultants originally contracted for fifty jurisdictions and within months were handling well

---

*This development has striking parallels to the impact of affirmative action upon the rise of human resources management and the professionalization of the personnel function. A comparison of the two developments should clarify further the history of modern personnel management and its contradictory relationship to technocratic reforms aimed at increasing opportunities and income of women and minorities. We are grateful to Ronnie Steinberg for calling this to our attention.

over a hundred. They had to adjust to the dispersed decision-making within the public sector. Administrators in the various cities, on the other hand, had to carry out highly technical procedures without understanding the broader context that would clarify their meaning and importance.[33] Personnel directors' faces get a kind of glazed look of wonderment when they try to describe the "hours and hours" they and their employees devoted to the process. But in the end, they had "an assessment, in most cases for the first time, of what our employees are actually doing."[34]

For many jurisdictions that had previously had no system at all and whose pay practices could only be explained historically, comparable worth had grown into a major transformation of management practices. Indeed, at least four metropolitan-area cities hired personnel directors in order to manage the study itself.[35] Several cities subsequently hired Arthur Young and Company or other consultants to help them develop a compensation plan using the data from their job analysis study.[36] A group of personnel directors, in need of peer support while working on the study, formed The Unknown Group (TUG) to meet every month. They invited outside speakers on some of the more technical aspects of comparable worth and job evaluation, but most important they provided each other with mutual support and practical help. They exchanged job classification hierarchies, for example, and discussed strategies for dealing with unsympathetic city councils or managers. Within this group, the variations in level of commitment to the concept of comparable worth fell at least in part along gender lines. All of the women, according to chairperson Irene Koski, believed that the process was worth it. And both men and women agreed that the new system would be more rational and logical once it was in place.[37]

Suburban Columbia Heights illustrates the minority case in which conservative politics triumphed over managerial agendas. In Columbia Heights the city council followed the recommendation of the mayor, an opponent of comparable worth, rather than that of the city manager, and hired Hay Associates instead of joining the MAMA study.[38] What Columbia Heights did not get, however, was a rationalized personnel and compensation plan. City manager Robert Bocwinski was unable to persuade his city council to fund a revision of city job descriptions.[39]

*Small Cities*

Small cities, many of which had neither administrative staff nor any personnel system, ran on the personal-relations-as-politics, as most small communities do. Most of Minnesota's towns have fewer than 20,000 people, and most of the state's 58 female mayors (out of a total of 855) and 518 female council members (out of a total of 3,443) were active in small towns. No doubt local considerations and personal politics defined their interest in comparable worth. In one small town, however, a committed woman on the city council promoted the issue in a way typical of the political process in a small town.

In Princeton, Minnesota, a town of 3,200 on the Rum River, comparable worth was implemented before the passage of the local law at the urging of a forward-looking Council Member, Faith Zwemke. Princeton had recently shifted away from a city clerk form of government to a professional city manager, who in 1981 encouraged the city council to use job evaluation. On the basis of the new job evaluation Zwemke and another Council Member did a comparable worth analysis of the Princeton public labor force. They discovered that three clerical workers were significantly underpaid, and in February 1984 the city council agreed to salary adjustments totalling about $10,000. One of the employees receiving a raise reported that "I finally feel I'm of some value, not just a number."[40] But, as a sympathetic male staff member pointed out, the three clerical raises had moved women above or "dangerously close" to police and street maintenance workers.[41] Indeed, the head of the police association announced that he would not sign a negotiated contract because "we weren't aware of the large increases given to the female employees."[42] Only continuous explanations by Zwemke convinced the police association, and the equally unhappy street maintenance workers, to accept the contract.

Many such townships had no employees or so few that they could simply fill out the required forms indicating that they had no inequities to report. Where there were inequities, the process tended to be technically simple, but it nevertheless occasionally touched off anxieties such as those in Princeton. In small cities, the separation of jobs from people in them is extremely difficult. Most, however, reported a relatively smooth process, aided significantly by the encouragement of the League of Minnesota Cities, technical assistance from the Department of Employee Relations, and the prior example of Princeton.[43]

*Counties*

The political structure of Minnesota counties is not unlike that of medium-sized counties. Counties may adopt one or more of five optional forms of government, including an elected county executive, a county manager, an elected at-large county board chair, a county administrator, and a county auditor-administrator. Whatever the form, it is the invisibility and unimportance of county elected officials to voters, the lack of a strong executive, and the power of administrators in this situation that define the implementation process in this unit of government willed to the United States by its early English settlers. Only 6.3% of the 445 county commissioners sitting in Minnesota in 1983 were women, and by virtue of their small numbers, and a much less supportive atmosphere for women, few were as powerful as the female council members in Minneapolis and St. Paul. One female county commissioner told us that it was pretty lonely for her as a woman on her county commission, and her support for comparable worth had not made it any easier.

From the beginning, counties as a whole were the least responsive type of jurisdiction and their compliance rate consistently lagged well behind all others. County boards tend to be more conservative than elected officials in other jurisdictions. In contrast to school districts, counties have multiple centers of authority and a highly complex labor force including such diverse responsibilities as law enforcement, prisons, social welfare, court systems, public health, and hospitals. Counties resent state and federal mandates in general and have a sense of grievance that they are regularly required to take on responsibilities for which they have no additional funds. In January 1986, when 80% of school districts and 63% of cities and townships had submitted pay equity reports to the state, only 37% of counties had done so.[44]

Because of the diverse responsibilities exercised at the county level even the smallest county has about eighty employees. Many, however, had no classification plan at all, and wage-setting occurred within separate departments, each department head "selling" the county board on the salary and other needs.[45] Nevertheless, the Local Government Pay Equity Act has generated a significant shift in county managerial practices as well. The number of counties employing individuals with designated responsibility for personnel functions has risen by more than 50% (from 20 to more than 30).[46]

The emphasis at the county level has been heavily oriented towards cost containment, a result of the influential leadership of Hennepin County (greater Minneapolis). Hennepin County contains 23% of the state's population and employs 8,000 people. Its sprawling bureaucracy is governed by a seven-member county board and a highly professionalized managerial staff. About half of the county employees are unionized into twenty bargaining units and seven of the largest of these (covering 75% of unionized employees) are represented by AFSCME. From the outset, proponents of comparable worth ran into active opposition on the part of professional managers and county commissioners.[47] Indeed, the impetus for the local law had come first from leaders in AFSCME frustrated by the county's adamant refusal to negotiate a pay equity agreement. Faced with a requirement to pursue a policy with which they deeply disagreed on philosophical grounds and whose costs they feared, Hennepin County personnel managers devised a set of highly influential policy guidelines. Following the example of San Jose, California, they chose to use the "balanced class" pay line instead of the "male" pay line as the standard against which other salaries would be measured, and to create an equity "corridor" extending 10% on either side of that line, within which salaries would be considered equitable. Thus, many traditional salary differentials, if they fell within the 20% "corridor," would be deemed equitable in perpetuity. Further, they agreed to raise low salaries to the bottom of the corridor and to exercise "reasonable restraint" in containing the rise of salaries in classes above the corridor, with the proviso that in no case would they pay more than 10% above or below market rates for any job class. The latter provision provided a formula for incorporating market considerations into wage policies that was at odds with state practice and Department of Employee Relations recommendations. Whereas the Department presumed that market considerations were relevant only for a few jobs in which scarcity of qualified applicants could justify significantly higher wages, Hennepin County proposed that the market could act as a "governor" on their comparable-worth-driven wage structure. Each of these measures subsequently has been adopted by other jurisdictions. Indeed, once Hennepin County announced them, many consultants began recommending them to their clients as well.[48]

Legal concerns and the negative example of St. Paul's experience with employee-based evaluation led to a set of policies regarding the evaluation process and the role of a consultant. Hennepin County's request for proposals specified that evaluation must be done by "an evaluation committee composed of competent professional experts with extensive experience in job evaluation."[49] The same expert evaluation committee would hear appeals, thus removing not only employees but management from the process. Two rationales supported these proposals. Managers feared that AFSCME would dominate any employee-based approach, upsetting other unions and making it extremely difficult for nonunionized employees to be adequately represented. They also wanted legal liability for errors or bias to rest primarily with the consultant.[50]

Following the lead of Hennepin County, many large counties chose cost-containing policies such as using the balanced-class or all-job line as their equity standard and drawing a corridor that enclosed that line. In most counties, however, where the cost of change was not excessive, the male line proved a less disruptive choice.[51] The presence of large numbers of female administrators, particularly in the social services, tended to raise the female and combined lines at the upper end significantly.[52]

Cost-containment efforts frequently had the effect of flattening the range of salaries at any given point along the chosen line. In Hennepin County raises, on the whole, went to lower-level managers and professions, and very few went to clerical workers, but Hennepin also marked as overpaid a number of professional positions (such as attorney) and traditionally male blue-collar job classes. The complexity (and perhaps the conflictual nature) of the study process itself can be measured in part by the 3,500 individual appeals which were made in addition to departmental appeals when job values were first released. As a result, the point values of 499 out of 503 job titles were changed (387 raised and 116 lowered).[53] The personnel director of Washington County said pay equity meant the "biggest upheaval any employer will see."[54]

## School Districts

In contrast to counties, school districts had strong executives and a large number of women, a situation not unlike that in the large cities and one associated with easier implementation. School boards are popularly elected, and choose their chairs from among their ranks. Each board works closely with its superintendent of schools, who, though an appointed person, has a job more visibly political and more susceptible to popular control than the job of the typical city manager.

Women have a long tradition of serving on school boards. The linkage between women and responsibility for the education of young children is so strong in the United States that school board suffrage was one of the few electoral privileges granted to women in the period before women's general suffrage. In 1983, women comprised 25% of Minnesota school board members. The Minneapolis School Board, like the Minneapolis City Council, saw women not only well represented but also well incorporated in the power structure. The cultural presumption of women's appropriateness for this role encouraged their full participation in most situations.

In sharp contrast to the reluctant compliance of counties, school districts consistently led the way. The success of school districts can be attributed in part to the strong leadership of the Minnesota School Boards Association, headed by Jean Olson, a member of the Duluth School Board and president of MSBA. The relatively easy job match, achieved by using models developed by Arthur Young and Company for small and large districts, facilitated compliance. In addition, some underlying attitudes and structural conditions predisposed many school districts to rapid implementation. School boards had considerable experience with federal and state program mandates. They also shared a commitment to "doing what is right." One official put it well, saying that school boards wished "to get an 'A'." The clear and focused mission of school districts, and a structure which places considerable discretionary power in the hands of a single top administrator, the district superintendent, also facilitated compliance.[55] Finally, the long-standing practice of paying teachers on a single scale meant that the largest group of school employees constituted a balanced class which reduced, at the outset, the potential financial burden.*

Perhaps the most common pattern, in conservative suburbs and rural areas, has been rapid compliance despite expressions of hostility to the policy. The large Anoka-Hennepin district had been a battle ground on the issue since a clerical workers' strike in 1981. In 1983, when secretaries demanded wages comparable to those paid to custodians, Superintendent Lewis Finch reiterated his firm opposition. "We're not comparing [secretary salaries] with anyone else's. . . . We should pay salaries that are market sensitive."[56] Nevertheless, just over a year later he proclaimed the district's intention to comply with the local government pay equity law "whether we think it's a good or bad law."[57] And indeed, the district proceeded with an Arthur Young study, decided to use the male trend line, and by spring of 1987 was "80% of the way to implementation except with the cooks."[58] Similarly, the Stillwater School District agreed to be an MSBA model district even though both the superintendent and the chairman of the board proclaimed their view that wages should be market driven and protested the lack of state funds for implementation.[59]

Personnel managers in schools, as elsewhere, however, also saw an opportunity to rationalize pay practices and strengthen their hands *vis-à-*

---

*Initially, teachers were wary of job evaluation and hoped to be excluded altogether. According to one leader of a teachers' union, teachers "would hate to see [a school district] dig into instructional funds to offset the costs for comparable worth." In addition, job evaluation held the possibility of dividing teachers. As the Superintendent of the Anoka-Hennepin School District put it: "The MEA [Minnesota Education Association] may not be too excited about the teaching positions being rated. Lo and behold, we may discover significant differences between teaching positions." While a few districts excluded teachers from their studies altogether, most decided that the law required the inclusion of all employees. In line with the preferences of teachers' unions, however, teachers were generally treated as a single class, thus avoiding invidious comparisons between different kinds of teaching. See *St. Paul Pioneer Press and Dispatch*, 2 January, 1985, p. 3NE.

*vis* unions. Gene Rucker, personnel director for the Rochester schools, declared that comparable worth was the "greatest thing since popcorn" because it "forces us to be good managers based on data, not power, biases, and personal relations."[60] In suburban Chaska, the decision to hire Arthur Young presented an opportunity to obtain a complete set of job descriptions and to correct a classification system that was "way out of whack." The credibility gained by employee participation seemed particularly important since the district had previously been unsuccessful in convincing clerical workers and teachers' aides to accept a reclassification. As the director of administrative services and personnel put it, "They saw a windfall; we wanted reclassification."[61]

### Conclusions

The implementation of comparable worth at the local level in Minnesota offers a fascinating contrast to the experience of the state, which was the model for localities. As a reform imposed on local jurisdictions by state elites, local implementation dramatically increased the scale of the effort, bringing new, often uninformed, suspicious, or hostile people into the process. As we have seen, this change of scale brought the typical problems associated with what Pressman and Wildavsky have called the "complexity of joint action": delays, multiple veto points, and responses in defense of current practices.[62] Indeed, Department of Employee Relations staff gave humorous, illustrated speeches across the country about the excuses used to delay or avoid implementation, ranging from the "ostrich" (if we don't do anything it will go away) to "Chicken Little" (implement pay equity and the sky will fall).[63]

The state law was proposed, passed, and implemented by a relatively small, tightly-knit group of people including women in key positions within the political structure supported by politically powerful women's advocates and AFSCME lobbyists. In contrast with the state experience, the local law has been implemented by a large and diverse group of managers and elected officials who had little or nothing to do with its initial passage. To the degree that the political leadership patterns associated with different types and sizes of jurisdictions could replicate the patterns that operated at the state level, implementation reflected the concerns of the law's sponsors. Specifically, the pattern of leadership in which significant numbers of women occupied decision-making positions within local power structures greatly enhanced the propensity to comply, the speed of compliance, and the likelihood that the analysis underlying pay equity policy would be accepted. But the process remained, for structural reasons, essentially different for local jurisdictions. Not only did the state have a job evaluation system in place at the outset, but also key political leaders were in a position to insist on a strategy of using that preexisting system rather than initiating an administrative overhaul.

Those who wrote the local law believed that the state's relatively smooth process could be replicated at the local level at a minimal cost of both money and effort. Their expectations were partially met, as nearly half the state's jurisdictions used the state job match with apparent ease.[64] This represents an important finding, a model for state-level technical assistance to small jurisdictions that would otherwise find comparable worth to be unduly technical and financially burdensome. What drafters of the legislation never imagined, however, were the dramatic changes it would precipitate in managerial practices and collective bargaining within moderate and larger-sized jurisdictions and the highly participatory process which many jurisdictions chose to use.[65] The result has been a series of paradoxical intended and unintended consequences. A policy intended to redress discriminatory wages ironically precipitated the use of technology that significantly increased managerial control in many areas. The participatory processes that were initiated in most medium to large jurisdictions also created a broad range of "stakeholders" who demanded a standard of fairness that amounted to pay for points rather than a remedy for discrimination. As a consequence, women in the lowest-paid categories *have* made significant gains in most jurisdictions, but so have a number of traditionally male-dominated job categories. And where the rising costs of such a distributive outcome have been burdensome, a variety of cost-containing mechanisms has served to restrain their impact, sometimes at the expense of those for whom such an outcome was originally intended.[66]

A local-level managerial revolution was perhaps the most startling unanticipated consequence. Most local jurisdictions had no job evaluation system in place; many did not even have job classification. Managers frequently had no accurate notion about what employees actually did on their jobs, and wage-setting followed historic patterns that tended to be informal and quite irrational. Where police and firefighters, for example, were the strongest, or the only, organized group, they would settle first and everyone else would get what was left.

During efforts on the local legislation, management and unions were fairly evenly matched in power, but during implementation local managers have often been more powerful than local unions, and the unionized labor force, where it has existed, has been far more fragmented. The local law clearly designated the choice of job evaluation system as a management prerogative subject only to a "meet and confer" obligation to employee representatives. In most cases this meant simply an informational meeting held after the decision had been made. In addition, subsequent pay policy decisions regarding the definition of job classes and job hierarchies, the appropriate pay line, the use of a corridor, and the timetable for implementation have also rested primarily with management.

Not only did a number of jurisdictions hire personnel specialists for the first time in order to implement pay equity, but also the resulting studies provided the necessary information for a new kind of management. Clear job descriptions and analyses of time spent on specific tasks permit a more rational and efficient allocation of labor resources as well as a more rational pay policy.* Furthermore, as in San Jose and Washington State, managers have also found that job evaluation studies and accompanying market surveys can be used to justify substantial increases in their own pay, in the name of comparable worth.[67]

The existence of this new body of information, defined primarily by managerial priorities, provides a new setting for collective bargaining. Unions supporting comparable worth understand the essential nature of this information because it documents precisely the inequity they wish to bargain to rectify. Managers, however, also see it as giving them a stronger hand in resisting the pressures of particularly powerful (and often male-dominated) unions. Unions have a decreased ability to exploit the irrationalities in the old system by shifting negotiation to a more political and less information-based terrain. A suburban city manager pointed out, for example, that police cannot claim "delivering babies" as a task they may regularly be called upon to perform once it is known that such occurrences have been quite rare in the metropolitan area in the last decade.[68]

Even in the highly politicized city of St. Paul, for example, while police obtained substantial raises on the grounds of comparable worth, firefighters cannot force the city to return their pay to parity with the police because the city's counsel maintains that to do so would force another round of raises for groups rated similarly to firefighters.[69] Pay equity also

---

*It should be noted, however, that these new possibilities were not universally welcomed. Some managers found themselves drowning in more information than they ever wanted to know, worsened perhaps by their own inattentiveness during the information-gathering sequences of the job evaluation process. In such cases it may well be that management and collective bargaining practices will quickly drift back to their prior patterns unless there are organized groups of female employees who insist on continued attention to pay equity and compliance with the state law. Interview with Bill Joynes, Golden Valley, Minn.

undermined the tradition of joint bargaining with clerical workers between the city of St. Paul and the St. Paul School District. To comply with the law, each jurisdiction had to conduct an *internal* comparison of wage rates, in addition to which city leaders were politically committed to pay equity while school board members were more concerned with cost. As a result, for the first time civil service workers with the same job title received different rates of pay from the city and the school district.[70]

Pay equity itself will remain a central issue in collective bargaining given the tendency of most jurisdictions to implement in two to four years. In addition, unions will continue to press for changes in pay policies such as the choice of pay line, the width of the corridor, and the meaning of "reasonable restraints" on wages that remain above the chosen line or corridor. Some of these issues will no doubt be tested in the courts, though the spate of suits expected after August 1, 1987, did not occur.* Only the city of Minneapolis has made these basic policies themselves the subject of collective bargaining.[71] If jurisdictions successfully implement a wage scale compressed around a single line, other predictions may also come true. Personnel Director Bob Ostlund of the Chaska School District, for example, anticipates that comparable worth may lead to coordinated bargaining, since the first group to settle will set the pattern for the rest, if reasonable relationships are to be maintained.[72] Both AFSCME and the Minnesota School Employees Association (SEIU), on the other hand, see comparable worth as something they will be bargaining over for the foreseeable future. They recognize the possibility that comparable worth could be a one-time fix that is subsequently undone in the future unless it is carefully monitored.[73]

The widespread and increasingly formal use of market surveys is also likely to have a continuing impact on wage-setting and collective bargaining. Such surveys had been common among larger jurisdictions but they received an additional boost from the wording of the local law, which designated comparable worth as "*a* primary" rather than "*the* primary" consideration in wage-setting. The Department of Employee Relations maintains that the law's requirement that local-jurisdiction wage rates bear a "reasonable relationship to similar positions outside of that particular political subdivision's employment" simply allows a jurisdiction to pay

*The expectation of successful litigation has been shaped in part by the changed legal climate since the Washington State case was reversed by the Ninth Circuit Court of Appeals. In addition, the quixotic suit by the Minnesota School Employees Association (SEIU), which resulted in very high legal costs to the union, and a series of decertification elections has made others more cautious. Interviews with Catherine Olson, Coon Rapids, Minn., 13 April 1987; James Fox, Minneapolis, Minn., 26 March 1987; and Nancy Crippin, St. Paul, Minn., 16 and 28 April 1987.

unusually high wages when market requirements make it difficult to hire a qualified person within the range established by an equitable pay plan. Legal advisors and labor relations consultants for the larger jurisdictions, however, have consistently interpreted the law as requiring a market study to be used alongside job evaluation in setting equitable pay rates.[74] Jurisdictions that have followed the pattern set by Hennepin County of using the market as a restraint on wage relationships established by job evaluation have been criticized by advocates of comparable worth. In essence, such policies reintroduce the historic discrimination embedded in the market into a plan designed initially to eliminate that discrimination.[75] The tensions between systematic job evaluation information and systematic market wage data remain an overt part of labor relations and labor practices.

Despite the strengthened hand of management occasioned by reclassification, job analysis, and market surveys, the involvement of thousands of local employees on evaluation committees presents a contrasting outcome, a large-scale experiment in employee participation. Levels of participation ranged from none, as in Hennepin County where the consultant was asked to do everything, to management only, as in the Rochester School District, to substantial employee involvement through evaluation committees trained by a consultant, and labor-management teams in which employee representatives sometimes included union staff.

At stake in these various arrangements was the credibility of the process and its outcome. A few managers believed only outside expertise could confer credibility.[76] Most felt that employee participation was the key and chose their consultants in part on that basis. Certainly employees who served on evaluation committees experienced the process of "buying-in" as they moved toward consensus on the relative value of different jobs.[77] But their role did not prevent, as many managers had hoped, a general outcry when the hierarchy of job values was published. In consequence, pay equity "took the blame" for the confusion and displacement known to accompany the implementation of new managerial systems and technologies.

Employee perceptions regarding the fairness or unfairness of the process derived from several key factors. Perhaps most important, they rested on a history of labor relations that was different in each jurisdiction. Outside consultants who functioned with clarity and competence also enhanced perceptions of fairness. Employee participation enhanced credibility, however, only when managers and consultants created a process within which their participation could be understood and where one group of employees could not be perceived as taking advantage of others. In several cases of very active employee and union involvement the resulting studies were unacceptable because the process as a whole became suspect. When consultants and managers did not set clear enough boundaries on the process or monitor it carefully, employee groups began to treat it as an extension of negotiation.[78] Where such a system worked as intended, however, administrators had the great advantage of shared responsibility and "blame" for the final results.[79]

When employees accepted the outcomes, however, they usually did so on the assumption that those above the line would not suffer pay cuts or freezes and that *all* jobs below the line (whether an all-jobs or a male-jobs line) would receive appropriate increases. The result has been a political situation in which most jurisdictions found it necessary to adjust the wages of male-dominated and balanced classes as well as female-dominated classes. The most spectacular example of these expectations occurred in St. Paul, where police marched on city hall to demand their "comparable worth."[80]

In the final analysis, however, there has been a significant shift in the allocation of wages to male and female public employees in Minnesota local governments. The jurisdictions that reported no inequities tended to be either very small—having only one or two employees, if any—or special jurisdictions (e.g., hospitals, nursing homes, and libraries), whose labor forces were either predominantly female or predominantly male, leaving little room for comparison. Strong majorities of school districts and counties as well as most larger cities did, however, report inequities along with plans to rectify them.* The following thirteen occupations represent 90% of employees eligible for pay equity increases according to reports to the Department of Employee Relations in early 1986: secretaries, other clerical employees, teacher aides, other school aides, cooks, other food service employees, non-nursing medical employees, nurses (RN, LPN), social services employees, library employees, city clerks and clerk-treasurers, and liquor store employees.[81] This list is fairly typical of the lowest-paid female employees in public employment, and indicates that the comparable worth policy would affect the groups that proponents had anticipated.

---

*In the reports received by DOER as of January 15, 1986, all counties and 86% of school boards indicated that they had found inequities. Larger cities remained unreported at that time, but the patterns in the metropolitan area and in the MAMA study indicate that inequities affecting female-dominated classes were routinely discovered there as well. See DOER, "Pay Equity in Minnesota Local Governments," St. Paul, Minn., 30 January, 1986.

A more specific example illustrates the very real impact which comparable worth policies can have. Preliminary figures from a suburban school district indicate that a health associate, in 1985–86, earned an entering salary of $6.21 per hour. If the associate worked full-time (40 hours per week for 39 weeks), which many did not, the salary would be $9,687.60 for the year or 86% of the poverty line for a family of four. Following the guidelines of its job evaluation and reclassification study, the district proposed that the minimum salary for health associates in 1986–87 be $7.75 per hour.[82] That would raise a full-time associate's yearly salary to $12,090 or 108% of the poverty line.

Because many jurisdictions found it politically and legally necessary to provide pay equity increases to male and balanced classes as well, the costs as reported to the Department of Employee Relations may not reflect the actual expense to local governments. Nevertheless, the Department reports indicate costs within the predicted range of 2–4% of payroll. The average cost, for jurisdictions reporting by January 1986, was 2.6% of payroll. Smaller cities bore proportionately higher costs because of their low salary base, while school districts provided the most consistently low costs (73% were under 2% of payroll). Counties and other larger jurisdictions, however, appear to have significant variation, depending both on their own previous pay practices and on a series of policy decisions regarding the choice of pay line and whether or not to use a corridor. For the Minneapolis School District, for example, the difference between the chosen course of an all-jobs line with a 7.5% corridor on either side and the male-jobs line without a corridor was tenfold. The former is expected to cost $900,000; the latter would have cost $9 million.[83]

In general, however, forecasts of financial doom have not been borne out in Minnesota. Between theory and practice there is agreement that wages for clerical workers and many health-care workers employed by local governments in Minnesota will certainly rise, despite ongoing struggles over how much. Wages of the highest-paid male workers may also decelerate, but against great pressure for their continued rise. Most of our informants agree that even the discussions of contracting out were already in the air before the issue of comparable worth appeared, and so far there do not appear to be significant disemployment consequences following implementation. Disemployment is most likely, however, in those areas where budgetary flexibility is lacking, such as school food services and some federally funded social services. Thus the most concrete goal of pay equity proponents, to put more dollars in the hands of the poorest-paid women, appears to be on the way to realization. According to one personnel director, the entire process has brought about a new awareness, an "acknowledgement of inequity even though grudging."[84]

A concern remains about the long-term enforcement and monitoring of a policy that has few if any penalties for noncompliance. This is particularly so in view of the higher level of conflict engendered by the implementation of pay equity at the local level in contrast to the state level. The courts may provide clarity, but while unions use the possibility of legal action for leverage in bargaining, few suits have been filed.[85] In 1987 the legislature imposed a financial penalty on school districts which failed to report a pay equity plan by October 1, 1987. It also required that plans "provide for complete implementation not later than December 31, 1991" and specified that "the plan does not have to contain a market study."[86] A similar law, applying to cities and counties, passed in the 1988 legislative session; it required reports by October 1, 1988, implementation by the end of 1991, and provided a penalty of 5% reduction in local government aid for failure to implement.[87] Many expect additional legislation in the future in the ongoing struggle for clarity about the practical meanings of pay equity for Minnesota jurisdictions.

# 7　Conclusion

With continued cooperative efforts on
the part of all those concerned, pay
equity will soon be a reality for public
sector employers in Minnesota.
*Commission on the Economic Status
of Women, 1988*[1]

The stories of intense conflict that pepper accounts of local leaders and employees as they reflect on the process of implementing
pay equity can be misleading. Those in the middle of the process, struggling with competing interests and having difficulty comprehending the
technology of job evaluation, used apocalyptic language: "agony and
pain," "the biggest upheaval any employer will see."[2] That specific kinds
of conflict accompany reclassification, job evaluation, and changes in pay
practices is unquestionable. Yet when public officials and managers were
specifically asked about how this conflict compared with other conflicts,
most agreed that implementing comparable worth was not unusually conflictual. The annual reports of jurisdictional associations also show that
comparable worth was just one of many issues on each government's
agenda. For example, the League of Minnesota Cities' report on legislative activity affecting its constituents averages about twelve pages each
year. Topics include courts, elections, environment, finance and revenue,
gambling, liquor and beer laws, pensions, personnel, planning and developing, public safety, transportation, and utilities. Under the heading of
"personnel" pay equity never consumed more than a few lines.[3]

The contrasting experience of local and state governments indicates further that implementation conflicts can be either exacerbated or minimized

by a series of policy decisions, but that conflict itself is part and parcel of public life. While local governments experienced more conflict than did the state, their struggles were primarily *internal,* did not spill over into the political arena, and were concentrated in a relatively brief period of time. By contrast, equity policies in other areas, such as busing, have remained highly politicized sources of conflict for decades. In the broader sweep of American history, the initial passage and implementation of comparable worth in public employment has been breathtakingly swift. It took sixty years of unceasing effort, for example, to end child labor.

The results of pay equity implementation in Minnesota are uneven and complicated. Employees, mostly women at the lowest ranks, received more money; managers in most cases emerged with more power. The implementation pattern of comparable worth both confirms and questions the research on equity policy that shows that committed elites create better equity policies, policies that are less open to sabotage during implementation, than do slow, participatory decision and implementation processes.[4] A recent review of successful busing programs shows, paradoxically, that fast-moving elites designed more durable systems than emerged from slower, more participatory debates.[5] The success of these elites may have rested not only on their speed and control but also on the hitherto unrecognized fact that they were not closely tied to technical analyses.

In terms of comparable worth, the political skills of an elite group of women at the state level, with allies in the union movement and the legislature, were highly effective in the passage of both pay equity laws. But the subsequent experience with implementation was dependent on specific configurations of political and managerial power, to the exclusion of most citizen groups. Managerial elites effectively changed the agenda away from wage justice and toward technocratic concerns. Once they had done so, even highly participatory processes yielded little genuine power for female employees (or males for that matter). Thus one must examine separately the gendered politics of political officials and of bureaucratic enforcers.

In this final chapter we analyze comparable worth as one of the legacies of two decades of struggle for women's rights that set the stage for new policy initiatives, trained leaders, and established limitations as well as possibilities for wage justice. The passage of Minnesota's two pay equity laws illustrates the increased power of women within political elites in the 1980s. The limitations of comparable worth, however, suggest the deeper democratic impulses within feminism and related social movements, and point to the inability of individualistic liberalism to fully recognize issues of participation, citizenship, community, and contribution to the public good. Against this backdrop, the practical realities of implementation expose the paradoxes of technocratic reform. In practice, comparable worth problematizes gendered work identities in a changing economy. What is the meaning and value of work and in particular of the service sector in an information economy? The simultaneous necessity and difficulty of using technocratic means to achieve a just and democratic social transformation remains a paradox at the heart of the issue of comparable worth. We conclude with an assessment of the broader reform context and a prognosis for the diffusion of comparable worth policies.

### The Vision of Comparable Worth

The political issue of comparable worth grew from the struggles of working women in the post–World War II era and it bridges the historic poles of feminist ideas in several ways. On the one hand it is a demand for equal treatment, a kind of economic ERA. It relies heavily on the bureaucratic state and on technocratic modes of implementation. On the other hand it suggests a connection between the devaluation of women's historic responsibilities within the family, the sex segregation of the labor force, and the low pay women receive. The premise is not, as in the case of protective legislation, that women *are* different but rather that they have been *treated* differently and that the cultural devaluation of women is itself imbedded in the structure of the labor market. It also proposes a solution that places direct economic resources into the hands of individual women.

As a legislative strategy, however, comparable worth has marked similarities with other reforms such as protective legislation. Essentially, it is a reform to be won through the efforts of a relatively small group of women most of whom will likely be middle-class. In Minnesota this included key leaders in the legislature, political appointees, and governmental insiders; women in unions; and leaders of a variety of women's organizations from the clerical workers in 9 to 5 to feminists in the National Organization for Women and mainstream activists in the League of Women Voters. These intersecting networks of female leaders assumed new and powerful roles within public life and politics.[6] Yet the importance of elite networks of political women in Minnesota as in other states highlights both the technocratic nature of comparable worth and its potential isolation from interested constituencies such as employees, unions, and the broader feminist movement as well as the general public. Indeed, large-scale public discussion can be harmful to the effort as it arouses right-wing ideologues who come flying to the defense of the "free market" and women's "natural" roles while using the technicalities of comparable worth to create a cloud of obfuscation. Political analysts Joyce Gelb and Marion Palley make a similar point when they argue that "it is sometimes possible to achieve significant change in the guise of incrementalism if the importance of a seemingly narrow issue is not recognized by key political actors."[7] At the same time, unless key figures in the implementation process (including the reform's intended beneficiaries) both understand and support the underlying goals, those broader possibilities may be subverted anyway.

Comparable worth in many ways raises fundamental ideological issues, which accounts in part for the vehemence of the opposition to it, once aroused. At a basic level comparable worth proposes a reordering of the ways women and minorities and the work associated with them have been valued by society. It challenges both a purely market-based definition of value (i.e. the value of a good or service is whatever the market will pay for it) and deeply rooted cultural presumptions about the value of women's labor within and outside the home.[8]

Comparable worth also promises a potentially fundamental transformation of women's lives by enhancing women's capacity to support themselves and their dependents in a time of deepening female (especially minority female) poverty. Most advocates focus on the importance of women's economic autonomy not only because of the threat of poverty but also because it would allow women to make life choices (e.g., education, work, marriage) more freely. Implicit in such an argument is the recognition that independent support is the foundation for full citizenship and participation in the broader community. In other words, political rights have little meaning unless women and minorities have the resources to act independently and to shoulder their share of communal responsibility. The liberal language of individual "rights," however, fails to capture this dimension.[9]

### Practical Realities of Comparable Worth

The vision of comparable worth emphasizes individual autonomy and wage justice, but the fact that comparable worth has been imposed in most instances as a top-down reform inhibits the dissemination of this vision even as it strengthens the possibilities of passage and complete implementation. The technocratic nature of its implementation in Minnesota and other states reshapes the original goals, adding new ones, and exposing underlying issues that the theoretical discussion of its possibilities may miss. These paradoxical outcomes include the addition of bureaucratic agendas and imperatives unrelated to the problem of discrimination, the divisive complexities of gender and race as they intersect with class hierarchies, and the technocratic limits on social transformation and social movement organization. We discuss each of these in turn.

*Bureaucratic Agendas*

The historical roots of comparable worth lie not only in the traditions of campaigning in behalf of female and minority workers but also in attempts by managers to rationalize wage-setting and labor allocation in large bureaucracies. This latter history brings to the issue a set of techniques and values that may conflict with those of comparable worth advocates.

For example, while the values of rationality and technical excellence certainly enhance the credibility of comparable worth, especially in the early stages, they shift the focus decidedly away from the problem of economically disadvantaged women and minorities. Proponents of rationalized wage-setting often raise the total bill for comparable worth by moving toward pay-for-points rather than increments primarily for job classes dominated by women and minorities. An appeal to such arguments achieved, in St. Paul for example, "comparable worth raises" for police, certainly not a traditionally underpaid female job. At the same time, Hennepin County demonstrated how to use technical expertise to reduce costs by moving away from the male pay line as a standard and by introducing concepts such as the "equity corridor" ranging from 5% to 15% above and below the designated line. Equity corridors certainly appear to formalize a new, but still lower wage scale for female-dominated jobs in public employment.

The need for both technical and political credibility frequently led jurisdictions to initiate large, costly, and thorough job evaluation and reclassification studies. Even before the issue of comparable worth arose, it was common wisdom among managers that any completely new job study, whether reclassification or job evaluation or some combination, was likely to be deeply unsettling to workers. Comparable worth, by making comparisons explicit and public and by changing job titles, job definitions, and job hierarchies, only intensified the tendency of such studies to arouse status concerns that would otherwise lie dormant. Furthermore, the democratic impulse behind comparable worth ironically finds its practical meaning in a system designed to enhance managerial control. Thus the impulse to "do it right" can result in a changed definition of "it", from comparable worth to something else altogether.

## Gender and Race v. Class

In theory comparable worth is not about class relations but about internal, horizontal equity between jobs of equal value. The technology used to illustrate gender- and race-based wage disparities, such as the ever present scattergrams, exposes the fact that gender and race hierarchies multiply class differences because they widen the gap between least- and most-paid. When gender- and race-based wages are raised to something approximating the white male norm, they intersect with traditional class relations as they have evolved among white males, disrupting some historic parity relations (e.g. between police and fire personnel) and revealing the gendered nature of job status. The latter has at least two dimensions of interest here: the status of blue-collar, male-dominated jobs and the status concerns of professionals, many of whom are women.

Many blue-collar, male-dominated jobs achieve status in part by their very definition as "manly work." Comparable worth in these cases appears threatening not simply because it may be achieved at some economic cost to similarly rated male-dominated jobs, but also (and perhaps crucially) because it disrupts a culturally prescribed gender hierarchy. Thus the anger of snowplow drivers, street maintenance workers, and firefighters clarified the degree to which their manliness was at stake in a scheme that threatened to equate them with female workers they thought of as subordinate. Indeed, in many cases the female-dominated jobs to which theirs were compared were precisely the kinds of work that their wives, daughters, and other female kin would do. The link between work hierarchies and familial patriarchy remained an implicit but ever-present subtext to many local debates just as it has in national, more theoretical discussions as well. Officials in one jurisdiction openly worried about whether they should pay a woman clerical worker more than her husband, who also worked for the city. In another case, Little Falls School District Personnel Manager James O'Toole negotiated raises for custodians, undermining the goals prescribed by their comparable worth study because in his view custodians, presumed to be heads of families, had a greater "need."[10]

The persistence of such attitudes, in the face of significant discrepancies between male and female wages, in turn, can precipitate considerable anger on the part of women towards male employees. A union activist in Contra Costa County, California, was shocked when she joined her union negotiating team and discovered what many men earned. "Window washers for the county make more than I do! A second-line supervisor of men makes $600 a month more than I do! There's no excuse that a janitor makes more than an eligibility worker! . . . They've been fed from *my* trough, mine and every other female-dominated job."[11] In Minnesota, such angry voices have remained relatively muted in deference to class solidarity and the crucial coalition built through AFSCME's dominance at the state level. At the local level, fragmented unions, little female organization, and the fact that comparable worth was imposed, not fought for, meant that most of the anger which received public expression was either male or managerial. The exceptions to this were the large jurisdictions where women had begun to fight for comparable worth before passage of the local law, most notably Hennepin County and Anoka-Hennepin School District. Even there, however, leaders were careful not to focus their grievances on their fellow workers.

The status of some professionals presents a more complex intersection of gender and status concerns. Professionals working in governmental bureaucracies find their concerns for independence and autonomy in constant tension with organizational necessity. They are a difficult constituency for unions, reluctant to be associated with nonprofessionals and with a conflict model of wage negotiation. In Minnesota, as in many other states, state-employed professionals withdrew from AFSCME to form an independent union, the Minnesota Association of Professional Employees (MAPE). Such professionals, *many* of them female, fear that comparable worth will diminish the distance (measured in salary and job points) between themselves and those just below them. Thus employee associations such as MAPE in Minnesota or the Public Employee Federation in New York tend to be opposed to or at least highly ambivalent about comparable worth.

On the other hand, female-dominated professions like nursing, librarianship, and dietetics have provided leadership in the struggle for comparable worth because in their experience gender is so explicitly a reason for their difficulty in obtaining the status, respect, and remuneration they believe they deserve. Their leadership rests further on the fact that their professions have increasingly become subordinated within large bureaucracies, resulting in restrictions on their independent judgment and authority. The most telling example, perhaps, is nursing, which since the

Second World War has moved decisively from the more independent (if poorly paid) work of the practical nurse in homes to the increasingly corporate hierarchy of massive hospitals.[12] Such a setting both reinforced the gendered subordination of nurses to doctors and administrators and provided the opportunity for collective action by nurses themselves.

## Impact on Collective Bargaining

The complexities of gender, race, and class status also make comparable worth a potentially divisive issue within and among traditional unions. Because the implementation of comparable worth has the effect of compressing wages, reducing the spread and possibly flattening the slope of the wage line, unions find themselves at odds, with different and competing definitions of their interests. Indeed, some male-dominated unions fear that comparable worth threatens gains won through bargaining in recent decades.

When comparable worth efforts become driven primarily by technocratic concerns they can change collective bargaining practices dramatically by reducing the scope of what can be bargained. Many managers in Minnesota clearly hoped that this would be the case, though strong unions and historic practices muted their efforts. In Oregon union concern about interference with collective bargaining derailed more than a year of work by the Task Force in State Compensation and Classification Equity even though the largest union was a strong supporter of comparable worth. The problem, as they saw it, was the identification of comparable worth with a massive reclassification of the state's labor force.[13]

The state of Minnesota, however, offers an alternative that successfully combines comparable worth and collective bargaining. Several factors made this possible. In the first place the process of job classification and evaluation and the pay equity law were not connected. With the former already in place, the latter simply required a reanalysis of existing information. Furthermore, the Minnesota State Employees Pay Equity Act had been carefully crafted to conform with existing bargaining practices, and it required a separate pay equity appropriation. Thus the policy appeared to provide an additional distribution of income rather than a *re*distribution of the wage bill from higher-paid (male) workers to lower-paid (female) workers. While the Department of Employee Relations was responsible for identifying job classes that should receive pay equity raises, the timing and rate of those increments remained in the province of collective bargaining. Even so, union leaders and pay equity supporters like AFSCME's chief negotiator Pete Benner recognize that comparable worth complicates their duty to represent fairly *all* of their members. With AFSCME's help, Minnesota managed to make that possible and it offers one of the most strikingly successful models available for other jurisdictions.

A different example comes from the city of San Francisco where comparable worth has been the subject of a political struggle between major unions and the Board of Supervisors on the one hand and the mayor on the other. At issue was the problem of cost.[14] In terms of method, however, San Francisco avoided many of the problems described above by using a "merged data approach," matching benchmark city jobs with job evaluation systems from four other jurisdictions (three California cities and the state of Washington, all of which had implemented comparable worth). This system, like the state job match used by many smaller jurisdictions in Minnesota, provided a quick route to the initial identification of underpaid job classes, after which the speed and timing of increments could be subject to collective bargaining.[15]

### The Transformative Possibilities of Comparable Worth

When measured against the egalitarian vision of economic justice for women and minorities that underlies the passion of most advocates, the concrete achievements of comparable worth in practice often fall short. Yet this may be an improper measure, fated to label any nonutopian outcome as a failure. For example, advocates like Alice Kessler-Harris argue that comparable worth offers a fundamental revaluing of women and their work.[16] Yet the use of preexisting methods of job evaluation by most jurisdictions implementing a comparable worth policy fails to meet this standard. Rather, it simply applies to women's jobs the *same* values and criteria that have been devised to rate traditionally male jobs.[17] In addition, the potential for changed consciousness and cultural values is muted when unions and managers believe that the success of the policy requires a low-key approach in order not to arouse division and hostility. In Minnesota this meant that 45% of employees who actually received comparable worth raises were unaware of that fact!

Similarly, the materially transformative possibility of comparable worth lies in its redistributive nature, its capacity to rearrange the wage bill, giving women and minorities a greater share. Yet the forces arrayed against any wholly or partially redistributive policy are great. Because redistributive policies *transfer* valued resources, establishing what are often viewed by participants as real long-term winners and losers, politicians are pressured to reconfigure policies in a more distributive manner, where a greater number of people benefit, but often without targeting those most in need. If *additional* monies can be made available, as appeared to be the case at the state level in Minnesota, then even a distributive policy can result in substantial gains for targeted classes. But in other cases a combination of pay-for-points and a series of cost-containment measures have clearly reduced the impact of comparable worth on the incomes of women and minorities.

Nevertheless, in Minnesota comparable worth has provided resources that significantly increase the capacity for autonomy and independence of women and minorities at the lowest end of the pay scale. As we have shown, the additional income generated by pay equity increments in Minnesota state and local jurisdictions substantially increased the incomes of clerical and health care workers whose earnings had been close to the poverty line wage.

As a reform rooted in union, civil rights, and feminist activism, comparable worth might also be seen as an important source of strength for social movements for economic justice. Some unions have found the *demand* for comparable worth to be a highly effective organizing tool. As numerous strikes and grass-roots efforts demonstrate, mobilization around this issue can be a democratic and empowering experience for women and minorities who rethink the value of their own work and challenge the hierarchy of values enshrined in the wage scale. Yet effective political advocacy has tended to remain in the hands of a relatively small political elite, and implementation appears highly subject to technocratic control. If in the most successful examples women are likely to receive increased wages with little knowledge about where they came from or why, their economic independence may be enhanced but their sense of group solidarity will not.

### Alternatives: Comparable Worth in Context

When measured against the predictions of opponents, comparable worth in Minnesota and elsewhere has not led to economic dislocations in the form either of significant disemployment effects or of exorbitant and inflationary growth in the total wage bill. In addition, as the state of Minnesota illustrates, comparable worth can be instituted with minimal disruption in large government (or corporate) bureaucracies which have professionalized their personnel functions and pay practices. Wherever there is a job evaluation system in place, the techniques for estimating inequities between male-, female-, and minority-dominated job classes are well established and simple. A second method that also serves to shift wages quickly and simply toward the lowest-paid women and minorities (but is closer to a solidarity wage than to comparable worth) is exemplified by the decisions of New Mexico and New Jersey to raise the wages of their lowest-paid workers *prior* to a comparable worth study. In either case there are clear advantages to separating comparable worth from the processes of reclassification and job evaluation, even though the results will remain problematic for proponents concerned about biases within job evaluation systems. Indeed, such a separation appears to be the only way to maintain a clear focus on remedying the historically low wages of women and minorities and to avoid giving primacy to technocratic concerns.

At the same time, comparable worth cannot bear the full weight of proponents' hopes for democratic change and wage justice. Clarity about what comparable worth as a technocratic reform can and does achieve can place it in its proper context as part of a broader strategy. What appear to be weaknesses, when measured against proponents' values, obtain only when comparable worth is discussed in isolation, as a single issue. Instead, comparable worth must be seen as a long-term strategy linked to a variety of other concerns. Comparable worth is a *procedural* reform—not the same as creating new individual rights and leaving individuals to enforce them in the courts. Like environmental protection, where one can never stop testing air quality regardless of specific victories, comparable worth will require constant vigilance.* If it reinforces hierarchy, activists must consider other, simultaneous ways to press for participation and power. If it is subject to other agendas, proponents must understand the implications of those agendas and oppose or ally with them consciously. If comparable worth legislation strengthens the hands of public managers, then organizing strategies that win comparable worth settlements directly through collective bargaining may offer a different set of possibilities. And all of these efforts will be enhanced if technical reforms can be described

---

* In Minnesota, the attempts to do this have taken two forms. One is additional legislation which provided penalties for local-jurisdiction noncompliance and identified more specifically the terms of compliance (i.e., market surveys were not required). Quantitative research now under way may clarify the degree to which local jurisdictions have in fact fulfilled the original legislative intent and provide the necessary evidence for further legislative initiatives. The second form of vigilance has been exercised through collective bargaining and the filing of a small number of court actions by unions, primarily AFSCME.

with a vocabulary that makes explicit the implicit claims to full citizenship and community participation.

Comparable worth may never provide the same satisfaction of broad mobilization that other issues, such as the ERA, do. The tendency towards elite domination (indeed the necessity for that once an initial legislative or collective bargaining victory has been won) and the complexities of implementation make that difficult. Key leaders and spokespeople frequently are union men (lawyers like Winn Newman, for example, and in Minnesota leaders of AFSCME: Pete Benner, Rick Scott, Roger Siegal), who must also maintain credibility with their male constituents. This advantages comparable worth as a coalition-building vehicle but removes it from the intense sociability of female-dominated and -defined social movements. The need for vigilance beyond initial victories, however, further clarifies the importance of linking comparable worth to a broad agenda for democracy and for wage justice.

Comparable worth policies will remain on the political agenda for the foreseeable future. A process has been set in motion in many public jurisdictions as well as private corporations (though the latter are unlikely to admit to it), and that process will continue to bear fruit. By August 1987 20 states and 166 localities (outside of Minnesota) had implemented comparable worth and 26 additional states were in the earlier stages of action.[18] Successful implementation in many locations, including Minnesota, provides models and spurs to further actions. And organizations of working women, including some of the fastest-growing unions (AFSCME and SEIU) as well as professional associations of nurses and librarians, will keep up a lively grass-roots pressure. Subsequent reform agendas will probably incorporate the broader understanding of wage discrimination introduced by comparable worth. And in a world in which women and men share productive work in the labor force in increasingly similar numbers, the pressure for wage justice will not abate.

# APPENDIX A

## Comparable Worth Interviews and Presentations

Aho, Kay, and Dwain Boelter, Personnel Decisions, Inc. Personal interview with Sara Evans. Minneapolis, Minn. 31 March 1987.

Anderson, Mary, Mayor of Golden Valley. Personal interview with Sara Evans. Golden Valley, Minn. 13 April 1987.

Andrew, Mark, Hennepin County Commissioner. Personal interview with Sara Evans. Minneapolis, Minn. 4 August 1986.

Baxter, Elaine, Representative, Iowa Legislature. Presentation at "New Directions in Comparable Worth" Conference, Minneapolis, Minn. 18 October 1985.

Benner, Peter, Executive Director, AFSCME Council 6. Personal interviews with Barbara Nelson. St. Paul, Minn. 4 June 1987 and 24 July 1987.

Berglin, Linda, Minnesota State Senator. Personal interview with Sara Evans and Barbara Nelson. St. Paul, Minn. 3 February 1987.

Bible, Dennis, Minneapolis Labor Relations. Telephone interview with Sara Evans, 28 July 1987.

Bocwinski, Robert, City Manager, Columbia Heights, and Linda Magee, Assistant City Manager, Columbia Heights. Personal interview with Sara Evans. Columbia Heights, Minn. 13 April 1987.

Boelter, Dwain. See Aho, Kay.

Boland, Lynn, Association of Minnesota Counties (AMC). Personal interview with Sara Evans. St. Paul, Minn. 8 May 1985.

Bowles, Sally, Personnel Director, Eden Praire (Minnesota) School District. Telephone Interview with Sara Evans. 29 April 1987.

Bravo, Ellen, Milwaukee Working Women/9 to 5. Personal interview with Barbara Nelson. Minneapolis, Minn. 20 February 1987.

Brennan, E. James, President, Brennan, Thomsen Associates, Inc. Presentation to Corporate Symposium on Pay Equity. New York, N.Y. 24 March 1987.

Briske, Linda, AFSCME, Washington County. Telephone interview with Sara Evans. 7 April 1987. And Byers, Phyllis, Negotiator, St. Paul Schools. Personal interviews with Sara Evans. St. Paul, Minn. 2 April 1987.

Byers, Phyllis, Negotiator, St. Paul Schools. Personal interview with Sara Evans. 7 April 1987. And Byers, Phyllis, Negotiator, Phillip Penn, Assistant Director of Personnel, and James Sargent, Director of Personnel, St. Paul School District. Personal interview with Sara Evans, St. Paul, Minn. 12 May 1987.

Ciccarelli, Reneta. See Hayes, Mary.

Crippin, Nancy, Executive Director, Minnesota School Employees Association. Personal interviews with Sara Evans. St. Paul, Minn. 16 April 1987 and 28 April 1987.

Dieter, Claudia, Compensation Analyst, Minnesota Department of Employee Relations. Telephone interviews with Barbara Nelson and Nancy Johnson, 15 July 1988 and 20 July 1988.

Erikson, Linda, Librarian. Hennepin County. Personal interview with Sara Evans. Minneapolis, Minn. 28 July 1986.

Farmer, Judy, Minneapolis School Board Member. Personal interview with Sara Evans. Minneapolis, Minn. 28 July 1986.

Fox, Jim, Arthur Young and Company. Personal interview with Sara Evans. Minneapolis, Minn. 26 March 1987.

Gregory, Bob, Australia National University and Central Bank of Australia. Personal interview with Barbara Nelson. Minneapolis, Minn. 11 May 1984.

Griffin, David, City Director of Personnel and Operations, Olmsted County, Minn. Telephone interview with Sara Evans. 13 March 1987.

Griffin, Gloria, Minnesota Women's Consortium. Personal interview with Barbara Nelson. St. Paul, Minn. 26 September 1986.

Grune, Joy Anne, National Committee on Pay Equity. Presentation at Meetings of the American Political Science Association. Washington, D.C., 30 August 1986. Personal interview with Barbara Nelson.

Haener, Dorothy, UAW Women's Department. Personal interview with Sara Evans. Detroit, Mich. 21 January 1983.

Haney, Mike, President, Minnesota Association of Professional Employees. Telephone interview with Barbara Nelson. 24 July 1987.

Hayes, Mary, St. Paul Clerical 2508 and Jerry Serfling, Business Agent, St. Paul City and Schools, and Reneta Ciccarelli, Local 1842. Joint personal interview with Sara Evans. St. Paul, Minn. 18 March 1987.

Hendrixson, Carolyn, Lobbyist, League of Women Voters of Minnesota. Telephone interview with Sara Evans. 3 April 1985.

Honmyhr, Judy, Personnel Director, Washington County (Minnesota). Telephone interview with Sara Evans. 6 April 1987.

Hoover, Eleanor, Human Resources Director, Minneapolis Public Schools. Telephone interview with Sara Evans. 28 July 1987.

Hubbard, Lisa, National Committee on Pay Equity. Telephone interview with Barbara Nelson. 13 July 1988.

Jackson, Steve, Acting Administrative Clerk, Princeton, Minn. Telephone interview with Sara Evans. 9 April 1987.

Jamnick, Joel, League of Minnesota Cities. Personal interview with Sara Evans. St. Paul, Minn. 8 April 1985.

Joynes, Bill, Metropolitan Area Managers Association. Personal interview with Sara Evans and Barbara Nelson. Golden Valley, Minn. 17 September 1986.

Keppel, Polly, League of Women Voters of Minnesota. Personal interview with Sara Evans. Minneapolis, Minn. 12 March 1987.

King, Geraldine, and Bill Michel, Ramsey County Public Library. Personal interview with Sara Evans. Roseville, Minn. 4 March 1987.

Kistler, Alan, Visiting Senior Fellow, Hubert H. Humphrey Institute of Public Affairs (and retired director of Organization and Field Services of the AFL-CIO). Personal interview with Barbara Nelson. Minneapolis, Minn. 29 May 1987.

Koski, Irene, Administrative Assistant and Deputy Clerk, Maple Grove, Minnesota. Personal interview with Sara Evans. Minneapolis, Minn. 6 April 1987.

Latimer, George, Mayor of St. Paul, Minn. Presentation at "New Directions in Comparable Worth" Conference, Minneapolis, Minn. 18 October 1985.

Lavin, William, City Manager, Granite Falls, Minnesota. Telephone interview with Sara Evans. 30 March 1987.

Lee, Jim, Minnesota Department of Employee Relations. Personal interviews with Nancy Johnson. St. Paul, Minn. 26 June 1987 and 8 July 1987.

Lindahl, Bob, Minneapolis Central Labor Union (CLU). Personal interview with Sara Evans. Minneapolis, Minn. 29 July 1986.

Lindenfeld, Tom, Executive Assistant to the President of the New Jersey Senate. Telephone interview with Barbara Nelson. Trenton, New Jersey, 16 February, 1986.

Lipman, Wynona, Senator, State of New Jersey. Presentation at "New Directions in Comparable Worth" Conference, Minneapolis, Minn. 18 October 1985.

Lutes, David, Minnesota Department of Employee Relations. Personal interview with Barbara Nelson, St. Paul, Minn. 9 October 1986.

Madar, Olga, Former President, Coalition of Labor Union Women. Personal interview with Sara Evans. Detroit, Mich. 10 December 1982.

Magee, Linda. See Bocwinski, Robert.

McRoden, Margaret, Vice-President, Minnesota Municipal Clerks and Financial Officers Association. Telephone interview with Sara Evans. 12 March 1987.

McWilliams, Jane, School Board Member, Northfield, Minn. Presentation at "New Directions in Comparable Worth" Conference, Minneapolis, Minn. 18 October 1985.

Meulebroeck, Tom, Chief Clerk and Financial Officer, Marshall, Minnesota. (Former President, Minnesota Municipal Clerks and Financial Officers Association.) Telephone interview with Sara Evans. 17 March 1987.

Michel, Bill. See King, Geraldine.

Miller, Clark, Control Data Corporation, Minneapolis, Minnesota. Telephone interview with Sara Evans. 11 March 1987.

Miller, Joyce, Amalgamated Textile and Garment Workers Union, Coalition of Labor Union Women; AFL-CIO. Personal interview with Sara Evans, New York, 7 February 1983; and personal interview with Barbara Nelson. Minneapolis, Minn. 21 April 1987.

Miller, Robert, Former Superintendent of Schools, Stillwater (Minnesota) School District. Telephone interview with Sara Evans. 8 April 1987.

Moody, Norman, Personnel Director, Beltrami County, Minnesota. Telephone interview with Sara Evans. 11 April 1987.

Nelson, Matt, Business Agent, AFSCME Local 517, Washington County, Minnesota. Telephone interview with Sara Evans. 8 April 1987.

Nelson-Gerth, Bonnie, Payroll Clerk/Bookkeeper, Princeton, Minnesota. Telephone interview with Sara Evans. 10 April 1987.

Niemiec, Joan, Minneapolis City Council. Personal interview with Sara Evans. Minneapolis, Minn. 30 July 1986.

O'Brien, Kathy, Minneapolis City Council Member. Personal interviews with Sara Evans and Barbara Nelson. Minneapolis, Minn. 21 July 1986 and 18 May 1987.

Olson, Cathryn, Employee Relations Director, Anoka-Hennepin County (Minnesota) School District. Personal interview with Sara Evans. Coon Rapids, Minn. 13 April 1987.

Olson, Jean, President, Minnesota School Boards Association. Telephone interview with Sara Evans. 18 March 1987.

Olson, Karen. See Smythe, Cyrus.

Ortwig, Al, St. Paul School Board. Telephone interview with Sara Evans. 10 March 1987.

Ostlund, Bob, Director of Administrative Services and Personnel, Chaska (Minnesota) School District. Telephone interview with Sara Evans. 9 April 1987.

O'Toole, James, Assistant Superintendent and Director of Human Resources, Little Falls (Minnesota) School District. Telephone interview with Sara Evans. 14 April 1987.

Penn, Phillip. See Byers, Phyllis.

Place, Karen, Seattle Department of Women's Rights. Personal interview with Sara Evans. Seattle, Washington, 1984.

Potter, Janet, Personnel Director, St. Cloud, Minnesota. Telephone interviews with Sara Evans. 7, 23 April 1987.

Queenslound, Kenneth, Superintendent, Blue Earth School District. Telephone interview with Sara Evans. 24 April 1987.

Reilly, Greg, Project Coordinator, Office of Employee Relations, New York State. Personal interview with Sara Evans. Albany, New York, 8 April 1986.

Riveness, Phil, Minnesota State Representative. Personal interview with Barbara Nelson. St. Paul, Minn. 18 September 1986.

Robinson, Wendy, 9 to 5, Minneapolis, Minnesota. Telephone interview with Sara Evans. 29 July 1986.

Rothchild, Nina, Minnesota Department of Employee Relations. Personal interview with Barbara Nelson and Sara Evans, and presentation to Duluth Women's Consortium, Duluth, Minn. 23 October 1984; Bonnie Watkins, personal interview with Barbara Nelson, St. Paul, Minn. 15 February 1985; and telephone interview with Barbara Nelson, 14 November 1986.

Scheibel, Jim, St. Paul City Council President. Personal interview with Sara Evans and Barbara Nelson. St. Paul, Minn. 16 September 1986.

Scott, Rick, AFSCME Legislative/Political Action Coordinator. Personal interviews with Barbara Nelson. St. Paul, Minn. 27 October 1984 and 25 September 1986.

Serfling, Jerry. See Hayes, Mary.

Siegal, Roger, Assistant Director AFSCME Council 14. Personal interview, St. Paul, Minn. 28 July 1986.

Sitz, Hazel, Personnel Director, Hutchinson, Minn. Presentation at "New Directions in Comparable Worth" Conference, Minneapolis, Minn. 17 October 1985.

Smythe, Cyrus, and Karen Olson. Personal interview with Sara Evans, Golden Valley, Minn. 14 May 1987.

Strauchon, Regina, University Personnel Department. Personal interview with Sara Evans, 29 July 1987.

Sylvester, John. Staff, Minnesota School Boards Association. Telephone interview with Sara Evans. 27 March 1987.

Teachworth, Lance, Minnesota Department of Employee Relations. Telephone interview with Barbara Nelson. 22 July 1987.

Thelen, Tom, League of Minnesota Cities. Telephone interview with Sara Evans. 30 March 1987.

Toenges, Rolland, Hennepin County Labor Relations. Personal interview with Sara Evans. Minneapolis, Minn. 4 August 1986.

Wagner, Fred, Director of Employee Relations, Rochester, Minn. Telephone interview with Sara Evans. 15 April 1987.

Watkins, Bonnie, Minnesota Department of Employee Relations. Personal interview with Barbara Nelson and Sara Evans, St. Paul, Minn. 1 November 1984; telephone interview with Barbara Nelson, 25 September 1986; personal interview with Barbara Nelson, St. Paul, Minn. 9 October 1986; personal interview with Sara Evans, St. Paul, Minn. 21 April 1987. See also Rothchild, Nina.

Wedel, Geraldine (Gerry), Minnesota Nurses Association. Telephone interview with Barbara Nelson. 24 July 1987.

Woods, Mary, National Committee on Pay Equity. Telephone interview with Nancy Johnson. 15 March 1988.

Wyatt, Addie, Amalgamated Meatcutters Union. Personal interview with Sara Evans. Chicago, Ill. 15 June 1983.

Zwemke, Faith, Mayor, Princeton, Minnesota. Personal interview with Sara Evans. Minneapolis, Minn. 1 May 1987.

# APPENDIX B:
## State Comparable Worth Activities and Characteristics[2]

| | Comparable Worth Activities[2] | | | | | State Characteristics | | | | | | |
|---|---|---|---|---|---|---|---|---|---|---|---|---|
| | Research/ Data Collection | Task Force or Commission | Job Evaluation Study | Comparable Worth Payments[4] | Collective Bargaining of State Employees Permitted[5] | Rank in Personal Income[6] | Rank in State and Local Tax Progressivity[7] | State Rank in Local Tax Burden (% of Pers. Inc.)[8] | Strength of Interest Groups in State Legislatures[9] | Political Culture[10] | Dominant Political Party[11] | Public Commission on Women[12] |
| Alabama | yes | | | | | 46 | 50 | 47 | strong | T | D | yes |
| Alaska | | yes | yes[3] | | yes | 1 | 9 | 1 | strong | I | D | yes |
| Arizona | yes | | | | | 30 | 20 | 7 | moderate | T-M | R | yes |
| Arkansas | | | | | | 47 | 25 | 48 | strong | T | D | no |
| CALIFORNIA[1] | yes | yes | | yes (neg.) | yes | 5 | 4 | 4 | moderate | M-I | D | yes |
| Colorado | yes | | | | yes | 8 | 8 | 20 | weak | M | R | no |
| CONNECTICUT | | yes | yes[2] | yes (neg.) | yes | 2 | 33 | 31 | weak | I-M | D | yes |
| Delaware | | | | | yes | 10 | 27 | 26 | moderate | I | R | yes |
| FLORIDA | yes | yes | yes | yes (neg.) | yes | 19 | 31 | 43 | strong | T-I | D | yes |
| Georgia | | | | | | 34 | 12 | 36 | strong | T | D | no |
| Hawaii | yes | yes | yes | | yes | 16 | 7 | 10 | strong | I-T | D | yes |
| Idaho | | | | | | 45 | 6 | 27 | moderate | M-I | | no |
| ILLINOIS | yes | yes | | yes (neg.) | yes | 9 | 41 | 28 | moderate | I | D | yes |
| Indiana | yes | yes | yes | | | 31 | 43 | 46 | moderate | I | R | no |
| IOWA | yes | yes | yes | yes (neg.) | yes | 28 | 15 | 30 | strong | M-I | D | yes |
| Kansas | yes | yes | yes | | | 13 | 29 | 37 | moderate | M-I | R | no |
| Kentucky | yes | yes | | | | 42 | 42 | 34 | strong | T-I | D | yes |
| Louisiana | yes | yes | yes[3] | | | 38 | 45 | 25 | strong | T | D | yes |
| Maine | yes | yes | yes | | yes | 37 | 35 | 13 | moderate | M | D | yes |
| Maryland | yes | yes | yes | | yes | 6 | 21 | 15 | moderate | I | D | yes |
| MASSACHUSETTS | yes | yes | yes | yes (neg.) | yes | 4 | 10 | 5 | weak | I-M | D | yes |

| State | | | | | | | | | | | | |
|---|---|---|---|---|---|---|---|---|---|---|---|---|
| MICHIGAN | yes | yes | yes | yes (neg.) | yes | 20 | 2 | 19 | weak | M | D | yes |
| MINNESOTA | yes | yes | yes | yes (neg.) | yes | 14 | 5 | 9 | weak | M | D | yes |
| Mississippi | yes | | | | | 50 | 49 | 29 | strong | T | D | no |
| Missouri | yes | yes | | | yes | 29 | 38 | 50 | moderate | I-T | D | yes |
| Montana | yes | yes | yes | | yes | 40 | 18 | 11 | strong | M-I | D | no |
| Nebraska | yes | yes | | | yes | 23 | 11 | 21 | strong | I-M | D | yes |
| Nevada | yes | yes | | | yes | 11 | 32 | 14 | moderate | I | D | no |
| New Hampshire | yes | yes | yes | | yes | 15 | 28 | 45 | strong | M-I | R | no |
| New Jersey | yes | yes | yes | yes (leg.) | yes | 3 | 24 | 23 | weak | I | D | yes |
| New Mexico | yes | yes | yes | yes (leg.) | (partially) | 43 | 19 | 12 | strong | T-I | D | yes |
| New York | yes | yes | yes | yes (neg.) | yes | 7 | 17 | 2 | weak | I-M | D | no |
| North Carolina | yes | yes | yes | | | 36 | 14 | 40 | strong | T-I | D | yes |
| North Dakota | yes | yes | yes | | | 25 | 16 | 32 | weak | M | R | no |
| OHIO | yes | yes | yes | yes (neg.) | yes | 24 | 26 | 49 | moderate | I | D | yes |
| OKLAHOMA | yes | | yes | yes (leg.) | | 32 | 36 | 41 | strong | T-I | D | yes |
| OREGON | yes | yes | yes | yes (neg.) | yes | 33 | 1 | 16 | strong | M | D | yes |
| PENNSYLVANIA | yes | yes | | yes (lit.) | yes | 26 | 34 | 24 | moderate | I | R | yes |
| RHODE ISLAND | yes | yes | yes | yes (lit.) | yes | 17 | 44 | 21 | weak | I-M | D | yes |
| South Carolina | yes | yes | | | | 44 | 39 | 38 | strong | T | D | yes |
| SOUTH DAKOTA | yes | | yes[2] | yes (leg.) | (partially) | 35 | 22 | 33 | moderate | M-I | R | no |
| Tennessee | yes | | | | | 41 | 47 | 42 | strong | T | D | no |
| Texas | yes | | | | (partially) | 21 | 46 | 44 | strong | T-I | D | no |
| Utah | yes | yes | | | | 48 | 23 | 18 | moderate | M | R | no |
| VERMONT | yes | yes | yes | yes (neg.) | yes | 39 | 13 | 6 | moderate | M | R | yes |
| Virginia | yes | yes | yes | | | 12 | 30 | 39 | moderate | T | D | yes |
| WASHINGTON | yes | yes | yes | | | 18 | 37 | 17 | strong | M-I | D | no |
| West Virginia | yes | yes | | yes (leg.) | yes | 49 | 40 | 35 | strong | T-I | D | yes |
| WISCONSIN | yes | yes | yes | | yes | 22 | 3 | 8 | weak | M | D | no |
| Wyoming | yes | yes | yes | | yes | 27 | 48 | 3 | moderate | I-M | R | yes |

(Notes to Appendix B on following page.)

## Notes to Appendix B

[1] Capital letters indicate states that had provided some kind of comparable worth payments as of August 1987.

[2] National Committee on Pay Equity: State Update, August 1987, "Summary of State Pay Equity Activity" (Washington, D.C.: August 1987), pp. 1–4.

[3] A state that meets the National Committee for Pay Equity's criteria for having a job evaluation study. See National Committee on Pay Equity, August 1987, p. 3.

[4] The abbreviations refer to the method by which comparable worth was achieved: "neg." for negotiation, "leg." for legislation, and "lit." for litigation. We are indebted to Lisa Hubbard of the National Committee on Pay Equity for sharing with us their preliminary analysis of the methods by which comparable worth was achieved in the early acting states. These categories do not capture the full range of activities undertaken in each state, and belie the complexity of political activity in each location where activist may have begun with one form of activity but ultimately used another. Telephone interview with Lisa Hubbard, National Committee on Pay Equity, by Barbara Nelson, 13 July 1988.

[5] Information on whether collective bargaining for state employees is permitted is for July 1985. Keon S. Chi, "Comparable Worth in State Governments: Trends and Issues," Policy Studies Review 5 (May 1986): 804–5.

[6] Rank in personal income is derived from "State Personal Income, 1982–1984: Revised Estimates," Survey of Current Business, 65:8 (August 1985), p. 18.

[7] Susan B. Hansen, "Extraction: The Politics of State Taxation," in Politics in the American States, 4th ed., Virginia Gray et al., eds. (Boston: Little, Brown, 1983),

pp. 426–7. Data are fpr 1979.

[8] Ibid., pp. 426–27. Data are for personal income in 1978.

[9] From L. Harmon Ziegler, "Interest Groups in the States," table 4.1, "Pressure Groups Reputed to be Influential, by State," in Gray, Politics in the American States, pp. 100–103. Data derived from Sara McCally Morehouse, State Politics, Parties, and Policy (New York: Holt Rinehart and Winston, 1981), no pages given.

[10] The abbreviations stand for types of political culture. "T" stands for traditional political culture; "M" stands for moralistic political culture; "I" stands for individualistic political culture. From Russell L. Hanson, "The Intergovernmental Setting of State Politics," figure 2.1, "Regional Distribution of Political Culture in the United States" in Gray, Politics in the American States, p. 32. Data derived from Daniel Elazar, American Federalism: A View from the States (New York: Harper and Row, 1972), p. 117.

[11] Dominant political party is derived by determining which party controlled the governorship, House of Representatives, and Senate during the four legislative biennia between January 1981 and January 1987. Data derived from The Book of the States (Lexington, Ken.: Council of State Governments, 1980–81, 1982–83, 1984–85, 1986–87); and Taylor's Encyclopedia of Government Officials, Federal and State (Dallas: 1987–88).

[12] Information on public commissions on women comes from State Information Book, 1987–88, ed. Gerry Jones (Rockville, Md.: Infax Corp., 1987).

# APPENDIX C

## Survey Design

In June of 1985, the Minnesota Center for Survey Research at the University of Minnesota fielded the Public Employee Survey designed and directed by the University's Comparable Worth Research Project. The survey covers 176 questions on work history; attitudes toward public employment; employee experiences in the workplace (with coworkers, superiors, subordinates); worker satisfaction and morale; information and attitudes about pay equity and experiences with the Minnesota pay equity policy; political beliefs; use of social programs; and socioeconomic and demographic information (including questions on the use of and need for child care arrangements). Before fielding the survey, the Comparable Worth Project contacted the Minnesota Department of Employee Relations and every public union and labor organization. Each person in the sample received two letters at work describing the project, prior to being telephoned at home. This telephone survey of 493 state of Minnesota employees is, to our knowledge, the only existing data set designed to assess the impact on employees of implementing a pay equity wage policy.

This survey design reflected two policies established by the state of Minnesota. State of Minnesota employees are not permitted to answer surveys or conduct personal interviews at work. In addition, due to privacy protection laws, the state of Minnesota does not release the home phone numbers of state employees. Therefore, only those people who returned a postcard indicating their home telephone number and their willingness to be interviewed were contacted by telephone. We contacted 1,000 employees for a target sample of 500; 652 people responded, of whom 588 were willing to be called (see table C.1). As part of the design, we quota-sampled the respondents (at the telephoning stage) to make certain that our final sample accurately represented the bargaining units in state employment in appropriate proportions.

TABLE C.1
**Responses to Request to Participate in the Public Employee Survey**

| Response Type | No. | % | No. | % |
|---|---|---|---|---|
| Responded to request | 652 | (65.2) | | |
| Said yes, used | | | 493 | (75.6) |
| Said no | | | 64 | (9.8) |
| Said yes, not used | | | 95 | (14.6) |
| Implicit no (no response) | 347 | (34.7) | | |
| Unknown | 1 | (0.1) | | |

183

TABLE C.2

**Comparison of Interviewees and Noninterviewed Contacts by Gender, Job Location, and Bargaining Unit**

| | 493 Interviewees (Those in Survey) | | 507 Noninterviewed Contacts (All Those Contacted but not in Survey) | |
|---|---|---|---|---|
| | No. | % | No. | % |
| *Gender* | | | | |
| Male | 254 | (51.5) | 269 | (53.1) |
| Female | 239 | (48.5) | 233 | (46.0) |
| Unknown | — | | 5 | (1.0) |
| *Job Location* | | | | |
| Twin Cities Metro Area | 261 | (53) | 295 | (58) |
| Greater Minnesota | 232 | (47) | 212 | (42) |
| *Bargaining Unit or other employment status* | | | | |
| Law Enforcement | 11 | (2.2) | 9 | (1.8) |
| Craft-Maintenance-Labor | 39 | (7.9) | 40 | (7.9) |
| Service | 40 | (8.1) | 46 | (9.1) |
| Health Care—Nonprofessional | 54 | (11.0) | 59 | (11.6) |
| Health Care—Professional | 8 | (1.8) | 5 | (1.0) |
| Office/Clerical | 92 | (18.7) | 101 | (19.9) |
| Technical | 41 | (8.3) | 44 | (8.7) |
| Correctional Guards | 8 | (1.6) | 16 | (3.2) |
| Professional Engineering | 11 | (2.2) | 15 | (3.0) |
| Health Treatment—Professional | 1 | (0.2) | 0 | |
| General Professional | 82 | (16.6) | 68 | (13.4) |
| Professional Residence Instructor | 3 | (0.6) | 3 | (1.0) |
| Supervisory | 41 | (8.3) | 43 | (9.1) |
| Confidential | 19 | (3.9) | 5 | (1.0) |
| Excluding work time | 4 | (0.8) | 22 | (4.3) |
| Severed | 1 | (0.2) | 1 | (0.2) |
| Managerial | 24 | (4.9) | 7 | (1.4) |
| Excluding all other | 6 | (1.2) | 14 | (2.8) |
| No bargaining unit | 8 | (1.6) | 9 | (1.8) |

The response rate to the letters requesting participation in the survey was high—approximately 65% of the 1,000 letters resulted in a returned postcard (see table C.1). In this respect, the survey design integrated a mailed questionnaire and telephone survey methodology. According to Backstrom and Hursh-Cesar, "a 70 percent completion [of a mailed questionnaire] is extraordinary" (Charles H. Backstrom and Gerald Hursh-Cesar, *Survey Research,* 2d ed. [New York: John Wiley, 1981], p. 118). Analyzing the characteristics of individuals interviewed and all those not interviewed but mailed initial letters, we found that the two groups appear to be very similar in terms of gender, job location, and of course, bargaining units (see tables C.2, C.3, C.4).

The final sample size is 493 interviews. The discrepancy from 500 is accounted for by members of prison guard bargaining units. Prison guards were more likely to be nonrespondents than any other employee group. They made up 3.2% of the non-respondent group, compared with 1.6% of the respondent group. Members of the prison guard bargaining unit make up 2.5% of the state's work force. At one state facility, no members of this bargaining unit returned cards. This is the only instance where a facility or unit did not reply.

TABLE C.3

**Comparison of People Who Returned Postcards with "Implicit No" Responses by Gender and Bargaining Unit**

|  | 652 Respondents | | 348 Nonrespondents (Implicit No) | |
|---|---|---|---|---|
|  | No. | % | No. | % |
| *Gender* |  |  |  |  |
| Male | 351 | (53.8) | 172 | (49.4) |
| Female | 301 | (46.2) | 171 | (49.1) |
| Unknown | — | — | 5 | (1.5) |
| *Bargaining Unit or other employment status* |  |  |  |  |
| Law Enforcement | 17 | (2.6) | 3 | (0.8) |
| Craft-Maintenance-Labor | 56 | (8.6) | 23 | (6.6) |
| Service | 59 | (9.1) | 27 | (7.8) |
| Health Care—Nonprofessional | 69 | (10.6) | 44 | (12.6) |
| Health Care—Professional | 10 | (1.5) | 3 | (0.8) |
| Office/Clerical | 110 | (16.9) | 83 | (23.9) |
| Technical | 66 | (10.1) | 19 | (5.5) |
| Correctional Guards | 11 | (1.7) | 13 | (3.7) |
| Professional Engineering | 20 | (3.1) | 6 | (1.7) |
| Health Treatment—Professional | 1 | (0.2) | 0 |  |
| General Professional | 99 | (15.2) | 51 | (14.7) |
| Professional Residence Instructor | 4 | (0.6) | 2 | (0.6) |
| Supervisory | 51 | (7.8) | 33 | (9.5) |
| Confidential | 21 | (3.2) | 3 | (0.8) |
| Excluding work time | 12 | (1.8) | 14 | (4.0) |
| Severed | 1 | (0.2) | 1 | (0.3) |
| Managerial | 27 | (4.1) | 4 | (1.2) |
| Excluding all other | 10 | (1.5) | 10 | (2.9) |
| No bargaining unit | 8 | (1.2) | 9 | (2.6) |

TABLE C.4
**Comparison of "Yes" Responses and "No" and "Implicit No" Responses by Gender and Bargaining Unit**

|  | 588 "Yes" Responses | | 412 "No" Responses | |
|---|---|---|---|---|
|  | No. | % | No. | % |
| *Gender* | | | | |
| Male | 313 | (53.2) | 210 | (51.0) |
| Female | 275 | (46.8) | 197 | (47.8) |
| Unknown | — | | 5 | (1.2) |
| *Bargaining Unit or other employment status* | | | | |
| Law Enforcement | 15 | (2.5) | 5 | (1.2) |
| Craft-Maintenance-Labor | 52 | (8.8) | 27 | (6.5) |
| Service | 46 | (7.8) | 40 | (9.7) |
| Health Care—Nonprofessional | 62 | (10.5) | 51 | (12.4) |
| Health Care—Professional | 10 | (1.8) | 3 | (0.7) |
| Office/Clerical | 102 | (17.3) | 91 | (22.1) |
| Technical | 52 | (8.8) | 33 | (8.0) |
| Correctional Guards | 10 | (1.8) | 14 | (3.4) |
| Professional Engineering | 19 | (3.2) | 7 | (1.7) |
| Health Treatment—Professional | 1 | (0.2) | 0 | |
| General Professional | 95 | (16.1) | 55 | (13.3) |
| Professional Residence Instructor | 3 | (0.5) | 3 | (0.7) |
| Supervisory | 49 | (8.3) | 35 | (8.5) |
| Confidential | 21 | (3.6) | 3 | (0.7) |
| Excluding work time | 10 | (1.8) | 16 | (3.9) |
| Severed | 1 | (0.2) | 1 | (0.2) |
| Managerial | 25 | (4.2) | 6 | (1.4) |
| Excluding all other | 7 | (1.2) | 13 | (3.1) |
| No bargaining unit | 8 | (1.4) | 9 | (2.2) |

# Notes

## Chapter One

1. Kathy O'Brien, interview with Sara Evans and Barbara Nelson, Minneapolis, 18 May 1987.

2. Advisory Committee on Pay Equity, "Report to the City Council," 6 August 1984, 2.

3. Joan Niemiec and Bob Lindahl, interview with Sara Evans, Minneapolis, 21 July 1986.

4. Kathy O'Brien interview; with authors, Minneapolis, 18 May 1987; Wendy Robinson, interview by telephone with Sara Evans, 23 July 1986; Jerry Serfling, interview with Sara Evans, Minneapolis, 18 March 1987.

5. Minnesota Statutes Annotated, Section 43A.01–43A.47 (West 1988).

6. Commission on the Economic Status of Women, *Pay Equity: The Minnesota Experience* (St. Paul: Commission on the Economic Status of Women, 1985), 15.

7. Minnesota Statutes Annotated 471.991–471.999.

8. Commission, *Pay Equity,* 18.

9. Research and Statistics Office, Minnesota Department of Jobs and Training, *Minnesota Non-Agricultural Wage and Salary, Employment, Hours, and Earnings, January 1980–December 1987* (St. Paul: Research and Statistics Office, April 1988). Estimates, based on a household survey, for total nonagricultural employment in 1987 are 1,929,526; for state government employment, 77,096; for local government employment, 204,045.

10. National Committee on Pay Equity, telephone interview with Nancy Johnson, January 1988.

11. *New York Times,* 17 November 1984, 15.

12. One business group, the Minnesota Associate of Commerce and Industry (MACI; now the Minnesota Chamber of Commerce and Industry, MCCI), consistently refused to return our calls. Whether this was a problem of internal communication or a disinclination to be interviewed is unclear. In Minnesota this group played a small role in policy making (see chap. 4).

13. American Association of University Women, "Pay Equity Action Guide" (Washington, D.C.: AAUW, June 1987), 5. Of the many definitions available, this seems to us one of the clearest, especially in relation to the definition of pay equity as "the goal of eliminating wage discrimination" in the same source.

14. This definition is drawn from Barbara J. Nelson, "Comparable Worth: A Brief

187

Review of History, Practice, and Theory," *Minnesota Law Review* 69 (May 1985): 1199–1200.

15. There are other, less frequently used approaches to comparable worth that emphasize returns to employees within a firm on human capital variables or that emphasize national aggregate occupational data. For the first approach, see Suzanne Donovan, "Comparable Worth Discrimination in the Private Sector: Can it Be Measured?" paper delivered at the Association of Public Policy and Management Meetings, Austin, Texas, October 1986; and Barbara Bergmann, "The Economic Case for Comparable Worth," in *Comparable Worth: New Directions for Research,* ed. Heidi Hartmann (Washington, D.C.: National Academy Press, 1985), 71–85. For the second approach, see Mark Aldrich and Robert Buchele, *The Economics of Comparable Worth* (Cambridge, Mass.: Ballinger, 1986).

16. See, for example, Commission on Sex Discrimination in the Statutes, *An Analysis of Wage Discrimination in New Jersey State Service* (Trenton, N.J.: Commission on Sex Discrimination in the Statutes, March 1983).

17. Department of Employee Relations, *Biennial Work Force Report: 1983–84* (St. Paul: Department of Employee Relations, 1985), 4; *Biennial Work Force Report: 1985–86* (1987), 5.

18. For examples of the price of medical services as a reflection of their original arrangements, see U.S. Congress, Office of Technology Assessment, *Payment for Physician Services; Strategies for Medicare,* OTA-H-294 (Washington, D.C.: Government Printing Office, February 1986), 70.

19. The definition of comparable worth evolved, over the course of the 1970s, from a looser conceptual frame focused on eliminating historic sex-based wage discrimination toward this tighter, more technological definition based on the use of job evaluation. It did so largely because job evaluation appeared from the outset as an important power resource for advocates. As a traditional management tool, it could be used to validate the claims of discrimination and to undermine the opposition's insistence that the implementation of comparable worth was simply impossible. See Donald Treiman and Heidi Hartmann, eds., *Women, Work, and Wages: Equal Pay for Jobs of Equal Value* (Washington, D.C.: National Academy Press, 1981), chaps. 4 and 5; Helen Remick, "Beyond Equal Pay for Equal Work: Comparable Worth in the State of Washington," in Ronnie Steinberg-Ratner, ed., *Equal Employment Policy for Women* (Philadelphia: Temple University Press, 1980), 405–48; Ronnie J. Steinberg, "'A Want of Harmony': Perspectives on Wage Discrimination and Comparable Worth," in Helen Remick, ed., *Comparable Worth and Wage Discrimination* (Philadelphia: Temple University Press, 1984), 3–27.

20. See, for example, Steven L. Willborn, *A Comparable Worth Primer* (Lexington, Mass.: D.C. Heath, 1986), 3.

21. See Lawrence Friedman, *A History of American Law* (New York: Simon and Schuster, 1973), 21–23; C. T. Onions, ed., *The Oxford Dictionary of English Etymology* (Oxford: Clarendon Press, 1966).

22. Barbara J. Nelson, "Women's Poverty and Women's Citizenship: Some Political Consequences of Economic Marginality," *Signs* 10 (Winter 1984): 209–31; Mary C. Dietz, "Context is All: Feminism and Theories of Citizenship," *Daedalus* 116 (Fall 1987):1–23; Mary C. Dietz, "Citizenship with a Feminist Face: The Problem with Maternal Thinking," *Political Theory* 13 (February 1985): 19–37; Linda Kerber,

*Women of the Republic: Intellect and Ideology in Revolutionary America* (Chapel Hill, N.C.: University of North Carolina Press, 1980).

23. Kenneth H. Bacon, "Future Pressures on Living Standards," *The Wall Street Journal*, 3 August 1987.

24. Richard McGahey, "The Rise and Fall of the American Postwar Socioeconomic Policy Consensus," paper presented at the Southern Historical Association Meeting, Charlotte, N.C., 13 November 1986.

25. Donald P. Schwab, "Using Job Evaluation to Obtain Pay Equity," in U.S. Civil Rights Commission, *Comparable Worth: Issue for the 80's: A Consultation of the U.S. Commission on Civil Rights, June 6–7, 1984*, vol. 1 (Washington, D.C.: Government Printing Office, 1984). Donald J. Trieman, "Job Evaluation: An Analytical Review," Interim Report to the Equal Employment Opportunity Commission (Washington, D.C.: National Academy of Sciences, 1979). Samuel Haber, *Efficiency and Uplift: Scientific Management in the Progressive Era, 1890–1920* (Chicago: University of Chicago Press, 1964). See also Linda M. Blum, "Possibilities and Limits of the Comparable Worth movement," *Gender and Society* 1 (December 1987): 394, and Roslyn Feldberg, "Comparable Worth: Toward Theory and Practice in the United States," *Signs* 10 (Winter 1984): 321–24.

26. For comparable worth advocates' and critics' views on job evaluation, see Donald J. Treiman and Heidi Hartmann, *Women, Work and Wages: Equal Pay for Jobs of Equal Value* (Washington, D.C.: National Academy Press, 1981); Treiman, "Job Evaluation: An Analytical Review"; Richard W. Beatty and James R. Beatty, "Some Problems with Contemporary Job Evaluation System," in Helen Remick, ed., *Comparable Worth and Wage Discrimination: Technical Possibilities and Political Realities* (Philadelphia: Temple University Press, 1984), 59–78; Ronnie J. Steinberg, Louis Haignere, Carol Possin, Cynthia Chertos, Donald Treiman, *The New York State Comparable Worth Study Final Report* (Albany, N.Y.: Center for Women in Government, 1985); Robert Livernash, ed., *Comparable Worth: Issues and Alternatives* (Washington, D.C.: Equal Employment Advisory Council, 1980); U.S. Civil Rights Commission, *Comparable Worth: Issue for the 80's*.

## Chapter Two

1. Caroline Dall, *Women's Right to Labor* (Boston: Walker, Wise, 1860), in *America's Working Women*, Rosalyn Baxandall et al., eds. (Random House, 1976), 80.

2. See Catherine White Berhead, Cynthia Chertos, and Ronnie Steinberg, "Pay Equity for Blacks and Hispanics in New York State Government Employment," in *Pay Equity: An Issue of Race, Ethnicity and Sex*, ed. National Committee on Pay Equity (Washington, D.C.: February 1987).

3. Eleanor Holmes Norton coined this phrase during her tenure as chair of the Equal Employment Opportunity Commission. It had gained general currency by 1984 when the U.S. Civil Rights Commission sponsored a consultation on the issue entitled "Comparable Worth: Issue for the 80's."

4. Republicanism by the middle of the nineteenth century bifurcated into communal and individualistic strands. In the latter, public life came to be seen increasingly as a violent and savage realm, parallel to the competitive entrepreneurial economy.

5. See Linda Kerber, *Women of the Republic: Intellect and Ideology in Revolution-*

*ary America* (Chapel Hill: University of North Carolina Press, 1980); Mary Beth Norton, *Liberty's Daughters: The Revolutionary Experience of American Women, 1750–1800* (Boston: Little, Brown, 1980); Nancy Cott, *The Bonds of Womanhood: "Women's Sphere" in New England 1780–1835* (New Haven: Yale University Press, 1977; and Mary Ryan, *Cradle of the Middle Class* (New York: Cambridge University Press, 1981).

6. Thomas Dublin, *Women at Work: The Transformation of Work and Community in Lowell, Massachusetts, 1826–1860* (New York: Columbia University Press, 1979).

7. See Alice Kessler-Harris, *Out to Work: A History of Wage-Earning Women in the United States* (New York: Oxford University Press, 1982), 49–56.

8. Mark Aldrich and Robert Buchele, *The Economics of Comparable Worth* (Cambridge, Mass.: Ballinger, 1986), 3–4. See also Kessler-Harris, *Out to Work*, chaps. 1–3.

9. Alfred D. Chandler, Jr., *The Visible Hand: The Managerial Revolution in American Business* (Cambridge, Mass.: Harvard University Press, 1977).

10. Margery W. Davies, *Woman's Place Is at the Typewriter: Office Work and Office Workers, 1870–1930* (Philadelphia: Temple University Press, 1982).

11. Ronnie Steinberg, *Wages and Hours: Labor and Reform in Twentieth-Century America* (New Brunswick, N.J.: Rutgers University Press, 1982), 3–13, 59–87; see also Lawrence M. Friedman, *A History of American Law* (New York: Simon and Schuster, 1973).

12. Quoted in *Growth of Labor Law in the United States* (Washington, D.C.: U.S. Department of Labor, 1976), 102.

13. Ibid., 36.

14. See Judith A. Baer, *The Chains of Protection: The Judicial Response to Women's Labor Legislation* (Westport, Conn.: Greenwood Press, 1978), chaps. 1 and 2.

15. There are many ironies in this domestic politics in the nineteenth and early twentieth centuries. Paula Baker has pointed out that as women turned the institutions they created over to government, men assumed control and volunteerism gave way to professionalism. In addition, the ideals of sisterhood based in middle-class culture frequently foundered in the face of class differences. See Paula Baker, "The Domestication of Politics: Women and American Political Society, 1780–1920," *American Historical Review* 89 (June 1984): 620–47; Barbara J. Nelson, "The Gender, Race, and Class Origins of Welfare Policy and the Welfare State: A Comparison of Workmen's Compensation and Mothers' Aid," in Louise Tilly and Patricia Gurin, eds., *Women in Twentieth Century Politics* (New York: Russell Sage, 1988); and Nancy Schrom Dye, *As Equals and As Sisters: Feminism, the Labor Movement, and the Women's Trade Union League of New York* (Columbia, Mo.; University of Missouri Press, 1980).

16. Samuel Gompers is a good example of a male unionist who subscribed to Victorian domestic ideology not only because he thought such a division of labor was natural but also because he feared the effects of a larger labor pool in driving down wages or making workers' demands for reasonable hours and conditions harder to win and enforce.

17. Baer, *Chains of Protection*, 17; *Growth of Labor Law in the United States*.

18. Baer, *Chains of Protection*, 10–11.

19. *Muller v. Oregon,* 208 U.S. 412 (1908). See Baer, *Chains of Protection,* 56–67, for an analysis of the *Muller* decision.

20. *Lochner v. New York,* 198 U.S. 45 (1905).

21. Quotes from "Declaration of Sentiments," Seneca Falls, N.Y., 1948, in Alice S. Rossi, ed., *The Feminist Papers* (New York: Columbia University Press, 1973), 416; and Sarah M. Grimke, *Letters on the Equality of the Sexes and the Condition of Woman* (Boston: Isaac Knapp, 1838), 10.

22. Charlotte Perkins Gilman, *Women and Economics* (Boston: Small, Maynard, 1898).

23. Marjorie Lightman, "Comparable Worth in Historical Perspective," paper presented at the Organization of American Historians' Annual Meeting, New York City, April 1986.

24. Barbara Bergmann, *The Economic Emergence of Women* (New York: Basic Books, 1986), 24–27.

25. See Valerie Kincaid Oppenheimer, *The Female Labor Force in the United States: Demographic and Economic Factors Governing Its Growth and Changing Composition* (Westport, Conn.: Greenwood Press, 1970), chaps. 2 and 5.

26. Roy Lubov, *The Struggle for Social Security, 1900–1935* (Cambridge: Harvard University Press, 1968).

27. Chandler, *The Visible Hand,* 468, 275–77. See also Samuel Haber, *Efficiency and Uplift: Scientific Management in the Progressive Era, 1890–1920* (Chicago: University of Chicago Press, 1964).

28. Haber, *Efficiency and Uplift,* 113. See also "Standardization of Public Employments," *Municipal Research* (November 1915), 10, 16–19, 31; "Standardization of Public Employment," *Municipal Research* (August 1916), 6–9, 98.

29. Merrill R. Lott, *Wage Scales and Job Evaluation* (New York: Ronald Press, 1926).

30. Quoted in Ruth Milkman, *Gender at Work: The Dynamics of Job Segregation by Sex During World War II* (Urbana, Ill.: University of Illinois Press, 1987), 81.

31. Dorothy S. Brady, "Equal Pay for Women Workers," *Annals of the American Academy of Political and Social Science* 217 (May 1947): 53.

32. Herbert R. Northrup, "Comparable Worth and Realistic Wage Setting," in U.S. Civil Rights Commission, *Comparable Worth: Issue for the 80's: A Consultation of the U.S. Commission on Civil Rights, June 6–7, 1984,* vol. 1 (Washington, D.C.: Government Printing Office, 1984), 94.

33. William Chafe, *The American Woman: Her Changing Social, Economic, and Political Roles, 1920–1970* (New York: Oxford University Press, 1972), 154–58, quote from 155.

34. See Milkman, *Gender at Work,* and Ronnie J. Steinberg, "'A Want of Harmony': Perspectives on Wage Discrimination and Comparable Worth," in Helen Remick, ed., *Comparable Worth and Wage Discrimination: Technical Possibilities and Political Realities* (Philadelphia: Temple University Press, 1984), 6–8. See also "Interview: Comparable Worth in the Forties: Reflections by Sylvia Scribner," *Women's Law Rights Reporter* 8 (Winter 1984): 105–7. Scribner was an organizer for UE at Thomas Edison and led the negotiations that eliminated wage differentials between women and men. Her interview vacillates between "comparable worth" and "equal

pay," but it appears that they demanded a revision of the company's job evaluation system on the grounds that the allocation of points systematically discriminated against women's jobs by assigning them lower points.

35. Kessler-Harris, *Out to Work,* 289–90. The figures, from Dorothy Brody, "Equal Pay—What are the Facts?" in *Report of the National Conference on Equal Pay, March 31 and April 1, 1952,* Women's Bureau Bulletin 243 (1952), 14–15, do not include domestic workers' salaries. If those salaries were included, women's earnings in 1939 would be 59% of men's and in 1950 45% (53% if domestic workers were excluded).

36. See Steinberg, *Wages and Hours.* See also Cynthia Harrison, *On Account of Sex: The Politics of Women's Issues, 1945–1968* (Berkeley: University of California Press, 1988), 96.

37. *Growth of Labor Legislation in the United States,* 221–52.

38. Leila Rupp and Verta Taylor, *Survival in the Doldrums: The American Women's Rights Movement, 1945 to the 1960s* (New York: Oxford University Press, 1987), chap. 7.

39. *Hearings before the Select Subcommittee of Labor of the House Committee on Education and Labor on H.R. 8898, 10266, Part I,* 87th Congress, 2d Session, 1962, 2–10, 17, 166.

40. Rupp and Taylor, *Survival in the Doldrums,* 176–78; Carl M. Brauer, "Women Activists, Southern Conservatives, and the Prohibition of Sex Discrimination in Title VII of the 1964 Civil Rights Act," *Journal of Southern History* 49 (1983): 37–56.

41. Donald Allen Robinson, "Two Movements in Pursuit of Equal Employment Opportunity," *Signs* 4 (1979): 413–17; Fern S. Ingersoll, "Former Congresswomen Look Back," in Irene Tinker, ed., *Women in Washington: Advocates for Public Policy* (Beverly Hills: Sage Publications, 1983), 196.

42. Rupp and Taylor, *Survival in the Doldrums,* 178.

43. Robinson, "Two Movements," 417–20.

44. 42 U.S.C. §2000(e)(1982). Section (h) of Title VII is referred to as the Bennett Amendment.

45. See Rupp and Taylor, *Survival in the Doldrums,* 178. For an example of jokes made about Title VII, see *New York Times* editorial, 12 August 1965.

46. Richard McGahey, "The Rise and Fall of the American Postwar Socioeconomic Policy Consensus," paper presented at the Southern Historical Association Meeting, Charlotte, N.C., 13 November 1986.

47. See Judith Hole and Ellen Levine, *Rebirth of Feminism* (New York: Quadrangle Books, 1971); Jo Freeman, *The Politics of Women's Liberation* (New York: David McKay, 1975). See also Rupp and Taylor, *Surviving the Doldrums,* who point out that some of the founders of NOW had connections to the National Women's Party, providing visible continuity to the suffrage movement. The NWP, on the other hand, responded ambivalently to this younger organization.

48. Sara Evans, *Personal Politics: The Roots of Women's Liberation in the Civil Rights Movement and the New Left* (New York: Knopf, 1979).

49. Claudia Goldin, "The Earnings Gap Between Male and Female Workers: An Historical Perspective," Working Paper No. 1888, National Bureau of Economic Research, Working Paper Series, Cambridge, Massachusetts, 1986, 22. On women's work expectations, see Steven Sandell and David Shapiro, "Work Expectations, Hu-

man Capital Accumulation, and the Wages of Young Women," *Journal of Human Resources* 15 (Summer 1980): 335–53.

50. Lester Thurow, *The Zero-Sum Society* (New York: Basic Books, 1980).

51. Lenore J. Weitzman, *The Divorce Revolution: The Unexpected Social and Economic Consequences for Women and Children in America* (New York: The Free Press, 1985), 323.

52. Diana Pearce and Harriette McAdoo, *Women and Children: Alone and in Poverty* (Washington, D.C.: National Advisory Council on Economic Opportunity, 1981).

53. Bergmann, *Economic Emergence of Women,* 27; Richard McGahey and John M. Jeffries, "Equity, Growth and Socioeconomic Change: Anti-Discrimination Policy in an Era of Economic Transformation," *Review of Law and Social Change,* 13, no. 2 (1984): 233–80; McGahey, "Rise and Fall."

54. McGahey and Jeffries, "Equity, Growth and Socioeconomic Change," 250.

55. McGahey, "Rise and Fall," 16–17.

56. See Linda M. Blum, "Possibilities and Limits of the Comparable Worth Movement," *Gender and Society* 1 (December 1987): 381–83.

57. See Evans and Boyte, *Free Spaces,* 146–48.

58. Joan M. Goodin, "Working Women: The Pros and Cons of Unions," in Irene Tinker, ed., *Women in Washington: Advocates for Public Policy* (Beverly Hills: Sage Publications, 1983), 140–47; Olga Madar, personal interview with Sara Evans, Detroit, 10 December 1982; Dorothy Haener, personal interview with Sara Evans, Detroit, 21 January 1983; Addie Wyatt, personal interview with Sara Evans, Chicago, 15 June 1983; Joyce Miller, personal interview with Sara Evans, New York, 7 February 1983.

59. Comparable Worth Project Newsletter, 3 (Winter and Spring 1983).

60. See Janet A Flammang, "The Implementation of Comparable Worth in San Jose," in Rita Mae Kelley and Jane Bayes, eds., *Comparable Worth, Pay Equity, and Public Policy* (Westport, Conn.: Greenwood Press, 1988), 159–90, and Helen Remick, "Comparable Worth in Washington State," in Kelley and Bayes, *Comparable Worth,* 223–36.

61. See Tinker, *Women in Washington;* Winifred Wandersee, *On the Move: American Women in the 1970s* (Boston, Twayne, 1988).

62. See Women's Bureau, U.S. Department of Labor, *Time of Change: 1983 Handbook on Women Workers,* Bulletin 298 (Washington, D.C.: Government Printing Office, 1983), 81–84, especially tables III-1 and III-2. The ratio did not reach 60% until 1981.

63. Quoted in Frances C. Hutner, *Equal Pay for Comparable Worth: The Working Women's Issue of the Eighties* (New York: Praeger, 1986), 154.

64. Quoted in ibid., 157.

65. Jenkins had led a battle against a proposed wage freeze in San Francisco in 1974 while working for the Service Employees International Union. There she argued that such a law "would freeze [women] into a pay rate that was set in an era of sex discrimination and would give them no right to bargain their way out of it." Quoted in ibid., 68.

66. Lisa Portman, Joy Ann Grune, and Eve Johnson, "The Role of Labor," in Remick, *Comparable Worth and Wage Discrimination,* 233; Alice Cook, *Comparable Worth: A Case Book of Experiences in States and Localities* (Manoa, Hawaii: Indus-

trial Relations Center, University of Hawaii at Manoa, 1985), 58–60; Hutner, *Equal Pay for Comparable Worth*, chap. 4.

67. See Jane J. Mansbridge, *Why We Lost the ERA* (Chicago: University of Chicago Press, 1986), chap. 5.

68. *Griggs v. Duke Power Co.*, 401 U.S. 424 (1971).

69. Quoted in Hutner, *Equal Pay for Comparable Worth*, 129.

70. 620 F. 2d 228 (10th Cir. 1980).

71. *IUE v. Westinghouse Electric Corporation*, 631 Federal Reporter, 2d Series, p. 1094.

72. Donald Treiman and Heidi Hartmann, eds., *Women, Work, and Wages: Equal Pay for Jobs of Equal Value* (Washington, D.C.: National Academy Press, 1981), ix.

73. Ruth G. Blumrosen, "Wage Discrimination, Job Segregation, and Title VII of the Civil Rights Act of 1964," *University of Michigan Journal of Law Reform* 12, no. 3 (Spring 1979): 399–502.

74. Treiman and Hartmann, *Women, Work and Wages*, x.

75. Ibid., 91.

76. Quoted in Hutner, *Equal Pay for Comparable Worth*, 83.

77. Janet A. Flammang, "The Implementation of Comparable Worth in San Jose," in Rita Mae Kelly and Jane Bayes, *Comparable Worth, Pay Equity, and Public Policy* (Westport, Connecticut: Greenwood Press, 1989), 160.

78. "Secretaries on Strike," *St. Paul Pioneer Press*, 30 June 1981, 1; Robert D. McFadden, "Yale Settles with Workers who Staged 10-Week Strike," *New York Times*, 20 January 1985, Y20.

79. *Pay Equity Newsnotes*, Summer 1987, 8.

80. Quoted in Linda M. Blum, "Possibilities and Limits of the Comparable Worth Movement," *Gender and Society* 1 (December 1987): 386.

81. Linda Erikson, personal interview with Sara Evans, Minneapolis, Minn., 28 July 1986; "County Pays Women Less, Study Indicates," *Minneapolis Star and Tribune*, 8 June 1983, 12B; Dennis Cassano, "Legislation Requested to Equalize Public Wages," *Minneapolis Star and Tribune*, 23 September 1983, 17A.

82. 452 U.S. 161 (1981).

83. Cook, *Comparable Worth: A Case Book*, 225.

84. 578 F Supp. 846 (W.D. Wash. 1983).

85. See Robert Livernash, ed., *Comparable Worth: Issues and Alternatives* (Washington, D.C.: Equal Employment Advisory Council, 1980). On presidential candidates see *New York Times*, 1 January 1984, section I, 1.

86. *New York Times*, 22 January 1984, section I, 1.

87. Julianne Malveaux, "Low Wage Black Women: Occupational Descriptions, Strategies for Change," paper prepared for the NAACP Legal Defense and Education Fund, January 1984. See also Judy Scales-Trent, "Comparable Worth: Is This a Theory for Black Workers?" *Women's Rights Law Reporter* 8 (Winter 1984): 51–58; Julianne Malveaux, "Comparable Worth and Its Impact on Black Women," *The Review of Black Political Economy* 14 (Fall-Winter, 1985–86):47–62; and National Committee on Pay Equity, *Pay Equity: An Issue of Race, Ethnicity, and Sex* (Washington, D.C.: National Committee on Pay Equity, 1987). Advocates associated with the National Committee on Pay Equity and the Center for Women in Government had

urged the application of comparable worth to wage discrimination based on race as well as sex since the late 1970s. See, for example, the testimony of Nancy D. Perlman and Ronnie Steinberg, Joint Hearings before the Subcommittees on Human Resources, Civil Service Compensation, and Employee Benefits of the Committee on Post Office and Civil Service, House of Representatives, *Pay Equity: Equal Pay for Work of Comparable Value—Part II,* Ninety-seventh Congress, Second Session, September 16, 21, 30, and December 2, 1982 (Washington, D.C.: Government Printing Office, 1982), 64–72, 539–60.

88. *New York Times,* 17 November 1984, 15. The impact of the gender gap on Republicans' reticence on comparable worth and equal employment opportunity issues was called to our attention by Ronnie J. Steinberg, who was interviewing key figures in the comparable worth controversy during that time.

89. *Wall Street Journal,* 12 April 1985, 60.

90. Ibid., 18 June 1985, 10.

## Chapter Three

1. Michael Evan Gold, *A Dialogue on Comparable Worth* (Ithaca, N.Y.: ILR Press, 1983), p. 8. Gold's book is set up as a conversation between advocates and critics of comparable worth.

2. Ibid., 9.

3. U.S. Bureau of the Census, Current Population Reports, Series P-60, No. 134, *Money Income and Poverty Status of Families and Persons in the United States: 1981* (Washington, D.C.: Government Printing Office, 1982), table 7; U.S. Bureau of the Census, Current Population Reports, Series P-60, No. 157, *Money Income and Poverty Status of Households, Families and Persons in the United States: 1986* (Washington, D.C.: Government Printing Office, 1987), table 7.

4. U.S. Department of Commerce, Bureau of the Census, "Male-Female Differences in Work Experience, Occupations, and Earnings: 1984," *Current Population Reports,* Household Economics Studies, Series P-70, No. 10, 1987.

5. Donald Treiman and Heidi Hartmann, eds., *Women, Work, and Wages: Equal Pay for Jobs of Equal Value* (Washington, D.C.: National Academy Press, 1981), 13–14.

6. United States General Accounting Office, "Options for Conducting a Pay Equity Study of Federal Pay and Classification Systems" (Washington, D.C.: Government Printing Office, March 1, 1985), 1.

7. Richard B. Freemen, "How Do Public Sector Wages and Employment Respond to Economic Conditions?" in *Public Sector Payrolls,* David A. Wise, ed. (Chicago: University of Chicago Press, 1987), 183–207.

8. U.S. Department of Commerce, Bureau of the Census, *1988 Statistical Abstract of the United States* (Washington, D.C.: Government Printing Office, 1988), Table No. 634. Current Population Reports, Consumer Income, Series P-60, No. 151, Issued April 1986, "Money Incomes of Households, Families and Persons in the United States: 1984" (U.S. Department of Commerce, Bureau of the Census), table 35. "Type of Income of Specified Type in 1984—Persons 15 Years and Over by Race, Spanish Origin, and Sex," 136. Because people of Spanish origin can be of any race, it is not

appropriate to add the percentage of Hispanic and Black transfer recipients to get a percentage of minority transfer recipients. Such addition would involve some double counting.

9. Peter T. Kilborn, "U.S. Whites 10 Times Wealthier than Blacks, Census Study Finds," *New York Times,* 19 July 1986, 1, 26; "Wealth, in Black and White," *New York Times,* 24 July 1986.

10. Bonnie Thornton Dill, Lynn Weber Cannon, and Reeve Vanneman, "Race and Gender in Occupational Segregation," in *Pay Equity: An Issue of Race, Ethnicity and Sex,* ed. National Committee on Pay Equity (Washington, D.C., February 1987), 20–21.

11. James N. Baron and William T. Bielby, "Organizational Barriers to Gender Equality: Sex Segregation of Jobs and Opportunities," in *Gender and the Life Course,* ed. Alice S. Rossi (New York: Aldine, 1985), 236, emphasis added.

12. Dixie Sommers, "Occupational Rankings for Men and Women by Earnings," *Monthly Labor Review* 97 (August 1974): 34–51, in Treiman and Hartmann, *Women, Work, and Wages,* 28.

13. Catherine White Berheide, Cynthia H. Chertos, and Ronnie Steinberg, "Pay Equity for Blacks and Hispanics in New York State Government Employment," in *Pay Equity: An Issue of Race, Ethnicity and Sex,* ed. National Committee on Pay Equity (Washington, D.C., February 1987), 99.

14. Barbara J. Nelson, "Women's Poverty and Women's Citizenship: Some Political Consequences of Economic Marginality," *Signs* 10 (Winter 1984): 230; Robert N. Bellah et al., *Habits of the Heart: Individualism and Commitment in American Life* (Berkeley: University of California Press, 1985), 142–63.

15. R. H. Tawney, *Religion and the Rise of Capitalism* (New York: Harcourt, Brace, 1926).

16. Jean Bethke Elshtain, *Public Man, Private Women: Women in Social and Political Thought* (Princeton, N.J.: Princeton University Press, 1981), 100–146; Lorenne M. G. Clark, "Women and Locke: Who Owns the Apples in the Garden of Eden?" in *The Sexism of Social and Political Theory: Women and Preproduction from Plato to Nietzsche,* ed. Lorenne M. G. Clark and Lynda Lange (Toronto: University of Toronto Press, 1979), 16–40.

17. Guido Calabresi and Philip Bobbitt, *Tragic Choices: The Conflicts Society Confronts in the Allocation of Tragically Scarce Resources* (New York: Norton, 1978), 17–24.

18. Gary Becker, *The Economics of Discrimination* (Chicago: University of Chicago Press, 1957), 31–37.

19. Henry J. Aaron and Cameron M. Lougy, *The Comparable Worth Controversy* (Washington, D.C.: The Brookings Institution, 1986), 19. Aaron and Lougy offer an excellent summary of the economic points at issue between pro- and anti-comparable-worth adherents.

20. Becker, *Economics of Discrimination,* 31–37.

21. Mark Aldrich and Robert Buchele, *The Economics of Comparable Worth* (Cambridge, Mass.: Ballinger, 1986), 79.

22. Ibid., 81.

23. Barbara Bergmann, "The Effect on White Incomes of Discrimination in Employment," *Journal of Political Economy* 79 (March/April 1971): 294–313, in Aldrich

and Buchele, *Economics of Comparable Worth,* 81–82; see also Gary Becker, "Human Capital, Effort and the Sexual Devision of Labor," *Journal of Labor Economics* 3 (January 1985): 33–58.

24. Mary Corcoran and Gregory J. Duncan, "Work History, Labor Force Attachment, and Earnings Differentials Between Races and Sexes," *Journal of Human Resources* 14 (Winter 1979): 3–20, in Treiman and Hartmann, *Women, Work, and Wages,* 22.

25. Solomon William Polachek, "Women in the Economy: Perspectives on Gender Inequality," in U.S. Civil Rights Commission, *Comparable Worth: Issue for the 80's,* vol. 1: 34–53.

26. Paula England, "Socioeconomic Explanations of Job Segregation," in *Comparable Worth and Wage Discrimination,* ed. Helen Remick (Philadelphia: Temple University Press, 1984), 33–35. Mary Corcoran, Greg J. Duncan, and Michael Ponza, "Work Experience, Job Segregation, and Wages," in *Sex Segregation in the Workplace: Trends, Explanations, Remedies,* ed. Barbara F. Raskin (Washington, D.C.: National Academy Press, 1984), 171–91.

27. Gold, *A Dialogue on Comparable Worth,* 7–14.

28. David Gordon, Richard Edwards, and Michael Reich, *Segmented Work Divided Workers: The Historical Transformation of Labor in the United States* (Cambridge University Press, 1982).

29. "Electrical Manufacturing," Hearings on the Codes of Fair Competition held under the National Industrial Recovery Act, Transcript No. 159, 19 July 1933, 100, 109, in Ruth Milkman, "Female Factory Labor and Industrial Structure: Control and Conflict over 'Woman's Place' in Auto and Electrical Manufacturing," *Politics and Society* 12 (1983): 168.

30. Jacqueline Jones, *Labor of Love, Labor of Sorrow: Black Women, Work, and the Family from Slavery to the Present* (New York: Basic Books, 1985); Cindy Sondik Aron, *Ladies and Gentlemen of the Civil Service: Middle Class Workers in Victorian America* (New York: Oxford University Press, 1987); Nannie May Tilley, *The Bright Tobacco Industry, 1860–1929* (Chapel Hill: University of North Carolina Press, 1948); John G. Richardson and Brenda Wooden Hatcher, "The Feminization of Public School Teaching: 1870–1920," *Work and Occupations* 10 (February 1983): 81–99; William David Michel, "The Development of Gender-Segregation in the Labor Force and Its Relation to Wage Rates: A Historical Study," M.A. paper, Hubert H. Humphrey Institute of Public Affairs, University of Minnesota, July 1986; and Sam Cohn, *The Process of Occupational Sex-Typing: The Feminization of Clerical Labor in Great Britain* (Philadelphia: Temple University Press, 1985).

31. Aaron and Lougy, *Comparable Worth Controversy,* 20.

32. England, "Job Segregation," in Remick, *Comparable Worth,* 36–38.

33. Milkman, *Politics and Society,* 162; Gordon, Edwards, and Reich, *Segmented Work, Divided Workers;* Richard Edwards, *Contested Terrain: The Transformation of the Workplace in the Twentieth Century* (New York: Basic Books, 1979). Milkman has argued that segmented labor market theories do not go far enough in elaborating the differences between all women and other marginal workers. She argues, quite correctly, that "the critical link between the family and women's paid work—ultimately the unique feature of women's relationship to the market—is simply absent" (162). See chapter 1 for a more complete analysis of this topic.

34. Treiman and Hartmann, *Women, Wages, and Work,* 40.

35. Peter B. Doeringer and Michael Piore, *Internal Labor Markets and Manpower Analysis* (Lexington, Mass.: Heath Lexington Books, 1971), 1–2.

36. England, "Job Segregation," in Remick, *Comparable Worth,* 39–40.

37. Treiman and Hartmann, *Women, Wages, and Work,* 33.

38. Ibid.

39. Aldrich and Buchele, *Economics of Comparable Worth,* 90.

40. O'Neill, "An Argument Against Comparable Worth," in U.S. Civil Rights Commission, 183. O'Neill did not include years of work experience or job tenure in her equations, as information on these variables was not available.

41. Of course there is a third hypothesis, which states that capital would be substituted for labor in the long run if comparable worth were implemented. See R. G. Gregory and R. C. Duncan, "Segmented Labor Market Theories and the Australian Experience of Equal Pay for Women," *Journal of Post Keynesian Economics* 3 (Spring 1981): 403–28.

42. Ibid., 425. Other economists reinterpret the results of Gregory and Duncan more gloomily, especially Aldrich and Buchele, who state that the unemployment rate for Australian women increased after 1971 by 0.4 points, representing an increase of 15%. (Aldrich and Buchele, *Economics of Comparable Worth,* 160.) Australian feminists are not fully satisfied with the national wage rate approach to solving the pay gap, wanting some sort of job evaluation as well. See Clare Burton, Raven Hag and Gay Thompson, *Women's Worth: Pay Equity and Job Evaluation in Australia* (Canberra, Australia: Australian Government Publishing Service, 1987).

43. Robert G. Ehrenberg and Robert S. Smith, "Comparable Worth in the Public Sector," NBER Working Paper No. 1471, 35.

44. Barbara R. Bergmann, *The Economic Emergence of Women* (New York: Basic Books, 1986), 190–91.

45. Donald Treiman writes that almost all job classification systems use some version of skill, effort, responsibility, and working conditions as the basis of compensable factors. The terms derive from the early National Electrical Manufacturers Association job evaluation plan and were adopted in the Equal Pay Act. Donald Treiman, *Job Evaluation: An Analytic Review,* Interim Report to the Equal Employment Opportunity Commission (Washington, D.C.: National Academy of Sciences, 1979), 32.

46. Herbert R. Northrup, "Comparable Worth and Realistic Wage Setting," in U.S. Civil Rights Commission, *Comparable Worth: Issue for the 80's,* 94.

47. Herbert Northrup, "Wage Setting and Collective Bargaining" in *Comparable Worth: Issues and Alternatives,* ed. Robert Livernash (Washington, D.C.: Equal Employment Advisory council, 1980), 107–36; and Donald P. Schwab, "Using Job Evaluation to Obtain Pay Equity," in U.S. Civil Rights Commission, *Comparable Worth: Issue for the 80's,* 83–92.

48. Barbara J. Nelson, "Comparable Worth: A Brief Review of History, Practice and Theory," *Minnesota Law Review* 69 (May 1985): 1209; Donald P. Schwab, "Job Evaluation and Pay Setting: Concepts and Practices," in Livernash, *Comparable Worth,* 77.

49. Nelson, "Comparable Worth," 1204; Gold, *Comparable Worth,* 50; and Treiman and Hartmann, *Women, Wages, and Work,* 117.

50. Ronnie J. Steinberg, "Identifying Wage Discrimination and Implementing Pay

Equity Adjustments," in U.S. Civil Rights Commission, *Comparable Worth: Issue for the 80's*, 99–116.

51. Richard W. Beatty and James R. Beatty, "Some Problems with Contemporary Job Evaluation Systems," in Remick, *Comparable Worth*, 59–78; Barbara Beno, "Comparable Worth: Re-Evaluating Our Mothers' Wage Scales," paper presented to Department of Sociology/Anthropology Faculty Seminar, Hofstra University, 27 November 1985.

52. David L. Kirp, Mark G. Yudof, and Marlene Strong Franks, *Gender Justice* (Chicago: University of Chicago Press, 1986), 169.

53. Ray Marshall and Beth Paulin, "The Employment and Earnings of Women: The Comparable Worth Debate," paper prepared for the U.S. Commission on Civil Rights, June 7, 1984, quoted in Elaine Johansen, *Comparable Worth: The Myth and the Movement* (Denver: Westview, 1984), 127.

54. Aaron and Lougy, *The Comparable Worth Controversy*, 29–36; Aldrich and Buchele, *Economics of Comparable Worth*, 113–29. Aaron and Lougy, cautious supporters of comparable worth, suggest that because different functional forms of the regression line show different specific relationships between equally valued occupations, comparable worth offers thorny problems of equity in implementation. But this problem is no different than noting that different job evaluation systems emphasize different job traits. The choice of form of regression equation is like the choice of job evaluation systems, something that management will want to keep control over and workers will want to bargain about. For a parallel discussion regarding air pollution, see Bruce Bender et al., "Choice of Functional Form and the Demand for Air Quality," *Review of Economic Statistics* 62 (November 1980): 38–43.

55. Michael Levin, "Comparable Worth: The Feminist Road to Socialism," *Commentary*, September 1984, 13–19; Jeremy Rabkin, "Comparable Worth as Civil Rights Policy: Potentials for Disaster," in U.S. Civil Rights Commission, *Comparable Worth: Issue for the 80's*, 187–95.

56. O'Neill in U.S. Civil Rights Commission, *Comparable Worth: Issue for the 80's*, 177–8.

57. Karl Pribram, *A History of Economic Reasoning* (Baltimore: The Johns Hopkins University Press, 1983), 14–15, our emphasis.

58. Saint Thomas Aquinas, *Summa Theologica*, in *Not in God's Image*, ed. Julia O'Faolin and Laura Martines (New York: Harper Touchstone, 1973), 131–32.

59. Alice Kessler-Harris, *Feminist Studies*, 5 (forthcoming, Winter 1989).

60. In Illinois, see Mark A. Emmert, "Public Opinion of Comparable Worth: Some Preliminary Findings," paper presented at the American Political Science Association meetings, September 1984, Washington, D.C. In Minnesota, see chapter 5 of this book. For U.S. data on employed persons, see the National Committee on Pay Equity, "NCPE Poll," *Pay Equity Newsnotes*(May 1985), 1; additional information provided from the Survey Codebook, made available by NCPE.

61. Karl Marx, *Capital* (New York: International Publishers, 1967), v.1. Karl Marx *Capital* (New York: International Publishers, 1967), v.3. Geoff Hodgson, *Capitalism, Value, and Exploitation: A Radical Theory* (Oxford: Martin Robertson, 1982), 55–71; Jon Elster, *Making Sense of Marx* (Cambridge: Cambridge University Press, 1985), 127–42.

62. Heidi I. Hartmann, "The Political Economy of Comparable Worth," paper de-

livered at the Conference on Alternative Approaches to Labor Markets, University of Utah, Salt Lake City, 12–13 October 1985; Heidi I. Hartmann, "Pay Equity for Women: Wage Discrimination and the Comparable Worth Controversy," paper delivered at the Conference on the Moral Foundations of Civil Rights Policy, University of Maryland, College Park, 18–20 October 1984; Joy Ann Grune, "Pay Equity Is a Necessary Remedy for Wage Discrimination," in U.S. Civil Rights Commission, *Comparable Worth: Issue for the 80's*, 165–73. A note on terminology regarding "work" and "labor" is useful. The conventional use of the word "work" means paid work. In this book we distinguish between three types of labor: productive activity for household use or exchange, performed in the market or at home (work); domestic labor (housework); and reproductive labor (the bearing and raising of children). See Barbara J. Nelson, "Family Politics and Policy in the United States and Western Europe," *Comparative Politics* 17 (April 1985): 351–71.

63. For a discussion of the role of choice as part of the ideological structure of families, see Rayna Rapp, Ellen Ross, and Renate Bridenthal, "Examining Family History," *Feminist Studies* 5 (Spring 1979): 174–200.

64. Mark Sproule-Jones, "Methodological Individuals," *American Behavioral Scientist* 28 (November/December 1984): 167–83.

65. Richard Sennett, *Families Against the City: Middle Class Homes of Industrial Chicago, 1872–1890*, (New York: Vintage, 1970), 120–49.

66. Polachek, "Women in the Economy," 49, but see England, "Job Segregation."

67. Nancy Barrett, "Poverty, Welfare, and Comparable Worth," in Phyllis Schlafly, ed., *Equal Pay for UNequal Work: A Conference on Comparable Worth* (Washington, D.C.: Eagle Forum Education and Legal Defense Fund, 1984), 25–32.

68. *EEOC v. Sears*, 504 F. Supp. 241 (N.D. Ill. 1980).

69. "Offer of Proof Concerning the Testimony of Dr. Rosalind Rosenberg," Defendant's Exhibit 3, Rosenberg version with notes, *EEOC v. Sears*, Civil Action No. 79-C-4373, U.S. District Court for the Northern District of Illinois, Eastern Division, par. 24; and "Written Testimony of Alice Kessler-Harris" (June 1985), *EEOC v. Sears*, pars. 2, 6, 13 in Ruth Milkman, "Women's History and The Sears Case," *Feminist Studies* 12 (Summer 1986): 376.

70. George Gilder, "The Relationship of Women to Wealth and Poverty," in Schlafly, ed., 1984, 91; Phyllis Schlafly, "Testimony on the Comparable Worth Bill," Testimony to the Compensation and Employee Benefit Subcommittee of the House Post Office and Civil Service Committee, 4 April 1984, in *The Phyllis Schlafly Report*, 18 (August 1984); and Allan C. Carlson, "Toward 'The Working Family': The Hidden Agenda Behind the Comparable Worth Debate," *Persuasion at Work* 7 (July 1984): 1–7.

71. Lester C. Thurow, *The Zero-Sum Society* (New York: Basic Books, 1980), 155–58.

72. See Linda Gordon, *Heroes of Their Own Lives: The Politics and History of Family Violence, Boston, 1880–1960* (New York: Viking Press, 1988); Nelson, "Family Politics and Policy in the United States and Western Europe"; George Gilder, *Wealth and Poverty* (New York: Basic Books, 1981).

73. Kristin Luker, *Abortion and the Politics of Motherhood* (Berkeley: University of California Press, 1984); Jane DeHart-Mathews and Donald Mathews, "The Cultural Politics of the ERA's Defeat," in *Rights of Passage: The Past and Future of the ERA*,

ed. Joan Hoff-Wilson (Bloomington: Indiana University Press, 1986), 44–53; Jane J. Mansbridge, *Why We Lost the ERA* (Chicago: University of Chicago Press, 1986). Mansridge shows that much of the anti-ERA organizing was carefully organized, as were the pro-ERA efforts.

74. Brigitte Berger, "Comparable Worth at Odds with American Realities," in U.S. Civil Rights Commission, *Comparable Worth: Issue for the 80's*, 65–71; and Aldrich and Buchele, *Economics of Comparable Worth*, 58–60.

75. *Christiansen v. Iowa*, 563 F. 2d., 353, 356 (8th Cir. 1977).

76. Jonathan H. Turner, "Theoretical Strategies for Linking Micro and Macro Processes: An Evaluation of Seven Approaches," *Western Sociological Review* 14 (1981): 4–15; Gregory McLennan, "E. P. Thompson and the Discipline of Historical Context," in *Making Histories*, ed. R. Johnson et al. (Minneapolis: University of Minnesota Press, 1982), 96–130; Ronnie Steinberg, " 'A Want of Harmony': Perspectives on Wage Discrimination and Comparable Worth," in Remick, *Comparable Worth*, 3–27; Sharon Toffey Shepla and Ann T. Viviano, "Some Psychological Factors Affecting Job Segregation and Wages," in Remick, *Comparable Worth*, 47–58.

77. Nancy F. Cott, *The Grounding of Modern Feminism* (New Haven: Yale University Press, 1987), 29.

78. Brigitte Berger, an opponent of comparable worth, represented the view that comparable worth will impose a national wage-setting bureaucracy when she wrote, "In spite of assurances to the contrary, a central system of government dictated wages appears to be the inescapable long range consequence of the currently advocated step process." Brigitte Berger, "Comparable Worth at Odds with American Realities," in U.S. Civil Rights Commission, *Comparable Worth: Issue for the 80's*, 70.

79. Jeremy Rabkin, "Comparable Worth as Civil Rights Policy: Potentials for Disaster," in U.S. Civil Rights Commission, *Comparable Worth: Issue for the 80's*, 187–95.

80. On the court and comparable worth, see Paul Weiler, "The Wages of Sex: The Uses and Limits of Comparable Worth," *Harvard Law Review* 99 (June 1986): 1728–1807.

81. Rosalyn B. Will and Steven D. Lydenberg, "20 Corporations that Listen to Women" *Ms* (November 1987), 45–52.

82. Suzanne Donovan, "Comparable Worth Discrimination in the Private Sector: Can It Be Measured?" paper delivered at the Association of Public Policy and Management meetings, Austin, Texas, October 1986.

### Chapter Four

1. Nina Rothchild, Duluth Women's Commission. Duluth, Minn., 22 October 1984.

2. Meeting of Senator Linda Berglin with the Association of Minnesota Counties. St. Paul, Minn., 15 February 1984.

3. Sidney Verba, "Some Dilemmas in Comparative Research," *World Politics* 20 (October 1976): 113, our emphasis.

4. Alexander L. George, "Case Studies and Theory Development: The Method of Structured, Focused Comparison," in Paul G. Lauren, ed., *Diplomacy: New Approaches in History, Theory, and Policy* (New York: The Free Press, 1979), 43–68;

Natalie Z. Davis, "Gender and Genre: Women as Historical Writers, 1400–1820," in *Beyond Their Sex: Learned Women of the European Past*, ed. Patricia H. Labalme (New York: New York University Press, 1980); Theda Skocpol and Margaret Somers, "The Users of Comparative History in Macrosocial Inquiry," *Comparative Studies in Society and History* 22 (1980): 174–97; Bonnie G. Smith, "The Contribution of Women to Modern Historiography in Great Britain, France, and the United States," *American Historical Review* 89 (1984): 709–32; Thomas J. Kaplan, "The Narrative Structure of Policy Analysis," *Journal of Policy Analysis and Management* 5 (1986): 761–78.

5. Some states, regardless of their current activity on comparable worth, have equal pay and fair employment practices laws that specify equal pay for something different, and arguably more, than equal work. For example Idaho, Kentucky, Maine, and Oklahoma have equal pay statutes passed between 1954 (Maine) and 1969 (Idaho) requiring equal pay for "'comparable work on jobs that have comparable requirements relating to skill, effort and responsibility.'" Advocates argue that laws like these permit comparable worth activities without necessitating new legislation, but that has not been the interpretation of most states with similar laws. See Virginia Dean, Patti Roberts, and Carroll Boone, "Comparable Worth Under Various Federal and State Laws," in *Comparable Worth and Wage Discrimination*, ed. Helen Remick (Philadelphia: Temple University Press, 1984), 243, from note 8, table 14–1, "Selected Characteristics of State Equal Pay Laws." Oklahoma relied on its 1963 equal pay statute, and in 1981 the state legislature appropriated funds to convert the state personnel system to a point-factor system. Mary Woods, National Committee on Pay Equity, telephone interview with Nancy Johnson, 15 March 1988.

6. We are indebted to Lisa Hubbard of the National Committee on Pay Equity for sharing with us their preliminary analysis of the methods by which comparable worth was achieved in the early-acting states. These categories—legislation, negotiation, and litigation—do not capture the full range of activities undertaken in each state, and belie the complexity of the political activity in each location, where activists may have begun with one form of activity but ultimately used another. Telephone interview with Lisa Hubbard, National Committee on Pay Equity, by Barbara Nelson, 13 July 1988.

7. Daniel Elazar, *American Federalism: A View from the States*, 2d ed. (New York: Harper and Row, 1972).

8. Political dominance of a state was calculated by the authors by the following process. For each biennium between January 1981 and January 1987 one point was given for Democratic control of the House of Representatives, Senate, or governorship. Scores ranged from zero for total Republican control of each "actor" to twelve for total Democratic control. Those states that had a majority of Democratic actors over the period were coded as Democratic. See Appendix B for details.

9. L. Harmon Zeigler, "Interest Groups in the States," in *Politics in the American States*, eds. Virginia Gray et al. (Boston: Little, Brown, 1983), 97–131.

10. Ronnie J. Steinberg, "The Unsubtle Revolution: Women, the State, and Equal Employment," in Steinberg, *Comparable Worth: A View from the States* (Philadelphia: Temple University Press, forthcoming 1988); and Ronnie J. Steinberg, "Identifying Wage Discrimination and Implementing Pay Equity Adjustments," in U.S. Civil Rights Commission, *Comparable Worth: Issue for the 80's: A Consultation of the U.S.*

*Commission on Civil Rights. June 6–7, 1984*, vol. I (Washington, D.C.: Government Printing Office, 1984), 99–116.

11. U.S. General Accounting Office, *Pay Equity: Status of State Activities* (Washington, D.C.: U.S. General Accounting Office, 1986).

12. The first discussion of comparable worth functioning like a solidarity wage is found in Sara M. Evans and Barbara J. Nelson, "Comparable Worth for Public Employees. Implementing a New Wage Policy in Minnesota," in *Comparable Worth, Pay Equity and Public Policy*, ed. Rita Mae Kelly and Jane Bayes (Westport, Conn.: Greenwood Press, 1988). Mary Ruggie, *The State and Working Women: A Comparative Study of Britain and Sweden* (Princeton, N.J.: Princeton University Press, 1984).

13. Private correspondence, Ronnie Steinberg to the authors, 10 May 1988.

14. Joanne Swartzberg, "Wisconsin—A Case Study of Comparable Worth," unpublished paper, Hubert H. Humphrey Institute, University of Minnesota, March 1986.

15. U.S. General Accounting Office Briefing Report to Congressional Requesters, "Pay Equity: Status of State Activities," GAO/GGD-86–141BR, September 1986.

16. Joan Acker, "Comparable Worth: The Oregon Case," in Ronnie J. Steinberg, ed., *Comparable Worth: A View From the States* (Philadelphia: Temple University Press, forthcoming 1988).

17. Hugh Winebrenner, "The Implementation of Comparable Worth in Iowa," *Policy Studies Review* 5 (May 1986): 863–70.

18. Acker, "Comparable Worth: The Oregon Case."

19. Daniel J. Elazar, *Cities of the Prairie* (New York: Basic Books, 1970), quoted in Citizens League, *Understanding the Quality of Public Life* (Minneapolis: Citizens League, n.d.), 23.

20. Millard L. Gieske, "Minnesota in Midpassage: A Century of Transition in Political Culture," in *Perspectives on Minnesota Government and Politics*, ed. Millard L. Gieske (Minneapolis: Burgess Publishing, 1984), 1–34.

21. The recent strike of meat processors ("P-9") was more conflictual than most of the recent strikes in Minnesota.

22. "State-Job Sex Bias Suspected," *Minneapolis Star*, 15 October 1974, 7c.

23. "State Panel on Women's Pay is Backed," *Minneapolis Tribune*, 11 February 1976, 6B.

24. "Study: Women Suffer Job Bias," *Minneapolis Tribune*, 8 November 1976, 1B.

25. Council on the Economic Status of Women, *Pay Equity and Public Employment* (St. Paul, Minn.: Council on the Economic Status of Women, March 1982), 10–11.

26. See *Minneapolis Tribune*, 9 November 1981.

27. The Council used the common research convention defining male jobs as having at least 80% male incumbents and female jobs as having at least 70% female incumbents. Aldrich and Buchele explain the methodology in this way: "In 1980 civilian nonagricultural employment was 43.2 percent female. An occupation in which women were represented in proportion to their numbers in total employment would therefore employ 432 women for every 1,000 employees or 432 women for every 568 men. If women are *overrepresented* by a factor of three [the common definition of overrepresentation], there would be 3 X 432 = 1,296 women for every 568 men—that is, the occupation would be 1,296/(1,296 + 568) = 70 percent female. Likewise, an occupation in which men were overrepresented by a factor of three would contain 3 X 568

= 1,704 men for every 432 women—that is, it would be 1,704/(1,704 + 432) = 80 percent male." Mark Aldrich and Robert Buchele, *The Economics of Comparable Worth* (Cambridge, Mass.: Ballinger, 1986), 130, n. 3.

28. Council on the Economic Status of Women, 1982, 28–32.

29. Rick Scott, comments as a panelist at the conference "New Directions in Comparable Worth: Minnesota and the Nation," Minneapolis, Minn., 19 October 1985.

30. "Quie Vetoes Bill Establishing 'Job Creation Conference,'" *Minneapolis Star and Tribune*, 24 March 1982, 6B.

31. Minnesota Statutes Annotated, Section 43A.01, Subdivision 3 (West 1988).

32. The authors are indebted to labor historian James Bialke for this information.

33. Minnesota Statutes Annotated, Section 43A.01, Subdivision 3 (West 1988), our emphasis.

34. For a discussion of the interest of the National Organization for Women in comparable worth during this period, see Jane Mansbridge, *Why We Lost the ERA* (Chicago: University of Chicago Press, 1986).

35. "Women at Work," *Business Week* 28 January 1985, 83.

36. James A. Emery, "An Examination of the Proposed Twentieth Amendment to the Constitution of the United States" (New York: National Association of Manufacturers of the U.S., August 1924).

37. In an important set of constitutional compromises, the Ninth and Tenth Amendments present a somewhat more richly elaborated relationship between the federal government, the states, and the people. Amendment IX reads "The enumeration in the Constitution, of certain rights, shall not be construed to deny or disparage others retained by the people." Amendment X reads "The powers not delegated to the United States by the Constitution, nor prohibited by it to the States, are reserved to the States respectively, or to the people."

38. C. Dallas Sands and Michael E. Libonati, *Local Government Law*, vol. 1 (Wilmette, Ill.: Callaghan, 1981), 1–4.

39. Ibid., 4–2. See also 1 Dillon, *Municipal Corporations* (5th ed., 1911), Sec. 237 at 450.

40. Sands and Libonati, *Local Government Law*, 4–14 and 4–15. See for Minnesota case law *Monaghan v. Armatage*, 218 Minn. 108, 15 NW2d 241; *Guaranteed Concrete Co. v. Garrick Bros.*, 185 Minn. 454, 241 NW588.

41. Sands and Libonati, *Local Government Law*, 4–5. See also California constitution, 1979, Art. XI, Sec. 8j.

42. Sands and Libonati, *Local Government Law*, 4–6 and 4–7. See also New York Constitution, Art. IX, Sec. 2(c).

43. Minnesota Constitution, Art. 12, Sec. 3,4; in Minnesota Statutes 1984, vol. 1, chap. 1–5.6, p. lxxxi.

44. Linda Berglin, personal interview with Sara Evans and Barbara Nelson, St. Paul, Minn., 3 February 1987.

45. "County Pays Women Less, Study Indicates,"*Minneapolis Star and Tribune*, 8 June 1983, 12B; Dennis Cassano, "Legislation Requested to Equalize Public Wages," *Minneapolis Star and Tribune*, 23 September 1983, 17A.

46. 578 F. Supp. 846 (W. D. Wash.).

47. "State Shrinks the Pay Gap," editorial in the *St. Paul Dispatch*, 27 July 1983, 6A.

48. "Squabble in the Sisterhood," *Minneapolis Star and Tribune*, 20 March 1983, 2C.

49. See *Minneapolis Star and Tribune*, 22 February 1984.

50. *Journal of the [Minnesota] House*, 24 April 1984, 9750; *Journal of the [Minnesota] Senate*, 20 April 1984, 6875.

51. Minnesota Statutes Annotated, Section 471.993, Subdivision 2 (West, 1986).

52. Ibid.

## Chapter Five

1. Robert Whereath, "Study Says State Women Live Longer, Know More, Earn Less," *Minneapolis Star and Tribune*, 26 September 1984, 3B.

2. Daniel A. Mazmanian and Paul A. Sabatier, *Implementation and Public Policy* (Glenview, Ill.: Scott, Foresman, 1983), 1–48.

3. Eugene Bardach, *The Implementation Game: What Happens After a Bill Becomes a Law* (Cambridge, Mass.: MIT Press, 1977), 66–84.

4. Nina Rothchild, Address to the Association of Minnesota Counties, St. Paul, 22 January 1985.

5. Randall B. Ripley and Grace A. Franklin, *Policy Implementation and Bureaucracy*, 2d ed. (Chicago: Dorsey Press, 1986), 95–101. For a discussion of policy types in political analysis, see also Raymond A. Bauer, Ithiel de Sola Pool, and Lewis Anthony Dexter, *American Business and Public Policy: The Politics of Foreign Trade* (New York: Atherton, 1963); Theodore J. Lowi, "American Business, Public Policy, Case Studies, and Political Theory," *World Politics* 16 (1964): 677–715; Theodore J. Lowi, *The End of Liberalism: Ideology, Policy, and the Crisis of Public Authority* (New York: Norton, 1969); Lewis A. Froman, Jr., "The Categorization of Policy Contents," in Austin Ranney, ed., *Political Science and Public Policy* (Chicago: Markham, 1968), 41–52; E. E. Schattschneider, *Politics, Pressures, and the Tariff* (New York: Prentice-Hall, 1935); E. E. Schattschneider, *The Semi-Sovereign People* (New York: Holt, Rinehart and Winston, 1960); Robert H. Salisbury, "An Exchange Theory of Interest Groups," *Midwest Journal of Political Science* 8 (1969): 1–32; and Robert H. Salisbury and John P. Heinz, "A Theory of Policy Analysis and Some Preliminary Applications," in Ira Sharkansky, ed., *Policy Analysis in Political Science* (Chicago: Markham, 1970), 39–60.

6. Ripley and Franklin, *Policy Implementation*, 115.

7. Redistributive policies, as their name suggests, rearrange the current distribution of existing resources, without adding additional resources.

8. B. H. V. Schneider, "Public Sector Labor Legislation—An Evolutionary Analysis," in *Public-Sector Bargaining*, ed. Benjamin Aaron, Joseph R. Grodin, and James L. Sterns (Washington D.C.: Bureau of National Affairs, 1979), 191–223 in David Lewin, "Public Employee Unionism in the 1980s: An Analysis of Transformation," in *Unions in Transition: Entering the Second Century*, ed. Seymour Martin Lipset (San Francisco: Institute for Contemporary Studies, 1986), 248–49.

9. Frank H. Cassell and Jean J. Baron, *Collective Bargaining in the Public Sector: Cases in Public Policy* (Columbus, Ohio: GRID, 1975), 6–7.

10. U.S. Bureau of the Census, *1982 Census of Governments, Volume 3, Public Employment, Number 2, Compendium of Public Employment* (Washington, D.C.:

Government Printing Office, 1984); Leo Troy and Neil Sheflin, *Union Sourcebook: Membership, Structure, Finance, Directory*, 1st ed. (West Orange, N.J.: Industrial Relations Data Information Service, 1985), in Lewin, "Public Employee Unionism," 243.

11. Harold W. Davey et al., *Contemporary collective Bargaining*, 4th ed. (Englewood Cliffs, N.J.: Prentice-Hall, 1982), 372, from table 15–1, "Public Union Growth, 1956–78."

12. Davey, *Contemporary Collective Bargaining*, 373–74.

13. Lewin, "Public Employee Unionism," 243.

14. Ibid; Richard Edwards, "Unions in Crisis and Beyond: Introduction," in *Unions in Crisis and Beyond: Perspectives from Six Countries*, ed. Richard Edwards et al. (Dover, Mass., and London: Auburn House, 1986), 1–13, esp. 2–3.

15. Council on the Economic Status of Women, *Pay Equity and Public Employment* (St. Paul: Council on the Economic Status of Women, March 1982), 14–15. Figures are derived from recalculations of information found in the table "State Employee Bargaining Units, October 1981." The work force represented in this table "includes full-time unlimited employees in the executive branch except the University of Minnesota, state university instructors and administrators, community college instructors, and state employees excluded from collective bargaining" (15).

16. Laura L. Vertz, "Pay Inequalities Between Men and Women in State and Local Government: An Examination of the Political Context of the Comparable Worth Controversy," *Women & Politics* 7 (Summer 1987): 43–57.

17. Inflation is measured by annual percent changes in the Consumer Price Index. U.S. Department of Commerce, *Statistical Abstract of the United States, 1987* (Washington: D.C.: Government Printing Office, 1986), 463, table 755. The average wage data were supplied by the Minnesota Department of Employee Relations from their records.

18. Commission on the Economic Status of Women, *Pay Equity: A Minnesota Experience*, (St. Paul: Commission on the Economic Status of Women, 1985), 14–15.

19. In 1980, the Census Bureau stopped distinguishing between farm and nonfarm families in their calculations of the poverty lines.

20. Mollie Orshansky, "Counting the Poor: Another Look at the Poverty Profile," in *Poverty in America: A Book of Readings*, ed. Louis A. Ferman et al. 2d ed. (Ann Arbor: University of Michigan Press, 1976), 67–115, quote from page 71; Martin Rein, "Problems in the Definition and Measurement of Poverty," in ibid., 116–31.

21. AFSCME Council 6, News Release, 25 July 1983.

22. Peter Benner, personal interview with Barbara Nelson, St. Paul, Minn., 11 July 1987; and Lance Teachworth, telephone interview with Barbara Nelson, St. Paul, Minn., 22 July 1987.

23. Minnesota Statutes Annotated, Section 43A.01 (West, 1984).

24. Mike Haney, telephone interview with Barbara Nelson, St. Paul, Minn., 24 July 1987.

25. Letter from C. T. to Nina Rothchild, 27 October 1983 (Department of Employee Relations Files, St. Paul, Minn.).

26. Letter from Nina Rothchild to C. T., 19 December 1983 (Department of Employee Relations Files, St. Paul, Minn.).

27. Geraldine Wedel, telephone interview with Barbara Nelson, St. Paul, Minn., 24 July 1987.

28. Lance Teachworth, telephone interview with Barbara Nelson, St. Paul, Minn., 22 July 1987.

29. A more extensive version of this analysis is available in Sara M. Evans and Barbara J. Nelson, "The Impact of Pay Equity on Public Employees: State of Minnesota Employee Attitudes Toward Wage Policy Innovation," Report to the Panel on Pay Equity Research, National Research Council, National Academy of Sciences, 15 November 1987.

30. For a more detailed analysis of employee responses to pay equity see ibid.

31. Michael Evan Gold, *Dialogue on Comparable Worth* (Ithaca, N.Y.: ILR Press, 1983) Joy Anne Grune, "Pay Equity Is a Necessary Remedy for Wage Discrimination," in U.S. Civil Rights Commission, *Comparable Worth: Issue for the 80's,* (Washington, D.C.: Government Printing Office, 1984), 165–75.

32. Geoffrey Cowley, "Comparable Worth: Another Terrible Idea," *Washington Monthly* 15 (November 1984): 54–57; Gold, *Dialogue on Comparable Worth;* June O'Neill, "An Argument Against Comparable Worth," in U.S. Civil Rights Commission, *Comparable Worth: Issue for the 80s,* 177–86; and Daniel Seligman, "'Pay Equity' is a bad idea," *Fortune* 109 (14 May 1984): 133–40.

33. Before fielding the survey, the Comparable Worth Research Project discussed the survey with the Department of Employee Relations and every public union and professional association bargaining for state employees. Each person in the sample received two letters prior to being called at home. As part of the survey methodology, respondents were quota-sampled (at the telephoning stage) to make certain that the final sample represented the bargaining units in correct proportions. For further information on the sampling process, see Appendix C.

34. DeWayne Cuthbertson, "Quiz Your Employees," *Personnel Administrator* 29 (November 1984): 126–28; Gordan S. Findlay, "A Modest Recovery," *Best's Review (Life/Health Insurance Edition)* 84 (October 1984): 80–82; Daniel Forbes, "Communicating Benefits Changes to Employees Explored at BI Conference," *"Risk Management* 31 (September 1984): 78–80; and Thomas W. Hourihan, "Help Employees to Understand Their Benefits," *Personnel Administrator* 28 (April 1983): 92–98.

35. Seventeen years' tenure with the state is approximately one-half standard deviation above the mean tenure.

36. Amy E. Sandberg, *Comparable Worth: Theoretical Effects on Retirement Pensions* (Minneapolis: Hubert H. Humphrey Institute of Public Affairs, M.A. paper, 1985). In Minnesota, the longer a person's state service, the higher the proportion of preretirement income replaced by pension. At every length of service, however, an increase in salary is proportionately matched by an increase in pension. Under the most common retirement situation, a person whose pension would be $500 per month when she or he retired could look forward to receiving $550 per month if the pay equity raise in her or his job was 10%.

37. State employees operate in a world that has three time-lines: the fiscal year which begins July 1, the contract year which officially parallels the fiscal year but which often does not begin until negotiations are completed several months after the fiscal year begins, and the calendar year on which state employees, like everyone else, pay their taxes. To make the situation more confusing, contract years are referred to

by the calendar year in which they begin, and fiscal years are referred to by the calendar year in which they end. We used the nomenclature most familiar to employees, asking them the size of their pay equity raises in contract year 1984, which was just ending.

38. Total equals 100.1% due to rounding error.

39. Only 52.5% of those earning $20,000 or less, and 55.0% of those with 12 or fewer years of education accurately reported their pay equity raise situation. In comparison, almost 93.7% of those earning at least $30,000 and 90.7% of those with at least 17 years of education accurately knew their pay equity raise status. (This last finding was jointly a function of the fact that these groups are disproportionately composed of men, and the fact that overall only 7.1% of men in the sample received raises.)

40. Arne L. Kalleberg, "Work Values and Job Rewards: A Theory of Job Satisfaction," *American Sociological Review* 42 (January 1977): 124–43; Clifford J. Mottaz, "The Relative Importance of Intrinsic and Extrinsic Rewards as Determinants of Work Satisfaction," *The Sociological Quarterly* 26 (September 1985): 365–85; Faye J. Crosby, *Relative Deprivation and Working Women* (New York: Oxford University Press, 1982); Graham Staines and Robert Quinn, "American Workers Evaluate the Quality of their Jobs," *Monthly Labor Review* 102 (January 1979): 3–12; and, Anthony F. Chelte et al., "Did Job Satisfaction Really Droop During the 1970s?" *Monthly Labor Review* 105 (November 1982): 33–36.

41. Kalleberg, "Work Values"; Angus Campbell et al., *The Quality of American Life: Perceptions, Evaluations, and Satisfactions* (New York: Russell Sage Foundation, 1976); M. A. Murray and T. Atkinson, "Gender Differences in Correlates of Job Satisfaction," *Canadian Journal of Behavioral Sciences* 13 (January 1981): 44–52; Clifford J. Mottaz, "Gender Differences in Work Satisfaction, Work-Related Rewards and Values, and the Determinants of Work Satisfaction," *Human Relations* 39 (April 1986): 359–78.

42. Randy Hodson, "Corporate Structure and Job Satisfaction: A Focus on Employer Characteristics," *Sociology and Social Research* 69 (October 1984): 22–49; Richard Edwards and Michael Podgursky, "The Unraveling Accord: American Unions in Crisis," in Edwards, *Unions in Crisis and Beyond*, 14–60.

43. Crosby, *Relative Deprivation*.

44. On the difference between general and specific satisfaction questions, see Barbara J. Nelson, "Client Evaluations of Social Programs," in *The Public Encounter: Where State and Citizen Meet*, ed. Charles T. Goodsell (Bloomington: Indiana University Press, 1981), 23–42.

45. Because of small cell sizes, most of the controlled cross-tabulations did not have $X^2$ statistics significant at the .05 level. The pattern of much higher levels of job satisfaction among Group 4 (yes reported, yes raise) than in Group 5 (no reported, yes raise) held constant when the cross-tabulation was separately controlled for sex, job tenure, education, and salary.

## Chapter Six

1. Large-scale implementation studies are rare, in part because they are so costly. See Paul Sabatier and Daniel A. Mazmanian, "Policy Implementation," in *Encyclo-*

*pedia of Policy Studies,* ed. Stuart Nagel (New York: Marcel Dekker, 1983), 151, 164.

2. We used a multiple-case substitutable design in choosing our localities. This means that where possible we initially tracked several jurisdictions with each constellation of characteristics, if possible. We chose this design because we wanted to build in as much variability as possible at the beginning of the study in case categories of jurisdictions responded in unforeseen ways. This did not occur, but in any design, especially a natural experiment where the researchers cannot manipulate any of the variables, it is important not to restrict the possible variation too greatly by the initial structure of comparison. The slight variation of number of jurisdictions studied that is reflected in our published work reflects these decisions.

3. Quoted in *St. Paul Dispatch,* 20 June 1984, 1N.

4. Peg Kalar, "Board Studies Comparable Worth Issue," *Fergus Falls Daily Journal,* 4 October 1984.

5. Commissioner Nina Rothchild to Personnel Administrator (form letter), St. Paul, Minn., 12 July 1984. Also Bonnie Watkins, personal interviews with authors, St. Paul, Minn., 9 October 1986 and 21 April 1987.

6. "Local Government Pay Equity—Informal Progress Report," Minnesota Department of Employee Relations, St. Paul, Minn. (January 1985).

7. Interviews with Bonnie Watkins and Dave Lutes, 9 October 1986, by Barbara Nelson.

8. Earl Larson, AMC President, "President's Report: Comparable Worth," *Minnesota Counties* 27:9 (September 1984), 2; handwritten note in DOER files to Bonnie Watkins describing a regional meeting in 1984 where many rural county commissioners heard about the local government law for the first time.

9. "Comparable Worth Extended to Local Levels," *Minnesota Counties,* 28:4 (25 May 1984); Dick Cox, "Comparable Worth's Ramifications," *Minnesota Counties,* 28:10, (21 December 1984).

10. Dick Cox, "Comparable Worth's Ramifications," *Minnesota Counties* 28:10 (21 December 1984).

11. Association of Minnesota Counties, "Personnel Consultant: Request for Proposals," St. Paul, Minn., 15 June 1984; Association of Minnesota Counties, "Comparable Worth Evaluation Service Available," 12 September 1984, in DOER files.

12. Earl Larson, "President's Report: Comparable Worth."

13. *"Minnesota County Platform: The Policy and Positions of the Association of Minnesota Counties:* As approved by the general membership of the Association of Minnesota Counties at the AMC Annual Conference, January 22, 1985," in *Minnesota Counties* 29:2 (22 February 1985), 19; Lynn Boland to Representative Peter McLaughlin, St. Paul, Minn., 7 January 1985, form letter with questionnaire sent to all Minnesota legislators, in DOER files; Lynn Boland, personal interview with Sara Evans, St. Paul, Minn., 8 May 1985.

14. Jean Olson, telephone interview with Sara Evans, 18 March 1987.

15. Minnesota School Boards Association to School Board members and Superintendents of Schools, "Re: Activity of Minnesota School Boards Association on Comparable Worth Law," St. Peter, Minn., 2 November 1984; interview with Jean Olson.

16. Minnesota School Boards Association, "Request for Proposal on a Comparable Worth Study" [St. Paul, Minn.], 5 September 1984.

17. John Sylvester, telephone interview with Sara Evans, 27 March 1984.

18. Interview with James C. Fox, Arthur Young International, Minneapolis, Minn., 26 March 1987; interview with Jean Olson; interview with John Sylvester.

19. Interviews with Faith Zwemke, Minneapolis, Minn., 1 May 1987; Joel Jamnick, St. Paul, Minn., 8 April 1985; Bonnie Watkins, St. Paul, Minn., 9 October 1987; Tom Thelen, telephone interview, 30 March 1987. See also "Equal Pay, New Business Subjects of City Meeting Here," *Herman Review,* 6 September 1984.

20. *St. Paul Dispatch,* 20 June 1984.

21. Ibid.

22. Frank H. Cassell and Jean J. Baron, *Collective Bargaining in the Public Sector: Cases in Public Policy* (Columbus, Ohio: GRID, 1975), 5–23.

23. Cyrus Smythe, "Comparable Worth Is an Attainable Goal," *Minnesota Cities* (November 1984), 38.

24. Interviews with Cyrus Smythe and Karen Olson, Golden Valley, Minn., 14 May 1987, and Bill Joynes, Golden Valley, Minn., 17 September 1986.

25. Interview with Bill Joynes, Golden Valley, Minn., 17 September 1986.

26. Interview with Kay Aho and Dwain Boelter, Personnel Decisions, Inc., Minneapolis, Minn., 3 March 1987.

27. For a discussion of the importance of fixers in the implementation process, see Eugene Bardach, *The Implementation Game* (Cambridge, Mass.: MIT Press, 1977), and Sabatier and Mazmanian, "Policy Implementation."

28. For a discussion of the importance of the incorporation of minority, and by extension female, elected officials into power structures, see Rufus P. Browning, Dale Rogers Marshall, and David H. Tabb, *Protest Is Not Enough: The Struggle of Blacks and Hispanics for Equality in Urban Politics* (Berkeley: University of California Press, 1984).

29. Commission on the Economic Status of Women, "Women Elected Officials in Minnesota," *Newsletter,* No. 111 (February 1987), 1.

30. George Latimer, panel presentation, Conference on New Directions in Comparable Worth, Minneapolis, Minn., 18 October 1985.

31. Interviews with Jerry Serfling, St. Paul, Minn., 18 March 1987; Jim Scheibel, St. Paul, Minn., 16 September 1986; Kathy O'Brien, Minneapolis, Minn., 21 July 1986 and 18 May 1987; Bob Lindahl, Minneapolis, Minn., 29 July 1986; and Joan Niemiec, Minneapolis, Minn., 30 July 1986; Latimer, panel presentation, 18 October 1985.

32. Bill Joynes, presentation, MAMA/University of Minnesota Employer Education Service Seminar, Supplementary Session, Brooklyn Center, Minn., 23 September 1986.

33. Telephone interview with Janet Potter, personnel director, St. Cloud, 13 April 1987.

34. Bill Joynes, "Reflections on Pay Equity or 'What Did You Do in the Comparable Worth War?'" *Minnesota Cities* 72:3 (March 1987), 6.

35. Ibid; interview with Dwain Boelter and Kay Aho.

36. Interview with James Fox, Minneapolis, Minn., 26 March 1987.

37. Interview with Irene Koski, Minneapolis, Minn., 6 April 1987.

38. Interview with Robert Bocwinski and Linda Magee, Columbia Heights, Minn., 13 April 1987; interview with Joel Jamnick.

39. Interview with Robert Bocwinski.

40. Telephone interview with Bonnie Nelson-Gerth, Payroll Clerk/Bookkeeper, Princeton, Minn., 10 April 1987.

41. Telephone interview with Steve Jackson, Acting Administrative Clerk, Princeton, Minn., 9 April 1987.

42. Joel Stottrup, "Equal-pay-for-equal-work idea part of city pay hikes," *Princeton Union Eagle*, 18 February 1984.

43. While most stories from small cities fit this model, there were cases both of recalcitrant and grudging compliance. Interview with Joel Jamnick, League of Minnesota Cities, St. Paul, Minn, 8 April 1985; telephone interview with William Lavin, city administrator, Granite Falls, Minn., 30 March 1987. The swiftest example of compliance was Hutchinson, Minn., which, using the Princeton model, completed its implementation on 1 January 1985. City of Hutchinson, Minnesota, "Local Government Pay Equity Reporting Form," [n.d.]; Hazel Sitz, Personnel Director, Hutchinson, Minn., panel presentation, Conference on New Directions in Comparable Worth, Minneapolis, Minn., 18 October 1985.

44. Minnesota Department of Employee Relations, "Pay Equity in Minnesota Local Governments," 30 January 1986.

45. Ibid.

46. Telephone interview with Judy Honmyhr, 6 April 1985.

47. Interview with Mark Andrew, Hennepin County Commissioner, Minneapolis, Minn., 4 August 1986. Personnel Director Chuck Sprafka and Labor Relations Director Rolland Toenges opposed comparable worth as "inconsistent with market forces." Rolland C. Toenges to Linda Erickson, Minneapolis, Minn., 11 January 1984, in "Status of Comparable Worth Issue in Hennepin County" (Minneapolis, Minn.,: Hennepin County Personnel Department, 9 April 1984).

48. A representative of Arthur Young and Associates indicated this pattern to us. Several managers and personnel directors in other local jurisdictions also pointed to the leadership role of Hennepin County in their interviews.

49. "Request for Proposals to Conduct a Job Evaluation Study of Hennepin County Classifications," 1985], 5.

50. Ibid., 6. Also interviews with Rolland C. Toenges, Minneapolis, Minn., 4 August 1986, and Commissioner Mark Andrew, Minneapolis, Minn., 4 August 1986; Chuck Sprafka, Hennepin County Personnel Director, panel presentation, MAMA/ University of Minnesota Employer Education Service, "Meeting to Exchange Ideas: Comparable Worth Compliance," Brooklyn Center, Minn., 23 September 1986.

51. Telephone interview with David Griffin, Olmsted County, Director of Personnel and Operations, 13 March 1987.

52. Telephone interviews with Judy Honmyhr, Personnel Director, Washington County, 6 April 1987, and Norman Moody, Personnel Director, Beltrami County, 11 April 1987.

53. Memo on "Final Results of Pay Equity Study" to All County Employe[es], from Dale Ackmann, County Administrator, Hennepin County, 7 May 1987.

54. Honmyhr interview.

55. Interviews with John Sylvester and Jean Olson.

56. *Minneapolis Star and Tribune*, 14 October 1983, 4B.

57. *St. Paul Pioneer Press and Dispatch*, 2 January 1985.

58. Interview with Cathryn Olson, Employee Relations Director, Anoka-Hennepin School District, Coon Rapids, Minn., 13 April 1987.

59. Telephone interview with Robert Miller, former superintendent, Stillwater School District, 8 April 1987; *St. Paul Pioneer Press and Dispatch,* 9 October 1985, 3NE.

60. Gene Rucker, panel presentation, MAMA/Labor Relations Associates, "Meeting to Exchange Ideas: Comparable Worth Compliance," Brooklyn Center, Minn., 23 September 1986. See also Gene D. Rucker, "An Approach to Compliance with the Minnesota Comparable Worth Act" (Rochester, Minn.: Rochester Independent School District No. 535 [1986]).

61. Telephone Interview with Bob Ostlund, Director of Administrative Services and Personnel, Chaska School District, 9 April 1987.

62. Jeffrey L. Pressman and Aaron Wildavsky, *Implementation,* 2d ed., (Berkeley: University of California Press, 1979).

63. See David Lutes and Nina Rothchild, "Compensation—Pay Equity Loses to Chicken Little and Other Excuses," *Personnel Journal* 65 (1986): 124–30.

64. This estimate is based on the fact that 52% of jurisdictions reporting by January 1986 had used the job match. Those outstanding, however, included most large jurisdictions in the Twin Cities metropolitan area and all those involved in the huge MAMA study.

65. Interviews with Bonnie Watkins, St. Paul, Minn., 9 October 1986 and 21 April 1987, and Representative Phil Riveness, 18 September 1986.

66. Arthur Young and Company surveyed 800 jurisdictions in February 1988 to determine some of the broad patterns in compliance with the Local Government Pay Equity Act. Only 195 responded, weighted heavily towards school districts (122 or 62.6%) and jurisdictions which chose to use outside consultants (151 or 77.4%). They found that 63.3% had chosen to use an all-jobs or balanced-classes pay line, 53.9% used a corridor, and 70.9% chose to adjust all classes that fell below the chosen line or corridor and only 28.5% adjusted only female jobs. Most had chosen cost containment methods for jobs paid above the pay line, ranging from salary freeze (14%), to slow increases (44.7%), lump sum payments (2.2%), two-tier wage schedules (1.1%) or a combination of these (16.2%). Only one jurisdiction reported a plan to lower salaries. Arthur Young and Company, "1988 Pay Equity Survey of Minnesota Jurisdictions, Final Results," Minneapolis, Minn., April 1988.

67. Ross Azevedo, interviewed on "Research Journal," KTCI-TV, 10 May 1988, and Research Proposal to the Center for Urban and Regional Affairs, University of Minnesota, 18 February 1988. Professor Azevedo is currently conducting a quantitative analysis of the pay equity reports and implementation plans submitted to the Department of Employee Relations by local Minnesota jurisdictions. His preliminary evidence indicates that while many jurisdictions have complied with the law with no apparent problems, in other cases "comparable worth requirements may have been used as a lever to justify raises for male dominated jobs and to undermine collective bargaining."

68. Interview with Bill Jones.

69. Conversation with council member Jim Scheibel, 28 July 1987.

70. Telephone interview with Al Ortwig, member St. Paul School Board, 10 March

1987; joint interview with Jerry Serfling, AFSCME Business Agent for St. Paul City and Schools; Mary Hayes, AFSCME Local 2508; and Renata Ciccarelli, AFSCME Local 1842; St. Paul, Minn., 18 March 1987; joint interview with Phyllis Byers, Negotiator; Phillip Penn, Assistant Director of Personnel; and James Sargent, Personnel Director, St. Paul School District; St. Paul, Minn., 12 May 1987.

71. Telephone interview with Dennis Bible, Minneapolis Labor Relations Director, 28 July 1987.

72. Rucker, panel presentation, MAMA/University of Minnesota Employer Education Service, "Meeting to Exchange Ideas: Comparable Worth Compliance," Brooklyn Center, Minn., 23 September 1986; telephone interview with Bob Ostlund, Director of Administrative Services and Personnel, Chaska School District, 9 April 1987.

73. Interviews with Nancy Crippin, St. Paul, Minn., 16 and 28 April 1987; Pete Benner, St. Paul, Minn., 4 June and 24 July 1987; Rich Scott, St. Paul, Minn., 25 September 1986; Jerry Serfling, St. Paul, Minn., 18 March 1987.

74. See Cy Smythe, "Comparable Worth: Compensation Inequities," parts I–VI, *Minnesota Cities,* November 1986–April 1987.

75. Interview with Kathy O'Brien, 21 July 1986; interview with Regina Strauchon, 28 July 1987.

76. This was the case, for example, in Beltrami and Hennepin Counties.

77. Interviews with Bill Michel, Roseville, Minn., 4 March 1987; Irene Koski, St. Paul, Minn., 6 April 1987; and Bill Joynes.

78. Examples of this problem were the Stillwater School District, Minneapolis, and St. Paul.

79. One example of this was the Little Falls School District, where the president of one employee union ended up handling most of the discontent with the job evaluation study, to Personnel Director James O'Toole's great satisfaction. Telephone interview with James O'Toole, assistant superintendent and director of human resources, Little Falls School District, 14 April 1987.

80. "300 St. Paul Police March on City Hall for Pay Hike," *St. Paul Pioneer Press and Dispatch,* 27 February 1987.

81. Department of Employee Relations, "Pay Equity in Minnesota Local Governments," St. Paul, Minn., 30 January 1986.

82. Chaska School District, "Proposed Classifications, Proposed Wages," and chart of positions with current beginning and maximum salary and bottom of the male corridor minimum and maximum salary by position, Chaska, Minnesota [August 1986], documents in the possession of Nancy Crippin, Minnesota School Employees Association.

83. Lee Anderson, "Pay Equity Study: Minneapolis Public Schools Special School District No. 1," Minneapolis, Minn., 1 July 1985.

84. Interview with Cathryn Olson, Employee Relations Director, Anoka-Hennepin School District, Coon Rapids, Minn., 13 April 1987.

85. The National Committee on Pay Equity reported in late 1987 that AFSCME had filed lawsuits against two Minnesota counties (Ramsey and Mille Lacs) for refusing to bargain for pay equity. In one of those, Ramsey County, they had reached a rapid out-of-court settlement. *Pay Equity News Notes,* Winter 1987, 4.

86. "Law Establishing a Financial Penalty for Non-compliance of Schools," re-

printed in Commission on the Economic Status of Women, *Pay Equity: The Minnesota Experience*, rev. ed. (St. Paul: Commission on the Economic Status of Women, 1988), 36.

87. Commission on the Economic Status of Women, "Session '88: Legislative Summary," *Newsletter*, no. 126, May 1988, 1.

## Chapter Seven

1. Commission on the Economic Status of Women, *Pay Equity: The Minnesota Experience*, rev. ed. (St. Paul: Commission on the Economic Status of Women, 1988), 19.

2. Janet Potter, telephone interview with Sara Evans, 13 April 1987, and Judy Honmyhr, telephone interview with Sara Evans, 6 April 1987.

3. *Minnesota Cities* 70 (August 1985) and 69 (August 1984).

4. Jennifer L. Hochschild, *The New American Dilemma: Liberal Democracy and School Desegregation* (New Haven: Yale University Press, 1984).

5. Ibid.

6. Our findings are congruent with the perspective of Ronnie Steinberg's study of comparable worth in the state of New York, "Women, the State and Equal Employment," in *Comparable Worth: A View from the States*, ed. Ronnie Steinberg (Philadelphia: Temple University Press, forthcoming, 1988). See also Ralph Smith, ed., *The Subtle Revolution: Women at Work* (Washington, D.C.: The Urban Institute, 1979); Ethel Klein, *Gender Politics* (Cambridge: Harvard University Press, 1984); Janet A. Flammang, ed., *Political Women: Current Roles in State and Local Governments* (Beverly Hills: Sage Publications, 1984); and Anne N. Costain, "Representing Women: The Transition from Social Movement to Interest Group," in *Women, Power, and Policy*, ed. Ellen Boneparth (New York: Pergamon, 1982), 19–37.

7. Joyce Gelb and Marian Lief Palley, *Women and Public Policies*, (Princeton: Princeton University Press, 1982), 10.

8. Alice Kessler-Harris, "The Just Price, The Free Market, and the Value of Women," *Feminist Studies* 15 (Winter 1989); see also Rosalyn L. Feldberg, "Comparable Worth: Toward Theory and Practice in the United States," *Signs* 10 (Winter 1984): 311–28.

9. Mary G. Dietz, "Learning About Women: Gender, Politics, and Power," *Daedalus* 116 (Fall 1987): 1–24.

10. Audience comment, panel on implementing pay equity by school boards, Conference on New Directions in Comparable Worth, Minneapolis, Minn., 18 October 1985; telephone interview with James O'Toole, Assistant Superintendent and Director of Human Resources, Little Falls School District, 14 April 1986. See also Linda M. Blum, "Possibilities and Limits of the Comparable Worth Movement," *Gender and Society* 1 (December 1987): 380–99.

11. Quoted in Blum, "Possibilities and Limits of the Comparable Worth Movement," 393.

12. See Barbara Melosh, *The Physician's Hand* (Philadelphia: Temple University Press, 1982).

13. See Joan Acker, "Comparable Worth: The Oregon Case," in *Comparable Worth:*

*A View From the States,* ed. Ronnie Steinberg (Philadelphia: Temple University Press, forthcoming, 1988).

14. See *San Francisco Chronicle,* 19 August 1985, 6; 23 August 1985, 2; 27 August 1985, 20; 31 August 1985, 4.

15. Memo from Albert C. Ambrose, Chief, Salary Standardization, to The Honorable Civil Service Commission, "Policy for Implementation of Charter Section 8.407–1, Compensation Adjustments (Includes Summary of Relevant Survey Data Used to Identify Pay Equity Differentials)," San Francisco, California, 30 January 1987.

16. Kessler-Harris, "The Just Price."

17. See Steinberg, "Women, the State and Equal Employment."

18. National Committee on Pay Equity, telephone interview with Nancy Johnson, 9 December 1987.

# Index